SOUL DOG

A MEMOIR OF SPIRIT, SMARTS, AND LOVE

Second Edition

Elisabeth Rose

Second Edition

ISBN: 979-8-9987060-0-4

This book is a memoir based on the author's recollections. Some names and
identifying details have been changed to protect people's privacy.

First Edition

Printed in the United States of America

Cover Design by Steven Novak
Author photo by Alby Lanser
Cover photo courtesy of the author

For my Grandfather, Richard Thiede,
who taught me that, like dogs, we are born lovable

Acknowledgements

This second edition of my first memoir, originally published as *For the Love of a Dog*, wouldn't have come to fruition without the encouragement of several key people. First, I want to thank Kim Witherspoon, agent at Inkwell Management, who believed in this manuscript from the beginning. She brought it to Patricia Gift, editor at Harmony Books, whose enthusiasm for the project was a true highlight in my life. Next, I'm grateful to my friend and fellow author Laura Mahaffey, who's been my tireless teacher, editor, critic, and cheerleader every step of the way. I owe thanks to my friends, family, and anyone who puts up with my dogs and writing. Lastly, I must honor the late David Hartwell, Senior Editor at Tor/Forge Books, who badgered me for this edition. I was too pig-headed to listen. David, my dear friend, you were right, and I miss you.

Contents

Preface to the Second Edition

What's New in the Second Edition

This edition restores scenes omitted from the original manuscript, particularly those starring my border collie, Pip. It also includes the original ending.

By the time the book came out in 2001, under the title *For the Love of a Dog*, I'd suffered seismic upheaval—a lost pregnancy, which shattered my family and my faith. Therefore, last minute, I asked for my editor's permission to rewrite the last chapter, which ended on a scene of me pregnant and playing Frisbee with my two border collies, Pip and Casey. After my life fell apart, I fell on hard times, which led me to rehome Pip, and I was too emotionally raw to disappoint readers who might ask about my new child, my husband, and Pip.

So I cut Pip scenes and replaced the final pages with a diplomatic summation of my divorce, then steered into an academic view of the human-canine bond. It was safe, analytical, and, according to some, disappointing. I had shut away my heart.

This version restores Pip to his rightful place. I offer you the original ending, "Everything Moves," in which he stars. It's true to who we were at the time, Pip deserves it, and readers deserve a vision of life, love, and hope. After all, our lives worked out in the end, just not the way I thought they were supposed to.

How Dog Training Has Changed

Although I changed the names and identifying details of several characters to protect their interests, this edition includes Bob Martin's real name. Not only has he passed away, I realize there was never any reason to conceal what he taught. He never needed me to shield him or apologize for him.

In the 1990s in Central Pennsylvania, Robert ("Bob") J. Martin, author of *Towards the PhD for Dogs*, was our most influential dog training instructor. Born in 1927, he trained German Shepherds, raised seeing eye puppies for 4H, and ran a school in the huge, well-lit basement of his home. Bob taught us to think of our families as wolf packs. When they misbehaved, we needed to put them in their place.

The summer of 1990, I sought his help with my border collie.

Kierney displayed dangerously erratic behavior, and the clock was ticking—I was seven months pregnant with my first child.

Today many oppose any form of punishment in dog training. My trainer friends and I are more Karen Pryor and Victoria Stilwell than Cesar Millan. Reward-based training works well for sane and healthy dogs in stable households where the humans have the necessary time, patience, and interest.

Recently two women walked into the dog club excited. They'd found *For the Love of a Dog* and read it. I regretted the scenes where I followed Martin's advice and said so.

To my surprise, however, they expressed compassion for me and shared their stories. As I listened, I realized this book gave us powerful bond out of the blue. I felt forgiven. Less alone. And they did too.

Why the New Title?

Back in the 1990s, my working title was *The Sidewalks of Heaven and Earth,* from the chapter of that name. Friends who knew me then still prefer it, but I'm not sure I even understand it. It also captures the everyday poignancy of walking our dogs through time. Dogs die and new dogs walk in their pawsteps. We die and new dog lovers take up the leash. But the dog-and-human love affair carries on.

A marketing team came up with *For the Love of a Dog* instead, and I agreed to it. I couldn't think of anything better. Until now.

Soul Dog tells you this is a story. It's the story of how I loved a dog so hard she became part of my soul. It's how she convinced me that either humans and animals all have souls—or none of us do. It's a fight for the worth and dignity of all nonhuman life.

If you've read this far, you're probably someone who loves animals as deeply as my friends and I do. I hope *Soul Dog* helps you feel vindicated for any moment you witnessed the personhood of another animal and someone made you doubt yourself. You can stop. You've found us now.

I also hope it helps you feel forgiven for any mistakes you've made along the way, especially when you were trying your best to do the right thing.

Soul Dog A Memoir of Spirit, Smarts, and Love

Chapter One

Compact Gods

One Sunday when I was about twelve years old, I stood in Reverend Van Dyke's receiving line after service, nervously chewing the end of my pigtail. The only child alone in line, I inched forward in the shadows between adult bodies, folding and unfolding my arms, phrasing and rephrasing the question I'd rehearsed for weeks as I gathered the nerve to approach the holiest person I knew. Not only was Reverend Van Dyke a large man, a white-haired, wisecracking, whiskey-drinking friend of judges and senators, he had once shut my father up. My father usually ridiculed everything and everyone, especially the pious. However, one Christmas Eve when, to please my mother, my father made an appearance in the church, Van Dyke greeted him, looked him slyly in the eye, and said, "Home for the holidays, Bob?" From then on, my father held Van Dyke in high regard. By approaching the one religious person my father honored, I felt as if I'd strapped on wax wings and flown toward the sun.

When my turn came, Van Dyke bent to greet me. Tossing my wet pigtail behind my shoulder, I gave him a firm handshake and asked, already fighting back tears, "Do animals go to heaven?" for I'd heard in Sunday school that they didn't.

"No, Honey," he said, and turned to shake the hand of the man behind me.

"Why not?" I said, even though I was a skinny, knobby-kneed, frizzy-haired girl, a nobody.

As if to entertain the adults in line behind me, Van Dyke bent toward me again, a beardless Santa. "Why, honey, they don't have souls."

"How do you know?" I said, my voice rising, because to me, he might as well have announced there was no heaven at all. If my wire-haired fox terrier Patches didn't have a heaven-bound soul, then I needed help that she didn't. Everything about dogs elated me. I loved them for barking at strange sounds. I loved the way their paws bob when they trot, the way their sides heave when they pant, the fact that

4

they move through the world horizontally. I loved the vulnerable, teetering way they hunkered to drop feces. My eyes needed a daily fix of dog-watching, my hands needed to shake rough paw pads, my forearms welcomed red tooth mark stripes from wrestling a puppy, and when I slept, my feet needed to feel the weight of a sleeping dog on them. At twelve, I knew this about myself. Having my own dog for about a year had confirmed it. If Patches couldn't have a soul, then I didn't want mine.

"How do you *know*?" I said.

"Animals can't reason," Van Dyke said.

The adults nodded and smiled sympathetically, maybe a little smugly too.

"Then do severely brain-damaged humans have souls?"

There was a ripple of alarm in his small audience, and Van Dyke lost his child-charming grin. "Of course they do!" he boomed, turning to pump the hand of the next in line. "Good to see you!"

"Then why don't animals?"

Exasperated, he looked down at me one last time. "I don't know," he said.

From that moment on through the rest of my childhood, I no longer believed in God, in an afterlife, or in the justice and wisdom of my elders. Van Dyke had let me down, had—ironically—failed to reason, and had shown me that a child's theological conflicts weren't worth his time. That small encounter affected me at twelve, because the relationship between God and Creation was the very center of my budding spirituality, and Van Dyke had nipped it. He left me adrift in a universe where rationality and authority fail, but where intuition and experience were to be squelched, hidden, and savored only privately, under a petticoat of shame. I couldn't call my secret knowing "faith" or "spirituality" or by any other church word, because Van Dyke had set in my mind two mutually exclusive contexts—church and nature. I was having none of the former.

Plus, my dad was relieved.

Unaware that my spirituality had merely been deflected, not snuffed out, I learned to meditate by dozing with my nose in the curls on my terrier's chest. Sharing a center of gravity with a rented horse was a kind of nirvana. Uncomfortable with the contradictions but caught up in the drama, I took on the mantle of improvised priesthood and performed funerals, well-attended by neighborhood kids and equally tearful whether for pet hamsters or for squirrels turned into cardboard on the road.

Still, no communion surpassed a romp with a dog. I'd wanted my own ever since the day, when I was four years old, a boxer taught me how to swim in the surf of the Ivory Coast, her blunt nose and seal-like face watching me above the waves as if her gaze alone could buoy me.

Years later, back in the United States, whenever I was lying on my bed, lonely, bored, or scolded, I imagined a lanky, short-haired, yellow-coated Sarah dog, the kind I'd seen in Ghana, trot across the hardwood floor to prod me with her nose. I'd imagine it so hard I could almost hear the click of of toenails.

Then on the Christmas of my eleventh year, as I stood walking a new Slinky from hand to hand, my little sister shrieked, "A puppy!" and a roly-poly Wire-Haired Fox Terrier pup scampered across the rug. My sister fell to her knees and scooped the puppy up, but I, stunned, dropped the Slinky and sank slowly to the couch. A dog. My dog. She was finally here. My parents, I told myself, will never regret this. Never will either of them have to feed her, or walk her, or discipline her. Never will I give them any reason to say, "I'm sorry we ever let you have that damn dog." The responsibility and the fear of how badly they could tease me now kept me seated on that couch for a good long moment. In fact, it surprised everyone, even me, that I didn't rush to the dog the way my sister had, but I was thinking, "We have the rest of our lives together."

The rest of our lives together lasted only six years, but we filled those six. In our neighborhood soccer was a game of eleven kids against one terrier. She played a fine game, dashing left and right, kicking the ball with her front paws and keeping it close with her chin. I tied her collar to my three-speed bike, a Raleigh Chopper with a banana seat, and she pulled it while I stood on the seat like a surfer. When it snowed, we went sledding. Patches pulled the sled all the way to the golf course where scores of people rode a rolling hill a half a mile long. At the top, Patches sat on the sled all by herself, waiting for me to give her a push, and when I did, she sat there, the back of her head, shoulders, and black saddle patch going down, getting smaller and smaller, until at the bottom when the sled stopped, she jumped off wagging her stubby tail, and pulled the sled back up the hill herself.

Determined to keep my parents from regretting her, I took her to a 4H obedience class and trained her several times a week—despite the family consensus that fox terriers were intractable boneheads. My parents had nicknamed her "El Stupido," "El Dumbo," and "Toad." At first, some of the more competitive kids in the 4H class, like the girl with a sheltie, wouldn't even look at us. Even the instructor shook her head at us a lot at first. Patches had introduced herself by pooping right in the middle of the room. During her long down-stay, she rolled over and kicked her legs in the air, scratching her back. Although she brazenly preferred life's gustier pleasures, such as attacking any dog larger than herself and humping the miniature dachshund, no one listened when I insisted that, like any class clown, she wasn't stupid, just uncooperative. She was like most people I knew: she'd only work if you gave her a good reason to.

Each summer at the 4H dog show, a show my parents never attended, Patches won obedience ribbons and trophies. One summer we entered a tricks competition, and she even upstaged me. I had taught her nine tricks, and we practiced them in the kitchen, in order, several times a day. We did simple tricks, such as shake, other paw, speak, roll over, twirl like a ballerina (spin on hind legs), and jump (jump over my raised leg). When the moment arrived, we strode to the center of the ring, and the crowd quieted. I gave the first command, and Patches whipped through all nine tricks, *without me*. She lifted, shook and lowered each paw, barked, rolled in the saw dust, stood on her hind legs and twirled, sprang back and forth over nothing. The judge almost fell backwards laughing, and the crowd, after a confused silence, burst into applause. When I failed to toss her a treat, Patches soloed the entire routine again. I was mortally embarrassed the way only a thirteen-year-old can be. I stood beet red and fighting tears. To me, it proved I was a terrible dog trainer, and the bond I cherished was a lie. She didn't need me and never really obeyed me.

I can't remember who came in third. I think the sheltie was second. I still have that first-place trophy. In fact, it's my only trophy.

I realized years later, Patches had more than obeyed me. She understood her role in the dog show. She took it on, owned it, and transcended it, performing much more than the puppetry I had planned.

Patches had become a neighborhood character, a four-legged Pippi Longstocking, a fanged Huckleberry Finn, a curly-haired Snoopy. I was always Charlie Brown, outdone again. If I wasn't doing something new with her, such as teaching her to climb trees, she had no interest in me. Sure, she slept on my bed at night and clawed my arm begging me to scratch her itchy, allergic skin. With the air of an impatient child, she'd kiss me whenever I asked. But I came to think that she loved me only for the tomboyish things I did. If someone else did those things, well then it was all the same. She seemed to need very little except freedom.

On Christmas Eve of my sixteenth year, Patches failed to alert us that the house was on fire. It burned while we slept, destroying furniture, wooden African dolls and Indonesian paintings and filling the rooms with so much dense and noxious smoke that we barely had enough breath to escape. The air reached nearly two thousand degrees at the ceiling; two silver candle sticks on the mantle melted. My grandmother was trapped in a second story bedroom, and the fireman who went up those stairs to save her was decorated.

Patches, who was downstairs where it started, had blown a classic opportunity to prove her worth. My parents didn't spare one wisecrack. Looking back, I'm not sure what they expected of her. To know the difference between a fire *in* the fireplace and a fire *next* to the fireplace? Their sarcasm always hinted at the expectation that she ought to leap through our lives like Lassie and make up for mistakes we'd made—such as failing to rig the house with smoke alarms and fire extinguishers. My father was a civil engineer. Wasn't he the one who should've known better?

Patches was just a dog, a bright, healthy, quintessential specimen of a fox terrier, nothing less, nothing more, muscular, fast, mischievous, adventurous, even murderous when we brought home hamsters. They escaped their Habitrail and disappeared into the nooks of the house. Patches the Ratter found them. I suppose I could say, in all honesty, that for my part I expected her to take up loving me where my parents, drained by their own witty warfare, left off short. I wished that Patches wouldn't want so much to run away. I wished she'd prefer my company to others. I wished she'd become a cautious, grateful, devoted dog—but still pull my Chopper, ride a sled, and keep a soccer ball from eleven kids. I wished she'd only hunt down a rodent and shake it till its blood sprayed the walls if I told her to. She was just a dog, and yet, like the humans in the house, she argued, she failed, she demanded, she fulfilled, she forgave. Perhaps her soul differed in degree from ours, not in kind. There were days, though, I didn't think she differed at all.

I had plenty of opportunities to ponder dog souls. On my paper route I befriended, tamed, and entertained every chained-up or penned-up dog. A German shepherd named Major started out as a terrifying guard dog. His owner kept him tied on a long chain inside a two-car garage with the door always raised. Major barked at me at first, but he let me pick up his tennis ball. He'd watch me throw it, then start barking again. A week or so of this led to a morning when he wagged his tail and barked at a much higher pitch when he saw me, as if he'd given me some thought overnight and decided I was all right.

About seven to nine years old, Major was trim, strong, full-coated, classically handsome. He possessed solid, functional hindquarters unlike the unnaturally angulated back ends of German Shepherds today. Having rearranged my paper route so that I delivered to Major's house last, I brought him toys and treats and sometimes spent a good hour playing catch and teaching him tricks.

Then one winter day Major wasn't in his garage. Instead, his owner, a small, stooped old man, was standing on the back step, shivering without a coat. The sight of him startled me, because I had only met this man a few times when I came around to collect payments for the newspaper. He just stood there, staring at me, pale, slouched, arms wrapped tightly around his waist.

"Where's Major?" I said.

"Poor Major's dead."

I gaped at the open garage, the grassy lot where he raced magnificently after his tennis ball. His absence was impossible. But his tennis ball was gone. His chain was gone. His water dish too.

"I knew you'd be upset," the man said, as if to explain why he had waited on his back step. He wiped the heel of his hand across his eyes. "Major is dead," he said, voice breaking, "and there wasn't anyone else to tell."

That moment has stayed with me, standing in the cold, the last newspaper almost weightless in my otherwise empty sack, trying to keep my new over-sized ten-speed bike upright, staring at an empty garage alongside an old man. It wasn't until many years later that I began to understand the man better, when I knew better that from his looks he was probably in his late seventies or early eighties, and I had a faint notion what life is like when you're elderly, living alone in a huge house in an American suburb. That probably wasn't the first time he waited for me—no, I had seen him watching from his window, had waved to him many times. He had watched me teach Major to "shake." He watched me scold Major, laugh at him, throw my arms around his dog. He had seen Major stand wagging his tail before I had even pedaled into view, and he had watched Major sit and stare when I rode away. When paying for the paper, he used to tip me well and thank me for being a good friend to Major.

And the first morning after Major's death, he waited outside for me because he knew something about me that I didn't yet know: I was the kind of person to whom such things could be told.

Without hearing, only feeling, I stood while the man told me things I'd never known about Major. None of the details mattered anymore. I forgot them immediately. Then I wobbled off on my bike, crying, the last newspaper still sliding around in my sack, a biscuit wedged in my jeans pocket. I was furious at the wind for lifting the bare tree branches, at the sun for brimming the rooftops, at my school for starting the next morning as if Major were alive. Major—I could hear his toe nails grab the macadam, could feel his wet breath on my hand, could see his mouth close earnestly when he watched me reach in my pocket. His deep fur rippled as he ran.

How dare death?

A ferocious, old, dirty white poodle mix tied to a dog house helped me recover. At first, every day he barked himself hoarse as soon as he saw me. I didn't know his name because no one was ever inside the old dirty white farm house to tell it to me. He always cringed and watched wild-eyed, but I knelt and left a biscuit on the grass before backing away. I did this every day, speaking softly, until his barking subsided, and he greeted me, tail wagging. Delivering the paper was safer for me then, and also more fun. Once he accepted me, I stopped by twice a day, on my route and on my way home from school, and he let me pet his cool, silky curls.

Before long, my visits got a little boring. Unlike Major, this dog was no dynamo. I'd arrive, put the news in the rack, sit on the grass, feed him his biscuit, and pet him. We'd watch cars pass, bees careen through the lilacs, a squirrel semaphore with its tail.

One day, a bit antsy, I rolled him over and shook his muzzle, inviting him to wrestle the way Patches loved to do. He chewed on my hand, and for a while, this was good. He dozed, his tilted head back far enough for his upper lips to sag, giving him a paleodontic grin. His teeth had blackened; he was old. I pressed his toes to study his claws, stared in some adolescent fascination at his furry penis sheath, and squeezed the leather of his ears and of my own, pondering cartilage, nerves, and skin. I was bored.

I spotted a stick, jumped up, and waved it at him.

He leapt backwards, wet himself like a scared puppy, and barked up a riot.

The next day he seemed to have forgotten our friendship. If anything, his barking was more frenzied than ever. He snarled, danced, gnashed his teeth, posturing like a school bully hiding the secret that his old man beats him at home. I concluded he'd been beaten with a stick. The following day I delivered the paper at dinnertime and rang the doorbell, braced for confrontation.

A woman answered, a woman who seemed too young to own an old house and an old dog.

My accusations failed me. "I made friends with your dog," I shouted over his barking, "but the other day I picked up a stick, and now he's afraid again."

"Yes," she said sadly. "Some kids once beat Whiskey near to death with a stick."

And so for me Whiskey's story became the first part of an on-going lesson that there is nothing more terrifying than being alive. It seemed obvious to me that humans weren't the only animals who cherished their own lives, but no one else I knew seemed to think so, or at least, no one else considered an animal's self-love to be a matter worth pondering.

Had Whiskey's owner reckoned with it, she might not have kept him tied in a front yard along a well-trafficked sidewalk near a grade school, at the mercy of wicked kids with sticks.

We can't know for sure whether we or other animals have souls. But we can be sure that both people and animals want to keep living. To put it another way, they have a powerful drive to perpetuate their own consciousness. We do have that much in common. Some argue that because the belief in the soul and the afterlife is universal to all cultures in all times, there must really be an afterlife. The universality of the belief, they say, is itself the proof. As for me, through my irreligious coming-of-age, I concluded that the universal notion of eternal life was more likely to be each individual's animal brain asserting its intention to keep on firing across its synapses as long as possible. Perhaps the soul is what you fear with, because the soul is the part of you that intends never to die.

One woman I know won't drive because she and her little boy were once in a car wreck. Whisky feared sticks, and a horse I once knew feared white shirts and being tied because he had once been tethered and scourged by a man in a white shirt. A man I know fears crowds because a circus pole once fell into the audience, killing someone right beside him. A dog once stung by a wasp hates any kind of buzzing. I'm afraid the building I'm in will catch fire while I sleep—before I go to bed I need to know how I'm going to get out without being able to see. Or breathe. Close your eyes. Hold your breath. Hurry. Where are the doors, where are the stairs, where are the windows, feel for the latch— can you open them blind? Now look. How far is the drop?

Almost any quirky fear has a good explanation, if you just listen for it.

To some, these eccentricities indicate phobias, post-traumatic stress disorders, trained Pavlovian responses, but to me, no matter what you call them, they indicate a kind of soul-smarts. If you want to live, why would you risk exposing yourself to something that once hurt or nearly killed you? The wish to live burns more deeply than our consciousness, made visible in the claw marks on the necks of people who have firmly decided, once and for all, to hang themselves. The brainstem learns independently, on the sly, how to survive. It remembers its lessons well, in defiance of reason. It compiles a ready wisdom, one kind of intellect among many we have in common with other creatures. If the soul flickers somewhere in our bodies like a wispy genie, maybe it's in our brainstem, our medulla oblongata, our animal brain.

Patches thought herself immortal. She was attuned to the eternity of each moment; nothing could separate her from the jauntiness of her own wit, muscle, and curls. Heaven is here and now, she seemed to believe, with something like the fervor of a saint. But I longed for more than here and now. I wanted to love God, but how could I love one that deemed my canine friends unworthy of Heaven? It was no lovable God who created an affinity between me and my fellow creatures and then nailed Christ on the cross and a No Pets Allowed sign on the pearly gates.

Years later, when I was a college undergraduate, I retained a thin, irrational ray of hope in the midst of my atheism. I clung to a line from Tennyson, "There lives more faith in honest doubt, Believe me, than in half the creeds." Sometimes, tentatively, surreptitiously, almost perversely, I'd let my imagination go slumming off to where there were souls and a Heaven, a realm as simple as Barbies and a Dream House. And invariably that journey would lead me back to Reverend Van Dyke and his mutually exclusive dichotomies: God and Creation, church and nature, reason and intuition, dogma and experience, humans and animals, adults and children. Probably men and women. For me, the dealmaker was dogs didn't have souls.

But Jesus said, "When you do it for the least of them, you do it for me," and weren't dogs "the least of them"? Wasn't God "the God of the *spirits of all flesh*?" Didn't kindly dogs come and lick the good beggar's sores? And what about His eye on that sparrow? Saving that sheep on the Sabbath?

My confusion seemed to suggest I was an unsalvageable sinner who suffered a great but nonetheless misguided love, like Paolo and Francesca. Patches and I would sweep around Circle Two of Hell for all eternity, on a phantom Raleigh Chopper banana bike and a sled.

In my studies of Western literature I ran across allusions to dogs and birth, dogs and death, dogs and eternity. Although references to dogs were nothing but passing details, they always made me perk up and sniff the wind. I was like a caged animal catching whiffs of my people, my dogs. Romulus and Remus, the legendary founders of Rome, suckled from my Great Wolf Mother. My dogs ran before Diana the Huntress, the patron of chastity and childbirth. Before I'd ever read a word about Lupus, the wolf-headed God of Death, I knew him. I wasn't afraid of the three-headed dog Cerberus, who prevented the living from entering the gates of Hades—like Psyche, I too would've known to distract each head with pieces of cake. Yet, no matter how it made me smile to run my fingers over my secret history, I had to discount it as the stuff of ancient and muddled minds, dead and debunked.

Much more often I was assigned the stuff of clear and canonized minds. I heard professors say things like, "Look how marvelously close Leibniz came to the truth about atoms." Something in me panicked at the idea that life might be nothing more than monads snapped together and humming like motorized Tinker Toys, even though monads were pretty cool. Although Philosophy was heavy anti-faith artillery, the missile that leveled me was fired in an Honors Sociology class.

The university's most accomplished and committed teachers always taught the Honors classes. The university gave them complete license in designing the curriculum. That meant the instructors invested more of their own interests, the students were more engaged, and the courses, often crossing disciplines, were difficult to categorize.

One morning our Honors Sociology professor scrawled a detailed chart on a blackboard that spanned an entire wall of the room. The unit gave us a brief overview of comparative religion. Here on the chart was the name of an ancient African tribe that had to cross a dangerous river to hunt, and below it was the name of their god, a river god. Here was the name of an American Indian desert-dwelling tribe; below it their most powerful god, the rain-bringer. Below the people of ancient Athens ran a list of a few of their gods, which read like so many characters in a soap opera, beautiful and powerful, peevish and passionate. Onward the chart went, around and around the globe, century after century, matched sets of people and their gods. It ended with the patriarchal Catholics of Rome and their great male Trinity: Father, Son and Holy Ghost.

"God did not create man in His own image," the professor concluded. "Clearly, *man* has created god in *his* own image."

The next scheduled office hour, I went to see the professor. I liked him. He seemed like a wolf or a husky—thick gray hair, thick gray beard, deep-chested, intelligent, energetic, and warm-hearted, both adventuresome and eager to serve his pack. I went to his office often because together we played tug of war with the sticks and bones of so many topics like dogs in the woods, dogs in the snow, dogs in a corn field, running and digging and rending. But after the chart on the board, I wasn't up to an intellectual romp.

"I'm stunned," I told him. "It seems so final."

"But this was old news to you."

"That's why I'm so shocked that it hurts," I said, ready to do whatever he thought we should do with it: run from it, bury it, tear it to shreds, piss on it. "I must've been hoping . . . otherwise."

I'd lost my honest doubt to bitter certainty.

I laughed, shaking my head, accepting my fate. "I'm jealous of people who believe in God."

He nodded. His broad shoulders sank against the back of his chair. "So am I," he said.

In twenty more years, I'll be just like him, I thought. I'll have let the gray in my hair come. A wolf-dog too, I'll always be on the move, fighting and playing and searching. I'll have my chance to be alpha. But my deepest craving was doomed to remain unsatisfied.

That day we sat a while, commiserating, and I felt a little better knowing that at least I was part of a noble tradition. Mine was the lot of the post-modern intellectual. I could lean my shoulder against the cold stone of rationality and heave it up the mountain, only to reach the summit and have it roll down again. And so, for lack of any other options, I cultivated existential courage and sour intellectual aggression, following in my father's footsteps. For my injuries, I won academic awards.

Things might have been different if I'd gone home to a sassy fox terrier who, every night, threw her might into breaking the spine of knotted sock.

The college years were dogless. When I left for West Chester University in Pennsylvania, my parents divorced. My father moved back overseas, and my mother took Patches and moved to Tennessee, too far for me to visit but once a year. I plotted and tried to budget and even looked at apartments, but could never figure out how a transient student with a small allowance could responsibly care for a dog. If I tried, too much could go wrong, and I might've had to part with Patches a second time.

Then, my sophomore year, my mother decided she couldn't keep my dog anymore. I got a letter telling me Patches had a plane ticket to Philadelphia. I had no car, no house, no time to think, and no options, but I found a way to pick her up at the airport. At my father's urging, I put a "free to good home" ad in the paper. The next day, a man showed up, said he was newly retired and would love nothing more than to spend the rest of his days adventuring in his new pick-up truck with a frisky fox terrier at his side. Two minutes after his arrival, the man had Patches tucked under one arm, a bundle of her toys, leads and dishes under the other, and he was walking out to his truck, throwing a "thanks" over his shoulder. And he carried the love of my life out of my life forever.

But he did leave me his phone number, address, and an invitation to visit any time.

A year later, I figured Patches wouldn't even recognize me, but I went to visit anyway. There was the pick-up truck, a well-kept house, a big fenced-in yard, dog toys and children's toys—I guessed for grandchildren. After missing her all year, I figured I was in for more heartache; she'd ignore me, her new life obviously richer than anything I'd ever given her. But when she saw me, to my surprise, she wagged her tail until she fell over frantic. Her happiness was so fierce she shrieked with every breath. The new owner and his wife stood by, eagerly telling me stories of their magical dog, asking if I wanted something to drink, but I couldn't hear, couldn't see anything except her familiar, bright, clean face, her cropped tail drumming the floor, her eyes fixed rhapsodically on mine.

"Thank God," she seemed to say, "you finally came." After running my hands over her trembling sides and pressing my cheek where it fit just right in the angle of her muzzle, I left abruptly and never went back.

Easier for me, it would have been, to pass the rest of my life thinking I meant nothing to her. As long as I could tell myself I had *imagined* she loved me things were easier. I could get another dog and imagine the whole thing all over again. There were no consequences for her, I could tell myself, because she was just an animal, and animals yearn for nothing loftier than eating, eliminating, and if the appropriate glands are in place, procreating. Now I knew that I had lost a blessing. I had been a lonely little girl and from among all great, strange teeming lives another mind had come to me, essentially by accident, had gotten to know my mind, had come to prize the time we spent together. She longed for it afterwards, just as I had. To her, the sight of me was cause for rejoicing.

Now I grieved twice as hard. Not only had I lost my friend, my vixenish little dog, so easy on the eye, so full of conviction that there was a hell of a lot worth living for, but she had lost me. Her loss compounded my loss, doubled it. I grieved that I hadn't been strong enough to trust my own intuition in a world that denies the personalities of animals for its own convenience. It's easier to deny the mental acuity and emotional complexity of the particular cat or horse we want to give away, or of the dog—a highly social animal—we keep isolated in a handy cement-and-chain-link run.

Regardless of an afterlife, on earth a soul is still of consequence. To deny that any other creature has one is to invite injustice. If we don't believe she has a soul, we never ask ourselves, "Does she feel pain?" or "Is she lonely?" If she doesn't have a soul, she has no need of communion, of fellowship, of exchanging thoughts and interests—she doesn't suffer. Not only was my little fox terrier, who would've ranked low on a canine intelligence test, capable of communion, she craved it. She gave and she received and she remembered giving and receiving and in so doing her little soul knew ecstasy and heartache.

And so I mourned her as if I'd been robbed of my own compact god.

One weeknight my senior year of college, I sat on my dormitory cot reading The Riverside Shakespeare, a book as dense and unwieldy as a steamer trunk. The now-familiar Elizabethan language eluded me. I was distracted by the effort of forgiving my boyfriend, Gavin, a tall, thin and handsome man from an Irish-American family. For two years I'd thought we'd marry, but now I had good reason to suspect he had cheated on me. My best friend, fellow horse-lover, and roommate Mary crouched at her desk, one narrow knee jigging with impatience, one hand working a pen, and the other a calculator. When I could concentrate on the text, it was only to read a passage and to hear it as though spoken by a wizened grandmother deep within me. I closed my smarting eyes; *where the greater malady is fix'd/ The lesser is scarce felt. Thou'dst shun a bear,/ But if flight lay toward the roaring sea,/ Thou'dst meet the bear i' th' mouth.* Upcoming exams and term papers and laundry surged against the hour, but I couldn't keep my chores in mind when such questions lashed at me: do I love my boyfriend, am I fair, am I just suspicious or is he untrustworthy, what exactly had he said, what should I have said, what did I want him to say, is he as unfaithful as he seems? *Ingratitude! thou marble-hearted fiend.*

The Riverside Shakespeare lay across my bony lap, lines of dialogue unrecanted, unchangeable, concise, freighted, and obscure, but still more decipherable than my lover. Cordelia and Lear are fixed in time, their flaws large and purposeful, their sight sometimes dim even

15

though they're articulate and full of promise, just as I and my lover were. *"We are not the first/ Who with best meaning have incurr'd the worst."* What hope was there for us when even Lear and Cordelia, who acted in good faith and spoke wisely, weren't able to avoid that last scene, when the king carries on stage the body of his one true-hearted daughter? Errors of judgment, errors of omission, plain old bad timing—and you get grief beyond endurance. Lear stoops over her body and cries out, *This feather stirs, she lives! If it be so,/ It is a chance which does redeem all sorrows/ That ever I have felt.* Losing my love, not to death but to unfaithfulness, ingratitude, an ending all the same, I closed my eyes again, felt the pressure of the book, heard the scratch of Mary's pen, knew myself grateful for Mary just because she was in the room, quietly moving.

A knock at the door, Mary's brother Joe came in, tall and dark, a shock of black hair over his brow, whistling and buzzing in one of his many cartoon voices that for Joe, somehow amounted to dignity—our own Fool. "Ready?" he said.

Tiny but defiant, pale and temperamental, a marked contrast to her brother, Mary rose from her desk and put on her jacket.

"Where are you going?" I said.

"The Neumann Th-b-b-enter," Joe sputtered like Daffy Duck. "It's a holy day."

"Can I come?" I said.

They blinked at me. For nearly two years the three of us had lived together, Mary and I in one room, Joe right across the hall. We ate most meals together, traveled, smoked cigarettes and drank beer together, sat up late talking. We said we loved each other. Mary was my best friend and Joe was Gavin's best friend. Mary and Joe, and their parents, siblings and grandmother, made me feel I was something of their late-edition cousin, born after Joe and before Mary, as if I'd been lost somehow and never seen until early adulthood when Joe, Mary, and I met in Killinger Hall, rather the way Jane Eyre stumbled upon her long-lost cousins on a stormy night on the moors. Loved and belonging, I would remain of course forever alien, not quite the same animal, a cross-bred, blond curls to their glossy black hair, atheism to their Catholicism. For their faith in God I'd shown only indifference bordering on hostility. Up until now we'd left that dagger sheathed.

"Why would you *want* to come?" Mary said, which at that time was an especially good question. I'd recently pinned a button on my denim jacket that read, "God is dead and I want his job."

In that split-second how could I tell her, or even tell myself, that it was because of the easy way Joe had walked into the room, patient and friendly, the way Mary, who was generally either frightened, ill, or furious, had jotted one last thing and left her desk without hesitation, smoothly rising, turning in obedience. I thought, how nice to spend one hour without question, to spend one hour doing something simple and good, for an hour, to be relieved of the burden of doubt. I wanted to take our two bodies, Mary's and mine, and walk them in the night air, to carry what we had in the room—that simple side-by-side abiding—to a holy place, balm for my feverish mind.

But what I said was, "I don't want to be alone."

They blinked at me one more time, then accepted my company. We walked together to a place they were tired of and where I had never been. They must have seen I was no threat that night, that my wit, which I sharpened compulsively, had been dulled by activities other than whetting it against the bovine stupidity of religion.

A gymnasium-like room, folding chairs, mumbling and kneeling, standing and mumbling again, here I was just an awkward outsider. I knelt a moment too late, bumbled the sign of the cross, stumbled through a faintly familiar prayer or two, *for our sakes He was crucified under Pontius Pilate.*

"Jesus died for you," an evangelist had once nagged at me, like a taunt, and I shot back, "Who asked him?"

Just when I was feeling more alienated than ever, people in front of me, beside me, behind me, all strangers, all turned and held out their hands. "Peace be with you," they said.

Puzzled and delighted, I'd barely recovered when they began filing into the aisle. I rose to follow, but Mary turned and whispered, "Wait here. You can't take communion. It's just for Catholics."

Two years before, in an effort to recover from a date rape, I got this wild idea that I'd go to confession. I prepared myself. I found the church. I found a priest out on the front steps craning his head to look down the street. And I asked to go to confession.

"It's Wednesday," the priest said, annoyed.

Shivering in the summer sun, fighting tears, I didn't understand.

"Confessions are on Saturday," he explained as if I were a hopeless dunce.

"I didn't know," I stammered, "I'm not Catholic."

"Oh!" he said. Now it made sense. He shook his head at how really stupid I was. "Confession is just for Catholics."

As if to prove to him how unsuitable I was, I burst into most unseemly tears. He showed me his back, walked up the steps, and through the doors of his church. The burden I hoped to leave behind became doubly more ponderous. I half-ran, half-stumbled back to campus, hiding my red and wet face as if it bore the marks of a leper.

Religion once again rejected me. I was the unsuitable one, the insolent one who argued all life has worth in the eyes of God, the one who didn't heed labels—not even those given to the days of the week. This time it left me sitting alone in a folding chair on a holy day in the badly lit Neumann Center, while Mary and Joe joined the smug, the comforted, the ones who belonged and believed and who filed past me, hands piously clasped, chins held high, in line to receive their mysterious gift.

I sat and thought, why not, for one moment, rest my tired mind, let it float? What would I risk? These crises with my boyfriend and my heavy course load were nothing compared to what I'd already survived, sexual assault, my parents' divorce, fire, my family scattered, my dog in a new home. All I had left in the world was the abstract wealth itemized on a computer printout: my grade point average.

Reason kept me safe. Analytical thinking earned me the respect and affection of the most influential professors. Intellect matched me with my academically glamorous boyfriend, whom I believed would be my husband—yet reason helped him lie to me. Reason was all I had left, but it wasn't enough, wasn't what I really wanted—it was a consolation prize. If I left it behind, just for a moment, and fell, I could always regain my footing—I'd pitted my wit against more formidable figures than my two religion-weary friends and their wee, pink-cheeked priest, old as a gnome, who looked his young parishioners in the eye and called them by name as he doled out the factory-stamped wafer he called "the body of Christ."

No, reason wasn't enough. There was more, I knew, because oceans had poured from the pens of Milton, of Donne, of Dante and Hopkins, and I had sailed them. My precious reason was a flimsy raft of sticks that I'd grabbed and lashed together with dissolving twine. If greater minds than mine believed in God, maybe, just maybe I didn't know everything. Besides, bitter certainty that God was dead had been a tiring position for me to maintain and probably wasn't worth the effort—it had made me a mean-spirited evangelist for atheism, compelled to rob dim, happy minds of their dim-witted peace.

When I dismantled people's faith, on what authority did I do so? Reason? Science? Annoyance? Or jealousy? How far did I really see? All things being equally nebulous, at least it was more pleasant to think that there might be places more beautiful and good beyond the fog on my horizon. I was exhausted trying to stay afloat on my splintering raft. And so, when Mary and Joe returned to their seats and knelt amid the sound of shuffling shoes, clanking metal chairs, and the drone, "the body of Christ, the body of Christ," I knelt on the cheap tile beside them.

I prayed, "God, if you exist, teach me to love."

A few people who knew me might argue that I already knew pretty well how to love. The old man who'd waited on his back step years before to tell me Major was dead might've said I was a loving child. And skeptics who knew me might zero in on the absurdity in the phrase, "God, if you exist," and argue that this was the beginning of intellectual corrosion, brought on by fatigue and repeated emotional abuse. My aunt, an apparently devout Episcopalian, phoned me in tears when she heard the news that I was joining the Catholic Church.

She said, "You used to be so *smart!*" Was it smarter to be Episcopalian? Some things would remain confusing.

My father had his own explanation for my ruin—Mary's brother, Joe, being the one male present at the moment of my conversion, must have brainwashed me.

Of my family members, only my paternal grandmother was glad. "I always liked Catholics," she said. Then again, she liked everybody. She gave me a plastic rosary and told me she'd found as a young woman walking through the chilly damp of a train tunnel. "It's a miracle I saw it in that darkness," she said, as if she'd been inexplicably lured into that tunnel just to find that rosary so that sixty years later she could bestow it on me, and only now did it all make sense. I took it as if it were given to me by a child, aware, as I bent to kiss her, that I was still too proud.

Eventually the pink-cheeked priest gave me a rosary too, one made of pressed rose petals. Although I treasured it, opened its little airtight case and sniffed it once in a while, I never said the rosary much. It bored me to empty my mind, frightened me to let it stand silent, like an abandoned beehive.

To be fair to my father, he did give me one moment of acceptance. Dead set against my holy idiocy, one day he marched up to me, a bourbon-on-the-rocks jingling in his hand, and slurred, "The three best men I've ever known were deeply religious." Before I could open my mouth to reply, he marched away.

Poor Gavin, himself a lifetime Catholic, having spent the last two years sharing a bed with me, was reluctant to bed alone. After we cried and argued many hours about the strictness of my newfound faith, he, by the grace of God it seemed to me, agreed to chastity. We accomplished what our friends said was impossible: we removed sex from a sexually active relationship without damaging it. Although we had been as sweet and graceful as twined otters, I was grateful for our little miracle of higher love.

In the year or so that followed, several people, in particular a couple of young, single men, argued that the Spanish Inquisition proved the Catholic church was too corrupt to serve as moral ground (which for the young men, was to say that because of the Spanish Inquisition, I should have sex with them). I don't know what happened to my brain once it felt that first holy flicker in the Neumann Center, but when people attacked my faith by flapping the Church's blood-stained history at me, I tended to fall silent and float. Accused of guilt by association, I never knew how to defend myself when I faced a verbal firing squad, especially when I seemed to them to be splashed in the blood of my spiritual ancestors—anti-Semitism, Renaissance witch hunts, the Crusades, the Albigensian horrors. I was, and still am, unequipped to fight this fight. As if from some distance in time and space, I heard again my own abandoned arguments against faith, felt again what I used to feel when I made them. I heard how angry and well-informed my attacker seemed to be, how intellectually deft. I noted how he warmed to his righteous task of ripping forth the moral inconsistencies, the self-contradictions of an institution that deems the Pope flawless. No matter how I replied, he would swoop for another weapon, say, pedophilia in the priesthood. He might have been right about it all. I wished I knew, but I simply was not prepared to devote years of my life to investigating and amassing the crimes of the so-called faithful, past and present, and then balancing them against the amassed crimes of allegedly faithless. At twenty-one, I couldn't begin to guess which side would tip, or what I should do in response. All I knew was that I'd chosen to be part of a nourishing little community of faith, made of two close friends and a priest I could respect. Why would I turn around and dismantle that?

And oh, there was more. Did I realize, the fervent young men asked, that faith is irrational (and therefore evil)?

That line of reasoning had been my own favorite path to steal along when I felt like bringing down one of the bleating religious. It's reckless to trust the Bible, which celebrates the slaughter of Israel's enemies and blames "the Jews" for Christ's murder; it's superstitious to pray, and it's just plain ludicrous to believe in God—a child's explanation of the inexplicable, a two-faced Santa Claus who pulls from his sack health and wealth with one hand, with the other pain, terror, and poverty. However, attacking faith on the grounds that it's irrational, I later realized, is a tautology, and therefore fallacious—faith is unquestioning belief, complete trust and reliance; we call it a "leap" because it catapults us beyond rationality. At the time, all I knew was that the person challenging my faith and I misunderstood each other. How could I bridge the distance between us without compromising myself?

I wondered about the motives he might have for attacking me. Faith might worry him because bad things have come from the faith of bad men. Maybe he thought faith might misguide him, embarrass him, invite ridicule from the likes of himself, or lose him some questionable pleasures. Faith appears to require submission to behavioral boundaries, a loss of freedom, and a relinquishment of control. It might weaken him. In much the same way that some believers thank God for everything from a promotion to a carbuncle cure, many unbelievers, perhaps unconsciously, credit their successes to the edge their atheism gives them. Opening their minds to faith might be taking scissors to Samson's hair.

Perhaps by attacking me, he was doing what I used to do when I confronted religious people—he was remaining loyal to his own previous declarations of disbelief and reassuring himself that he was free, in control, and unchangeable. Maybe, as I used to do, he was whistling in the great dark night of the Void—the tide, as Loren Eiseley called it, that swirls "like vapor just beyond the edge of the lamp at evening and similarly out to the ends of the universe." Standing in the electric light of reason, peering at the night through the glare of Darwin and DNA, he believed he was facing the dark more stoutly than those of us who went to church to eat the opium of machine-pressed wafers. The very nature of darkness, however, is that there's always more to it than meets the eye of man.

Why had I become Catholic?

I didn't know, couldn't quite say. Sometimes I tried anyway. "Well, I do know it didn't have anything to do with the Spanish Inquisition," I would say. "Something happened to me that I guess hasn't happened to you. In a moment of despair, I prayed a desperate, nonsensical, little prayer, 'God, if you exist, teach me to love.' In the seconds that followed I experienced some sort of physical change—does faith produce pheromones? Something like adrenaline shot through my legs, burned in my middle, flared like elation. In fact, the core of me lit, right near my stomach. It felt like a readiness, determination, confidence, passion. I must have flushed; my eyes must've shone. The feeling came suddenly, as if I was an accidental medium possessed by a ghost. I suppose it must be what's called the Holy Spirit. Inhabited by the sensation of this spiritual entity that wasn't me, I felt I'd never be alone again. I believed that whenever I needed, I could siphon from this presence the strength, comfort, wisdom, and compassion for which I'd been thirsting. I'd have it to give not just to myself but to others around me. I felt like I was better off. I feel like I'd become a more valuable member of the community. I was unchanged, still myself, and yet I had been forgiven, I felt my dignity shored up. I'm free to wander far from my little candle of sorts, if I choose. Near, and I seem to see well and I'm stronger; far, and I'm disoriented, proud, self-reliant, and prone to despair, but it always turns out I've never strayed as far as I think I have. I can agree with every reason you've given to hate the Church, and I can probably think of a couple more you forgot. Maybe my small prayer and the sensations that followed were a psychotic episode that obviously continues to affect me—I don't know. Frankly, I don't understand it, but whatever it is, I'm not going to let you argue me out of it. I'm probably addicted to it the way kleptomaniacs are addicted to adrenaline, runners to 'runner's high,' and daredevils to the flirtatious wink of death."

The few who'd respectfully listened forgave me for my faith. My fiction writing mentor, Paul West, bristled and sniffed, as though he thought this cub might grow into a lion like himself, except that she sometimes had about her a worrisome, alien scent. Maybe she consorted with dogs.

After Mass at the Neumann Center, I stunned Mary and Joe by asking to join the Catholic Church. In my naiveté, I thought, from studying Western Literature, that the Roman Catholic Church was the Original, the other Christian sects mere political or theological deviations, and therefore younger, not as tried, not as true, not as meaty should I really want to sink my academic fangs into this subject. Besides, as a natural heretic, destined to deviate, I sensed I'd be safest if I started as close to Christ as I could literally get—the apostolic succession, a two-thousand-year shoulder tap. Mary and Joe took me to meet the pastor—an elderly, gnome-like, but fresh-faced Irishman named Monsignor Kelly. He offered to teach me catechism downtown, in the same old stone church that two years before had turned me away in tears.

"Unconscionable," the Monsignor said when I told him the story. The priest who rejected me was gone.

Once a week, I was Monsignor Kelly's over-eager student. I read a lesson from the outdated and juvenile *Baltimore Catechism* and returned to him triumphant, pinching between my fingers the thread that would unravel the fabric of Christianity and unafraid to pull it. I scoffed at his God: "*The Baltimore Catechism* says that He denies heaven to the virtuous pagan." So I, a twenty-one-year-old heretic with little to lose, dared the wise and patient Monsignor to defend Him. Each week I found a chasm I couldn't or wouldn't cross, and each week Monsignor Kelly, pink and blue-eyed, white-haired and gentle, filled the chasm in. Patiently, he'd begin, "The Jesuits say . . ." or "Since Vatican II . . ." proving that the landscape was a wide-open plain upon which my mind could gallop, zigzagging like a foal.

Finally, I asked him, "Do animals have souls?"

"Catholics believe that they do, yes."

Chapter Two

The I in the Sparrow

My four college years at West Chester University, I thought at the time, were the rock-bottom, animal-starved years, when getting snubbed by a campus squirrel was enough to make me hang my head. I had a car (mainly so I could drive to Penn State to visit Gavin), a man near West Chester let Mary and me exercise his two quarter horses, and Mary had two old horses at her parents' farm in Lancaster county, so we sometimes sneaked off for horse-time. Horseback riding was an impetuous escape from paper. But however down-and-out animal-poor, I at least had the occasional horse-fix, plus Mary's sensuous penciled horse drawings taped to our cement-block walls. I didn't know how good I had it.

Once I finished my Bachelor of Arts degree, I moved to State College, PA, to attend graduate school at Penn State, where Gavin was already studying Electric Engineering. Although I occasionally had him around, we both led hectic academic lives, and I craved more companionship than I got. Having done the grown-up thing and rented myself an apartment instead of a dorm room, I found myself waking up to nothing but a newscaster's eyes twitching to the CNN TelePrompTer. The only pets my lease allowed were fish or birds, because both are ostensibly much tidier than cats and dogs—I guessed that my landlord had never owned a bird. Since I'd spent most of my life in house full of parrots my mother cared for, I assumed myself experienced enough to commit the next fifty years of my life to a human-parrot union. But a graduate student stipend was nothing in the way of a parrot-dowry, which can run up over a thousand dollars.

Therefore, on one of my first afternoons in State College, when I went out to buy a plastic spatula, a box of trash bags, a cheap phone, a bath mat, and a potted vine to hang in my single window, I picked up a pair of finches in a tiny metal cage and put them on my book shelf. Dubious potential for companionship, I knew, but at least something would be moving around in my apartment other than me, the cockroaches, and a newscaster's eyes. They would do as temporary substitutes until the day I could get myself a fox terrier.

The male finch was sleek, each feather a minuscule scallop of brown, fawn and white. His throat was marked by the bright red slash that gave his species the name "cutthroat." With no mark on her neck, his mate was not much fancier than a common female sparrow, just cleaner. Whenever I moved, they startled and battered the cage, then clung to their upper perch, little breasts heaving. Worried they'd die of panic, I settled on the fold-out couch that doubled as my bed. Slowly I opened a book and moved only to turn a page. By dinnertime, the male was clanking from perch to bars and back with no more wit and will than a pendulum. At nightfall, I covered the cage with a cloth, a courtesy I knew comforts a frightened bird, but these two, at their first sight of a descending cloth, nearly bloodied themselves on the bars.

In the morning I woke to an almost insect-like tweet, much like the ringing of my cheap landline phone, which I'd already dubbed "the cricket." I wondered if the sound was a cockroach. I'd heard they could sing like crickets. The faint, squeaking metallic sound, like the wheel of a doll's shopping cart, had a musical structure: a refrain, a rest, a refrain. I jumped up and answered my new phone. No one was there. The squeaking persisted. In fact, it was such a high pitch as to be nearly inaudible. I stood still and turned my head to locate it. The bird cage.

I pulled the cover off the cage so slowly I barely breathed. The two sat rigidly silent on their perch. Then I backed away and sat myself on the floor to watch.

In a moment the male straightened his bird-bent legs until he stood almost sand-piper-like, ruffled his chest, and began bobbing up and down hard, doing painfully rapid squats, his chest feathers rippling while he made mighty of his watery little song. His head turned back and forth like a sprinkler jet, spraying our world with his song. The tune went forward and back: tweedle-deedle-HAIRNT! HAIRNT!-deedle-tweedle. Rest. Repeat. I phoned Gavin and described the operatics. When he'd witnessed them himself, he named the bird Pavarotti.

Within a few days, Pavarotti's hen was ill. No doubt about it, she rested flat on her belly in the food dish, which was the highest and most stable place for her to perch. Shivering and squinting, she looked like a caricature of a flu-bitten human. I took her to the vet, who took a molecule of blood and pronounced her lungs infected. I was to inject liquid penicillin into her beak several times a day; in other words, I was to traumatize the sick bird every few hours, which I did dutifully, but one morning found her dead on the paper anyway, Pavarotti silent.

The tiny thing had suffered and died, and I blamed myself. I knew that, like parrots, cutthroat finches weren't native birds and needed to be sheltered from drafts of alien air. I had thoughtlessly carried her home in the thin cardboard box the pet shop gave me. It was summer, but how long did I have her outside? Had I fed her properly? I bought a book on finch care and a bird magazine with an article on finches. According to their recommendations, I'd covered the basic survival needs well enough. But finches in stores have often been badly stressed before they ever get stuffed into the flimsy box that reads "I've found a new home!" The article told me the whole bird merchandising process was shameless. The price of the bird, twelve dollars at the time, reflected a mark-up to compensate for mortalities in transit and on pet store shelves. Whether bred in the United States or captured and shipped from Africa, my cutthroat hen had really cost less than two dollars. I had paid the bird market to kill six birds so that I could buy one. Her time with me had probably been her healthiest.

However, I had given her very little to thrive on. Although among the smallest of all pet birds, finches require a great deal of flight space. They don't live long unless in a flock, which almost implies that if not allowed to fly and to interact with other finches (i.e., to use their bodies and minds), they grow pathologically depressed. The handbook recommended a minimal flight cage of six-foot width and two-foot height and depth, per pair. To increase hygiene and add a sense of security, I read, all cage walls should be solid, parasite-resistant wood with a mesh front. I, however, had never seen a flight cage for sale and certainly couldn't afford one. I put the handbook down, went over to the cage, and opened it.

Given that finches are well-known for dying of loneliness, they're usually only sold in pairs, which is the pet stores' one cost-effective concession to the personhood of their wares. Therefore, until I could find a single female, Pavarotti lived with me, loose in my studio apartment. He spent most of his day flying from the curtain rod to the upper bookshelf and back, as high as he could get without hitting the ceiling. He never fluttered into the bathroom or the kitchenette, but he would, if I were sitting still, land beside me on the rim of my lampshade, or even hop on my rug and tug the yarn with his beak. The yarn-tugging got to be a vigorous exercise routine for him, almost violent, his claws scraping the carpet audibly as he yanked.

It fascinated me to have him on the rug, a pogo-ing Tom Thumb in a trim brown overcoat. He explored the carpet as if he'd just inherited an estate. Occasionally he found something to eat. Once he hunted down a spider. Sometimes, with a pang, I could see that he was doing his best to live robin-like. He must've been a territorial ground-feeding bird, a lifestyle thousands of cutthroats were probably living on the continent of Africa alongside humans who ignored them the way I did robins. There might be people there who'd think it a crime to cage a cutthroat, a free bird—I'd heard that in other parts of the world, people kept as their exotic caged birds our robins, our nuthatches, our blue jays.

The better I knew him, the more I regretted the opportunity to know him, because it meant he lived in a small room in an alien climate at the mercy of my limited finances and my amateur finch-keeping skills, which, however, were improving. Pavarotti sang. He called to the birds outside. Twice, he landed on my head, and once on my stomach while I was exercising on the floor. I found myself trying to think of ways to buy him a ticket to Africa. Then one day I saw in a pet shop a female cutthroat who had lost her mate. By now I loathed the pet shops that sold finches. I'd hear shoppers in there, people as ignorant as I had been, choosing a finch because it'd match their new couch, or buying a canary for the kitchen window as if it were a feathered wind chime. A few times I'd had the unpleasant honor in a pet shop of being the one to notice little feathered corpses among cage-bottom debris. With Pav's happiness in mind and telling myself I was rescuing her, I brought Betty home to her mate.

As soon as Pav saw her he attacked her. In fact, if my eyes weren't deceiving me, he raped her. Then he left her alone while she straightened her feathers, collected her bird-thoughts, and surveyed his estate. At the other end of the curtain rod, he was maniacally bobbing and singing and making me wish I were deaf in the upper frequencies. To my disgust, Betty quickly forgave him the rape and the music and joined him on the curtain rod. She did keep about two inches between them whenever he tweedled and bopped toward her. By nightfall, she allowed him to preen her neck. This he performed devotedly, something he had rarely done for his first hen, almost as if he had regrets. I couldn't blame Betty for giving in so soon. What choice did she have for comfort in this strange place, understandably much more afraid of me than of him, a cutthroat like herself?

So I found myself thinking such unconscionably anthropomorphic thoughts, however natural such musings might have been considering that I was alone a lot studying the work of D. H. Lawrence. It was one thing to have a priest give my belief in animal souls the go-ahead, another to undo more than a decade's denial. Besides, I could suppose them to have souls and still grant them no consequence, their lives amounting to no more than the blink of a firefly, evanescent and worthless, bubbles and chaff.

"Lesser souls," Monsignor Kelly had qualified. "The Church believes animals have lesser souls."

Gavin was studying Philosophy as well as physics and electrical engineering, so I expected him to insist that birds are almost reptilian, capable of not much more than cold-blooded ganglionic responses to stimuli. However, he seemed genuinely interested in my stories of Pav's and Betty's affair, watched them absorbedly for long stretches and told their stories himself to our otherwise rational academic friends, who, it turned out, often had bird stories of their own to tell. It made me think that, just as there are certain situations in which it's appropriate to use slang, there are allowable levels of anthropomorphism in certain informal settings, especially in ours, where we students were denied animal contact. Maybe it was a form of nostalgia.

What worried me was these otherwise scientific people sometimes seemed to assume that birds had personhood. When they spoke they had an illicit air, as if they were escaping on an intellectual underground railroad. They weren't joking, and the point of every story was the same: birds are people too.

Such talk secretly thrilled, but also worried me—these two little bird-people were my responsibility. Another thing worried me as well, a question a friend had posed: "How can you take such good care of these finches, and yet still eat chicken, especially knowing how they're raised?"

Like anybody else, I hate having my inconsistencies pointed out. Well, I didn't know how chickens were raised, and so this friend, a meat eater, was thoughtful enough to describe chicken-rearing and slaughter so graphically that for weeks afterward I was fairly uncomfortable with any talk of the personhood of birds. To prevent the pinch to my conscience, I took to studying Pavarotti's and Betty's behavior more and more carefully, searching for reassuring signs that they were *not* people; they were nothing but my bio-chemical toys. I went on with my morning routine of putting a chicken into the crock pot, which I loved to do because the cooked meat slipped from the bone and sank. When I came home, the skeleton floated conveniently on top of a succulent chicken stew.

But one morning from the other room came a new sound, a papery flapping. Head down, Pav was fluttering his wings like a chick begging for food. I watched as I got ready to shower. In this submissive posture the big guy sang to Betty, landing in the shadowy spaces between the tops of my books and the shelf above them, making a baby-chick's raspy cry. He'd disappear between the books and the wall, rasping, and Betty followed. While I showered, Pav dozed by her side preening her neck, the two tucked atop the *Complete Short Stories of Mark Twain*. By the time I was dressed and heading out, he'd gone back to work trying to rid the carpet of its yarn. I had to ask myself, what did human lovers do that was so different?

We sweet-talked to each other, echoes of a mother to her baby. And wasn't kissing reminiscent of mouth-feeding? The finches' mating act itself, as anyone who has ever witnessed it will tell you, is embarrassingly familiar. Later that day when I came home to my chicken stew, I saw that Pav had finally pumped up enough muscle to free some yarn from the carpet. He was heartily ripping it up and carrying it to the potted vine in the window where he and Betty now spent their nights, down near the soil, under the leaves. They were making themselves a nest. What was I longing for Gavin to do, but to marry me, and help me start a family? In fact, I had chosen an apartment over a dormitory because I was eager for homemaking. A little envious of Betty, I wanted a man like Pavarotti who would, for my sake, fight a giant carpet for its yarn.

I drew these parallels between myself and my finches even though I knew better. There's something threatening about empathy for animals. Some people seem to think that it might make them sappy, compassionate to the point of impotence, unable, say, to build a hospital because the proposed site is a field where brown rabbits hop under the delicate shadows of Queen Anne's lace. Yet today we know better than to assume that human characteristics and animal characteristics are mutually exclusive. TV nature programs show us that our disregard for the complex and hauntingly "human" needs of animals is driving many to extinction. Of course, these shows also add that our self-centeredness is the key to the salvation of these animals. An episode warns us, urban sprawl threatens an admirably hard-working species of bee. Without that bee, we won't have enough Florida oranges to meet grocery demands. As we change the channel, cynicism steals in—is the threat real, do we care about animals and environments, or are these nature programs popular only because as we sit beside our ozone-depleting air conditioner, snacking on a rainforest-ruining burger, watching our state-of-the-art TV, we like to wallow in a little guilt?

Rare is the human brain that can contain it all. For me, it came down to the simple fact that each night I grew a little more uncomfortable lifting the chicken skeleton out of the crock pot while in the other room, Pav and Betty chirped lovey-dovey to each other.

Not long after I began to consider that even tiny birds had complex and individual self-interests, I stopped eating chicken, then eggs, then all animal flesh, and I left Gavin, who, resolutely attached to his fledgling life in the dormitory, would not fight giant carpets to bring me yarn for our nest. Also, it turned out that his acceptance of my sudden chastity was less a miracle than a magic trick—behind the curtain he had hidden stand-ins, sexual stunt doubles, exactly as I'd feared all along.

A year and a half later, I married Joe Schall, who was, like me, a favorite student of the acclaimed novelist Paul West. Joe was a physically imposing intellectual I had caught sneaking out of the ivory tower on his way to daily Mass. In the apartment we rented, we made an aviary of one bedroom, with several finch species, potted fig trees, perches, nest boxes, a water bath, a sand bath, plus a yard-sale couch for us fans of avian soap opera.

One night, our mentor Paul West lingered on that couch, eyes glittering with Westian wit and wonder, watching them as they shot and stuck to their perches like darts, turned and fired off their weightless cannonball bodies again, masters of thin air. After passing several long minutes uncharacteristically silent, Paul said, "Air is like water. It always regroups as if you've never been. Your birds are playing at the game called Being Present at Your Own Absence. When they glide forward they've gone beyond themselves and left no trace."

He noticed that the birds, using the air with diminutive nonchalance, didn't seem to mind being present at their own absences, for when they landed they turned around to look at the span of unaffected air they'd just crossed. "We humans are the only ones preoccupied by absence."

"Oh, no," I said. "Absence is all they think about; they're bent on staying present." I told him they weren't looking at the empty air, they were looking at him. "They're ready to dodge when you try to stuff one of them in your mouth."

Paul was charmed to learn that, like his novel's Rat Man of Paris tenderly lining his love's trash bin with a plastic bag, Joe had designed for my birds clever guano-catchers—little shelves beneath each perch—which he lined with paper and changed once a week.

With all the clean space, foliage, sunshine, nest boxes, seed, sand, and chopped fresh vegetables, it was inevitable that our zebra finches, a notoriously prolific species, should raise three broods a year. Rudy was a traditional zebra male with his back striped black and white, an open vest of orange dotted white, a black and white ringed tail, two clownish orange cheek patches and a big red bill. His hen, Jill, was the more unusual zebra, solid white, not albino, just white with an orange beak. Their young joined the flock and paired up incestuously, but never—although they went through most of the motions—actually raised young of their own; evidently a captive flock allowed only one breeding pair. However, female finches regularly lay unfertilized eggs, just as chickens do, and we would find eggs as smooth and small as misshapen pearls, laid, as if with a sense of humor, in the bird bath, on the window latch, on a fig leaf. Once we found one on the telephone receiver.

What fascinated me most when watching these successive generations of homemakers was that each one was unique. Larry, for instance, had a different song, something of a gravely CHONK-kitty-CHONK-kitty-CHONK, nothing like his father's becketta-BACKa! becketta-BACKa! becketta-BACKa! BAY! BAY! BAY! And nest-building was an activity they performed whether or not they were breeding, as if they enjoyed the luxury of four finch-sized walls and a soft bed for its own sake. As the other young ones did, Larry went about nest-building clumsily, making none of the practiced, decisive choices of nest material his father automatically made. Larry turned a bit of string in his beak, dropped it, peeled a thread of bark from a fig tree, dropped that, as if he were discovering the joy of nest materials, the glee of a sharp beak, and then finding how good it was to fly with a blade of dried grass in his beak, how right to wrestle it into the dark nest box where Claudia rasped and chirruped to him, how aimless to carry a length of straw to a perch and break it with his claw. Gradually, his activity became more purposeful, and he and Claudia chose a nest box, stuffed it with string, and slept in it.

Never did I see any of them behave in a way that could be called strictly instinctual. Long before he'd arrived in my home, Rudy, the zebra patriarch, had bungled and gradually honed his nesting skills. Every fledgling's first bath, first taste of sand, first landing on Pavarotti's nest box was an accident, a timid act of curiosity, a bravely executed mistake. Larry put thread on perches, on the windowsill, in the bath, on Claudia's back. They all behaved this way, as if they, like humans, simply did every little thing their minds and bodies could do with whatever happened to be around. To me, their curious, playful, blundering progressions toward self-awareness looked like some kind of faith—in themselves, in their environment, in their tomorrows. When they stumbled, they changed their behavior, almost as though they nursed a growing awareness of finch right and finch wrong. Eventually, through trial and error and some heed to whatever fears and pleasures arose, the young zebras, male and female, all discovered that nesting would put to happy use all they were capable of, but they each found out in their own ways and developed their own styles.

Inevitably one would annoy another. The offended finch squawked and attacked until the accused learned to behave or the plaintiff learned to put up with it. Thus our flock of finches developed its own code of behavior, a morality, a culture, an avian democracy. Our multi-species flock needed some sort of melting pot mentality simply to reduce the stress between such varied lifestyles. Probably several years older than any other finches in the aviary, Rudy and Jill did little except tend their eggs and their chicks. Rudy attacked any finch who interfered or who distracted him by, for example, splashing it up a bit too exuberantly in the bath. The tri-colored nun, Agnes, and her new companion, Oscar, spent most of their time trembling on the highest corner perch, and the other finches ignored them. Comparatively aggressive and even hateful, Pavarotti nursed long-standing grudges, never forgiving Schubert for claiming the wicker nest box, reviling Jill for her successful motherhood. His mate, Betty, we never got to know very well, since she spent all her strength keeping Pavarotti calm. If she angered him, say, having tapped beaks with Rudy, he'd snatch her out of the air by her tail and dangle her screaming from his perch. A bit of an idler, Larry liked to sit in a patch of sunlight with his younger siblings, often volunteering to coach and feed them. Schubert policed the seed dish, Randy and Roberta explored the inside of cages and dressers and cupboards, and Ginny loved to frighten herself by escaping to other parts of the house. I suspect she was searching for a handsome stranger, a new single zebra male with his own wide-open estate.

30

Whenever we entered the room we caused mass hysteria, finches batting the ceiling, conking into walls and windows, tumbling through fig branches, clawing each other for the highest perch. Once settled on these perches or on each other, they froze and watched us, calm as long as they were well above our faces—they never seemed to realize that we had hands that could reach above our heads, even though we'd often used those hands to snatch them off the perches when they needed medicine or a trip to the vet's. Yet they had comprehended things much more complicated than that, such as how to get in and out of the flight cages and how to pull nesting string from the dispenser. I had to wonder whether the idea of hands might be far too strained to the mind of a creature who met the world with beak and wings.

But despite the fact that I'd been told it was theologically acceptable, in some circles, to suppose all animals had souls, it still seemed outrageous to think that a finch might have an idea to strain, that it might make assumptions about another animal based on its own experiences—might avia-morphize—that it might have mirror-neurons and an imagination. My tiny birds might have looked at me and seen a creature with a face, therefore with eyes to hunt them, a mouth to kill them and the will to do so. But no hands. It's the shape of that mistake that provokes me to wonder.

I was always agonized by their fear of me, so strongly did I care about them. They didn't find the game of Being Present at Your Own Absence amusing, and when it occurred to them that their absence might become permanent, and it often did occur to them, they hurled their fragile bodies this way and that, screaming their muted screams. Nothing panicked them more than being caught, boxed, and carried out of that room. It grieved me to have to do it. Having assumed the right to be the sole parents in the flock, Rudy and Jill mercilessly overpopulated the room. Therefore, I had to torture their young by snatching them out of the air and out of their familiar lives.

Other zebra pairs mated, nested, and even laid eggs, but never did another zebra hen become a mother until Jill developed cancer. Rudy therefore tossed her aside for his daughter Claudia, an agreeable, competent finch in soft, classic, zebra-hen gray, with a bright, contrasting orange bill. Like her brother Larry, she had helped raise many of her younger siblings. She'd been nesting with Larry for a long time. Rudy's relentless fatherhood even forced me to turn over young birds to a pet shop. I chose the most sympathetic finch shop I could find, but still, taking them there felt only slightly more noble than flushing them down the john or frying them up Spanish-style, whole, plucked, and split down the middle.

It would've been nice to have a pet that wasn't terrified of me, maybe one I could touch without fear of accidentally killing it. The finches were far more intriguing—and distressing—than they were companionable. They nested and governed their airborne democracy without my participation. We didn't even interact. We didn't talk.

31

Still, I must've been meeting their needs well, because, to my surprise, after a few years, Pavarotti and Betty incubated fertilized eggs too. It was a surprise and and an honor because cutthroats don't normally breed in captivity. I was elated by the proof that my finchkeeping pleased Pavarotti. Diligently he and Betty built their nests, baby-talked to each other, and warmed their eggs, and I watched with excitement. However, shortly after hearing the tell-tale cheeping in the nest, I found a chick mutilated on the floor, one writhing in the soil of a potted plant, another left in the sun to burn slowly. Their blue-lidded eyes, loose pink skin, and unformed limbs shocking me no less than finding a human fetus, a severed hand, a bare, wet, twitching heart. At first, I figured Rudy was playing King Herod the First, but then I saw it was Pavarotti himself. Apparently, Pav's estate only made him comfortable enough to be a good father to eggs, not to new birds, new males who might usurp him.

Infanticide was just the beginning.

A pair of tri-colored nuns in a pet shop enchanted me, not so much with their contrasting colors, white with a jet-black hood and rich mahogany wings, but with their shy clumsiness. The politics of the animal trade aside, I could spare them further pet shop traumas and give them a safe, tender place, so I bought them. A day or two later, Joe and I went away for a weekend, leaving all the birds a couple of dinner plates heavy with seed and water. Quarantined in another room, the nuns had a small cage with a deep dish of seed and a large full water bottle. One of our neighbors, who was from India, promised to check on the birds daily. I showed her the aviary, then took her to the room where the two new nuns, blasting terrified around the cage, would stay until they proved healthy enough to join the others in the aviary.

"Oh, we have these in India," she said, wrinkling her nose, unimpressed. "They live in the bushes. They're really timid. They're everywhere but you never see them."

She later claimed she checked on the birds as promised and noticed no trouble. However, when we came home, I found one of the nuns dead and the other panting and teetering, its overgrown nails barely gripping the perch. The answer flashed upon me at my first glance—the water bottle was still full—they didn't know how to drink from it—one dead and the other dying of thirst! I ran for a water bowl. As soon as I opened the cage the bird zipped to the rim and drank—in that one moment, unafraid of me, meeting her bear in the mouth.

Female cutthroats are prone to getting "egg bound," which is often fatal. One day Betty died with yolk streaming from her cloaca. The wicker nest turned out to be a nasty trap for finch toes, which hobbled many a bird before we discovered where all the toes were disappearing to. All the birds tended to respiratory infections in this alien climate, and I took them to the vet, spent money, caught and medicated them, and sometimes they lived. Because of her cancer, a tumor on her back, Jill had gradually lost her mate, her role as First Hen, and slowly, her flight. Ostracized at seed dish and bath, she was free to eat and drink only when no other bird cared to notice that she was trying to survive. Joe grew fondest of her, maybe because his own mother had raised thirteen children and now had cancer too. Joe spent hours collecting twigs and constructing finch-sized ladders so Jill could climb from her favorite perch to the food and water, to a tree, and to the window for sunshine. By the time she lost all ability to fly and relied on those ladders to live, Pavarotti started ripping feathers out of her back.

The very day we decided to remove her from the bird room altogether, she died in a freak accident. When Joe left the room while in the middle of cleaning it, she must've fallen to the floor, and, unable to reach any of her ladders, hopped out of the room (which she had never left before), down the hall to the rim of the bucket of cleaning solution, and fell in. Reading a book just a few feet away, I had heard every desperate splash but mistook the sound for Joe wringing out the sponge. Dear tiny white Jill drowned in that bucket. Several people have since nodded at her story, soberly remarking, "Yes, she committed suicide."

After Jill died, Joe decided that we turn my finches over to a parrot breeder who kept, along with dozens of other bird species, a few finches in cubbyholes built into her basement wall. Unable to argue with him, because he had slowly taken over the cleaning and feeding against my will, I submitted. I let him give them all away, even my Pavarotti, my first and my last, my long-abiding, nasty feathered friend. I often regretted it, especially when I thought of them confined to those little wooden boxes. What had I heard during my eavesdropping on finch conversation that made me fear so much for them?

Now they inhabit my nightmares. I dream I'm busy, I'm packing for an outing or fussing over a meal before guests arrive, knocking around a house that I've lived in for years yet never seen before. I intuit my way through doors, down halls, around furniture, from room to room leading to stairs and more rooms. I find a wall decorated with sheets of mirrored glass cut into the shapes of birds. I pause, delighted by the ingenious jigsaw carving. I can see myself in the bird-mirrors and think, "These will fascinate our guests." I hurry along and stumble into a cluttered storage room—boxes, cages, dead fig trees still rooted hard in their dried-out pots. Guilt jolts me like the zap of a cattle prod—I've forgotten my birds for *years*! I hear tiny lungs panting, tiny claws skittering. I can't find them—the junk and the cages are the very colors of their feathers—what seems to be a bird is a pile of guano with feathers stuck in it; another is just a dirt-clotted rag. I rifle through the clutter—oh! there's a dead bird, oh! not *Claudia*! another! Who? But a feather stirs! She lives! The head turns slightly, the claw twitches, I can hear a faint rustle. Hurry for water! Another room and more filth, more guano, tangled cages—silent but for the whisper of one stirring feather, the intimation of a last breath.

Chapter Three

All the Animals Dreaming

When I first moved to State College, Pennsylvania, back when I was still a graduate student living in my own apartment, I met an extraordinary woman. She was young but recently separated from her husband, who'd been her high school sweetheart. Struggling against her rural Pennsylvania upbringing, she was all strength and sanity and breasts—she had two small children, a toddler and an infant. But none of this was what made Missy extraordinary.

I met her at a pet shop halfway between campus and my apartment, where I stopped in almost daily on my way home. I bought nothing there, not even seed for my finches—this shop sold bird seed infested with moth larvae. But the shop was open and warm on chilly evenings and offered a respite from term papers and back-biting colleagues and the little note a professor scribbled on the bottom of a shoddy bibliographic review of mine: "You ought to rethink your career." In that shop, I could put down my briefcase and stop pretending I didn't miss having a dog.

I mostly ducked in to escape the rain—it always seemed rainy outside. The store was small, dark, dusty, and cluttered, but served as a social space for other locals. We sat on the floor or the counter to chat the time away, not even pretending to shop. I immediately absorbed Central Pennsylvania twang and melded myself to a group starkly different from the scholars whose lifestyle I'd chosen.

Missy came into the pet shop several times a week, babies in tow, to buy supplies for her six or eight enormous fish tanks and brag about her horse and wolf. She bragged so much, it wasn't long before I didn't believe she had a horse, a wolf, or eight fish tanks. In fact, if I hadn't seen the two little girls myself, I might not have believed she had children. It was impossible that Missy, who had no money and no prospects and no husband and two kids, owned a two-thousand-dollar, second-level dressage, nine-year-old quarter horse. She herself admitted she barely knew how to ride.

That seemed strange to me.

"I bought him for spite," she said. "When we was kids I always told my cousin I'd have a horse one day, and she laughed in my face."

When I mentioned I used to ride horses in college, Missy blurted, "You wanna shareboard?" She needed help paying the board and keeping Shannon in riding form. "He gets to dickin' with me when he needs ridden, and I just don't have the time." She hooked a thumb at the baby in the carrier.

So we went out to the barn. There was Shannon, an actual quarter horse. He had a deep coffee-colored coat and a tar-black mane. His tail was long enough to make him look like he'd just thundered out of a medieval poem.

Missy gave me ground rules: I couldn't ride him for the first two weeks. During that time, I had to observe her tack him up and exercise him. I had to agree to take lessons, I could never tie him up, I'd have to be the one to clean his penis sheath, and I couldn't wear white. All of these peculiar rules were more than acceptable—except I couldn't afford to shareboard. I could maybe swing it for a few months using my tax refund. I decided that I'd do such a good job taking care of him that I'd make myself indispensable. When I finally ran out of money, Missy would let me keep working with Shannon for free.

Something more than spite motivated Missy to keep Shannon when she could barely feed her babies, something even greater than her love for horses—her love of boasting. Missy could boast Shannon's price and training, his extraordinarily long tail that dragged the ground, his temper and grand neuroses. Even though I was paying Missy for my time with Shannon, Missy seemed to think of me as someone she hired and paid, not just to care for her horse but to listen to her stories. Talking almost nonstop, Missy told stories about Shannon, about her wolf (which I never saw) and her dangerous, drunken, foolish asshole of a soon-to-be-ex-husband. She once published an article in a fish magazine about how she was the first to get an obscure salt water fish to spawn, and this she told me over and over because I was getting a graduate degree in English and hadn't published anything. She was funny. Colorful. Devilishly outspoken. After a few weeks, it was clear I was the one doing all the barn work—I was paying Missy for the privilege of working as Shannon's equestrian nanny. She called me almost daily for reports of him, then apostrophized about her boss, her husband, her demonically competitive cousin.

I loved it.

My friendship with her horse became separate from friendship with Missy. In some ways more satisfied by the greater demands of tending a horse's body over tending a dog's, I picked his hooves, oiled the tack, untangled his mane and tail, dragged a shedding blade across his coat, scraped bott eggs off his legs, and cleaned his penis sheath, (one of the most shocking chores I've ever performed.)

Gradually discrepancies arose between Missy's characterizations of him and my experiences with him. Sure, at first he nearly cracked my shin when I tried to comb his tail, just as she said he would. Just as she said, he ran away from me in the pasture. The first time I came in wearing a white T-shirt, he nearly broke his own skull rearing in the stall. But I wasn't Missy. I didn't enjoy telling stories about what an uproarious pain in the butt Shannon was. Soon Shannon gave me different stories to tell.

I slipped into a "don't-mind-me" mode that once taught the mean dogs on my paper route to trust me. Within two weeks, Shannon came when I called him off the pasture, no matter what color I was wearing. He dozed when I "dicked" with his gothic tail. Shannon and I spent a lot of time standing around breathing together. When he saw me, he'd swagger across the pasture and blow gently into my face, and I'd blow into his wide velvet nostril, and then we wouldn't look directly at each other again, because that's how much we trusted each other. Shannon was a good dog.

One day, as I lugged the saddle through the dark, narrow, winding barn with a low ceiling, originally intended for cattle, who don't lift their heads the way horses do, I thought, this is silly, tacking up in the stall when the cross-ties are right next to the tack room. When I got to Shannon's stall, I looped his lead once around the door latch. No reaction. The next time I was out there, I did it again, with a slip-knot, and leaned into his shoulder until he backed up and felt himself tied. Nothing. I tied slip-knots in the stall, along the fence post, in the practice ring, on bolts in the outside wall, and finally I clipped him in the cross-ties and tacked him up like an ordinary horse.

I was more frightened of Missy finding out than of Shannon kicking down the barn. Missy was a little bit scary, as big as her stories, even though she was only five feet tall. Missy had the power to make absurd declarations into fact. For instance, Missy was fat when I met her and swore to me that she was actually a toothpick wearing pregnancy fat—lo and behold, in the space one month she transformed into a stick figure cartoon of her former self. Missy was like The Dungeon Master in a weirdly realistic game of Dungeons and Dragons. If I dared revise her Shannon portrait, she might scribble something fabulistic over my changes: "Shannon hates being tied and when some idiot English major bitch tied him he bit her head right off and trampled her dead body before tearing down the barn and breaking his neck, dead." And lo, it would be so.

Shannon himself was a physical manifestation of Missy's spite against her cousin. So I hid from her the fact that I was listening to Shannon and not to her. But what was the point? I was running out of money. "I have to quit," I said. "I've been pouring my tax return into this, and now it's all dried up."

"You can't quit," she said. "Shannon really likes you. He's been pleasant lately." Then it occurred to me: She's telling other people stories about me! *I talked this English major Milquetoast into training my Shannon. She knows squat, but she's turning into a pussycat.* She asked me to keep working with him anyway.

I beamed for days. The Dungeon Master liked my version of Shannon. Apparently, I was better at revising horses than I was at writing bibliographic reviews.

However, Shannon had an opinion of his own in these matters. Before Missy or I met him, Shannon had been some Olympic hopeful's dressage horse, or so Missy said. Sometimes I figured he didn't like white T-shirts was because he preferred his rider in top hat and tails. More breath-taking than ballet and usually performed to classical music, dressage is a hoity-toity riding style that requires the horse to make complex maneuvers—such as lengthening or collecting stride and making lateral movements—in response to his rider's subtle hand and leg commands. Neither Missy nor I was subtle enough for Shannon. The only time I ever saw Missy self-conscious was in the saddle. "My legs are too short," she said, glancing at my much longer ones. Perhaps she enjoyed bragging to others that she had a duped long-legged, mild-mannered, unpublished English major into soothing her tall and contrary horse for her. In the saddle, she looked not only afraid that somebody would blow a whistle, cry foul, and whisk her off that fancy horse, but that Shannon too might decide her unworthy and dump her.

Once on his back myself, I understood. He *would* dump her. Of course, I had more to fear because I had bluffed my way up there, having lied about my dressage training—I hadn't even heard the word before. I lied only because at that point I would've done anything to be near any conversable animal besides an academic.

When I met him, Shannon's turns were exaggerated by the few years he'd spent as a champion barrel racer, but otherwise he performed dressage rather like a concertmaster barely tolerating us kazoo players. Although having long legs can make dressage easier, mine didn't do me much good at first—Shannon lost his patience and threw me off all the time. I couldn't even "ask for a stop." We walked, and I asked and asked, *andaskedandasked*, and he dumped me. He made a brisk, low dip with his shoulder that set me right on the ground. Although according to my instructor I learned rapidly, I was never a quick enough study for Shannon. During flying lead changes I leaned on the bit with too much weight in one stirrup, and he'd flatten his ears, whip the reins from my hands, and dump me. But Shannon loved me—he'd veer away from the gravel of the ring and gently shrug me onto the grass. His affection for me seemed to make my kindergarten dressage more painful to him, as if the more he liked me the more he expected of me, or as if he came to feel *guilty* for getting annoyed with me. Finally my riding instructor suggested we try learning something new to both of us, such as hunt seat.

To me riding lessons were not a means to a trophy, but more like dog obedience classes, which simply teach you how to talk to your dog. Or they were like the Spanish classes I took when I was studying in Spain—you could kick out the classroom door and *use* what you'd learned. I'd picked up a lot of horse speak in the stall alone with him, but there were so many more things to discuss out there in the ring, if only he were more patient. Or if only I had enough money to take lessons more than once a month. We had miles of State Game lands to talk about, but according to Missy, trail rides were out of the question because Shannon would spook and rear and break my skull on a tree trunk before tearing into the forest to get shot by deer hunters.

However, after my success with cross-ties and white T-shirts, I was getting bold. First, I took him on trail in groups with other horses and riders. He did spook and rear, but he seemed *sensible* doing it—or was I just that prone to emotional contagion? At first, Shannon kept one ear cupped to my voice and asked me every step of the trail, "What was that? A chipmunk dashed across the path! That boulder's crouched and ready to spring! That-there's a carnivorous tree!"

For my empathy to do us any good, I had to heed my own feelings as well as his and to decide whose made more sense at the moment. Many riders, perhaps including Missy, make the mistake of being afraid of the horse's fear—true, a frightened horse can kill you. But rapport with a horse partly means overriding his mood with your own. Emotional contagion is what horses are all about. The trail was safe, and I was not afraid, so I imparted my calm to him—I didn't clamp my legs around him in case he bolted, but instead, sat lightly, legs slipping as his sides rolled. Since horses are reliably empathetic, as long as I stayed calm, Shannon stayed calm.

"I'm afraid!" he said.

"I know," I could tell him, "but I saw the fox too, and I'm not afraid." I'd assert my calm as a baffle to his emotional storms.

If I let the reins go slack, he could pay attention to the forest and not to my clumsy bit-work. True, my instructor might've tsk-tsked, perhaps recommending quite the opposite, and true, he was likely to stay calm if I were calm, but he was also an independent thinker, an honest doubter, and couldn't be completely at ease until he'd checked out the forest for himself. Lengthening the reins, relinquishing most of my control to him, I "gave him his head." After a few weeks, he walked on our favorite path half-asleep, with his bottom lip lax and swinging. Even when the two of us went trail riding without anyone else, he stopped asking me what everything was.

One day, months later, we went out alone. Halfway along our now-familiar trail, he threw his head up and said, "Something's there!"

He wouldn't go forward without knowing what it was, but he couldn't turn his back on it either. We were stuck. I had some options—I could drive him forward with my heels, give him a few good welts with the crop, threaten to break his palate with the bit, yank him into a swirling pretzel the way my instructor had taught me to do when he was obstinate. But I knew him well enough by then to understand that while Shannon might be an irritable snob and a coward, he was not a fool. Repaying trust with trust, I dismounted and lifted the reins from his neck like a leash. I walked before him, step, by step, searching and talking, getting a little frightened myself. Around the bend, what should stand before us but a bee hive, a great big man-made beehive, whirling with bees, deposited on the trail like a pod from outer space.

"Shannon," I said, "this is definitely something."

After sharing a minute of communal staring, Shannon and I relaxed. I got back in the saddle, and we squeezed right past it.

As the years passed and I got to know some of the other riders at the stable, I understood better than ever Missy's self-consciousness in the saddle. I knew why she rarely rode. The stable is like a country club, and someone with nothing but a passion for horses is lower than a caddie. It became clear to the others that Missy was "horse-poor," and I was even poorer than that. I wore torn jeans, tattered garage-sale boots, and a borrowed helmet. I rode either bareback or on a borrowed saddle. I could afford lessons only infrequently. The others probably caught on that I only paid in labor. They never saw me at riding competitions, which require entry fees, trailering costs, and the right duds. The other women in the barn, the ones with eight-hundred-dollar dressage saddles and the latest jodhpurs, the ones who owned and trained their own exquisite young mounts, knew that Shannon was royalty and Missy and I were not. *They* belonged on Shannon's back. If anyone was going to cry foul and whisk Missy out of her saddle, it was one of these people.

However, my instructor told me I had one thing that none of the wealthy riders could buy—ectomorphism. On the ground I looked like Olive Oyl, but in the saddle, I was a pony club princess. Dressage is the ectomorph's sport; the judges strongly favor those who possess the elegance of a long, lean frame. The other women took me on as if I were Cinderella in ashes. Taking lessons made things worse—I got better.

"You're a natural," my instructor said. "There's a show coming up just a few miles from here. You should enter."

I was tempted, but what would I wear? How would I get Shannon there? Where was my fairy godmother?

And why did I go out to that barn in the first place? I didn't have time for it. I had term papers to write and a pile of student papers to grade. Every day in that barn I was an impostor, speaking a language no other human in the barn spoke, loving Shannon as if he were my dog. I'd even taught him to heel.

I was living a language with Shannon; we were merging our two voices, mine of sound, his of body, inventing our own pidgin. Shannon expected me to talk to him like an Olympic dressage rider, and as a dressage conversationalist, I could only frustrate him. We had a language barrier. But, I could defer to his good sense, and he to my kindness; we had faith in each other. By the end of three years, three years interrupted by my exams and financial troubles, Shannon the Horrible, Shannon the Perilous, Shannon the Snob, let me ride him like a burro. I went to fetch him in the pasture and rode back to the stable bareback with nothing but a halter on his head. I even rode him bareback on trail. I snuck a couple of bareback jumps in the ring, just for the ragged tomboy hell of it. Shannon was my friend.

When I got married I moved to an apartment right near the barn. I could walk there daily if I wanted to, but I was still an overworked graduate student. Impelled by the encouragement of Paul West, I rethought my career, officially dropped out of the Ph.D. program and entered the Creative Writing program, which didn't require bibliographic reviews.

In the new program, I met another fiction writing professor, Peter Schneeman, who wore cowboy boots to work just as I did. He'd actually had been a cowboy, out West. When Peter heard me talk about my friendship with Shannon, he gave me a book that argued that animals and their trainers share language, *Adam's Task: Calling Animals by Name*, by Vicki Hearne, a horse and dog trainer and an assistant professor of English at Yale. The book vindicated me both in the barn and in the English Department. In the barn, I might've been poor and unschooled, but now I was sure I was really talking to horses at least as well as the other riders were. Thanks to Vicki Hearne, I knew the time I spent with Shannon wasn't anti-intellectual; rather it called into play much of what I'd learned, not just in graduate school, but throughout my life, as a student, a teacher, a daughter, a lover, a writer, a human animal on a planet alive with animals.

Shannon didn't take well to my longer absences. If I'd been gone a week ,he'd scowl at me with flattened ears, toss his head when I tried to slip on the bridle, and shrug me out of the saddle and onto the grass. I didn't blame him; I knew how much routine meant to him—I was becoming less a fixture in his life than an interruption.

Then Missy ran off with a new man and left her two-thousand-dollar horse behind. That's because, as it turned out, she couldn't take Shannon—she owed George, the owner of the stable, several months of back board. Shannon was collateral. After a couple of months George started saying, "Missy owes me more than that horse is worth." After a year, George could legally consider Shannon his own, and when that happened, and it was sure to happen, he promised to sell Shannon to me.

"Even if Missy wins the lottery and pays me," he said, "she can't afford the cost of trailering him to Missouri. Wait a few more months and you can have him for a song."

Well, I didn't even have a song. And if I couldn't afford shareboarding, I sure couldn't afford full board and vet and farrier bills.

Yet, now that Missy was gone and Shannon was in limbo, a change had come in the way George and the other riders viewed me. I was no longer a possible competitor or an undeserving impostor, but as a kind of mascot, Shannon's stablemate. I had earned the same status as the nameless female Siamese cat who dropped from the barn rafters to the top of Shannon's stall door and rubbed herself against his chin. It was okay to be just an adult tomboy hanging out at the barn doing my best for Shannon. People smiled at me. Maybe all along they'd been less judgmental than I feared. They seemed concerned about me, almost as though they could guess that, whenever Missy swore she was going to move him to Missouri, I'd break down in the stall and cry on Shannon's neck. They shared money-saving tips, showed me how to give Shannon his inoculations myself, and recommended shareboarders, almost as if he were mine already. But he wasn't, and I couldn't forget he belonged to Missy, the Dungeon Master, she who actualized the impossible.

However, if there were justice in the world—and the women at the barn seemed to feel there was—Shannon and I would not be parted.

One day George claimed he was taking legal possession of Shannon. Unable to stand the suspense, I went home, called Missy, and asked what she was going to do.

"I bought him once before, didn't I?" she said. She didn't have a job and her new boyfriend was out of work. She was also trying to finagle a way to have her eight fish tanks shipped out to her (I never found out what happened to her wolf). "It would really help if you'd find two people to shareboard."

"Yes," I said, "I guess it would." Two people paying board would stop Missy's debt from rising and she could start to pay it off. Why would I help her do that? Shannon seemed convinced the best fate for him was to pass the rest of his life in the pasture in his herd of fellow geldings.

Missy got no help from me, but she didn't need it. Somehow, the Dungeon Master found another woman to shareboard—in fact, a colleague from the university. The woman was excited, had a lot of questions. I tried to be helpful. Then, about two weeks later, I saw her in limping in the hallway. She had a cast on her leg. Shannon had kicked her in the shin—she never went back to the barn.

I'm afraid I took pleasure from this woman's mishap. It's not the broken bone I enjoyed, but the evidence that Shannon loved *me*—he hadn't cocked a hoof in my direction for years. It may clear the conflicts between owning or renting live property and cultivating a friendship with an animal. But it also showed I was right to worry that

Shannon had unpleasant days ahead—he didn't like getting to know new people, didn't like his routine changed. Once Missy paid off George, it would grieve Shannon to be carted up and towed over a hundred miles away from this old dark barn and this hillside, reeling day and night with crows and killdeer, barn swallows, insects, nighthawks and bats. His pasture was a rise in the middle of a wide valley from where you could see storms blow in from the north. Belgians stood like flesh-and-blood battle tanks across the street, pigs screamed and stank hidden away in a shed at the bottom of the hill, and to the west lay hundreds of acres of forest. Because of me, Shannon had tasted its leaves.

For some reason I kept going out to the barn. I'd walk across the geldings' pasture until the grazing horses lifted their heads. One of them, the coffee-colored one with the impossibly long tar-black mane and tail, lifted his face and swung toward me, his head low and bobbing, his mane brushing the grass. He broke into a trot until he reached me, then spun himself broadside. His neck curved around me, he lipped my pockets for carrots, he blasted his wet breath into my hands, he blew softly into my face, and his big, black, glossy eye gazed into mine.

One day as I put his halter on and started toward the barn, I asked myself, what do I want now from the barn, the tack, the riding lessons? I took off the halter and just stood in the pasture with him. Then, for the next few late spring weeks, all I did at the farm was stand in the pasture with the geldings. I watched the killdeer run and listened to them cry like displaced seabirds. The flies swarmed on warm days, and the grass thickened to a darker green. The horses ripped grass and ground their teeth. I moved slowly along with the herd for about half an hour, around the time I'd be getting choked up knowing that either Missy would win the lottery or George would sell Shannon out from under me. Either way I was going to lose my mighty friend.

Without Shannon, I would also lose my right to stand on this hill, the highest spot in the valley from where you could see storms blow in. Everything was changing fast and for the worse: the neighboring fields were for sale, some zoned commercial, some residential. Across the street, the Belgians, those timeless giants, had suddenly disappeared, their pasture leveled to raw dirt.

One day Shannon's Siamese cat came mewing through the grass— she liked rubbing herself against all those stationary legs. I carried her back with me as I left, burying my face in her vibrating side.

And then there was this black dog, George's border collie, Sweep. George loved telling me how Sweep zigzagged the pasture all day slaughtering ground hogs. I'd see her slinking against the fence, eyeing the horses like a starved pygmy panther. Black with a white blaze on her muzzle and a white stripe running underneath her from her chin to her tail tip—a upside-down skunk—Sweep would see me coming, know I was heading out to the pasture, and try to block me. She'd stare me in the face. When she had my attention, she'd twitch her eyes off to the side, as if trying to make me look at something. Finally I noticed a deflated soccer ball hidden in the deep grass. I figured out that I was supposed to kick it, which I did more and more often, until Sweep started waiting for me with her soccer ball by the front drive.

One day I spent so much time playing with her that I never made it up the hill to the pasture. There I was, thumping that dull old soccer ball with my yellow yard sale boots when George approached. He said, "Missy paid me."

The two of us shared a moment of silent astonishment. We watched the distant herd of geldings nose its way across the hillside. I couldn't quite tell which coffee-colored horse was Shannon.

"Now she just has to come up with trailer fees," George said.

I shrugged and, for a moment, blinked back furious tears. Shannon would soon be spooking at white T-shirts, kicking people who dicked with his tail, using cross-ties to demolish barns, and freaking out in the woods until deer hunters shot him just to shut him up. It was over for me, likely I may never ride again, and very likely I would never have another chance to love a horse. I finally managed to say, "She'll come up with the money."

"Of course," George said.

Sweep yapped at me. I'd left the soccer ball idle too long.

"She's pregnant," George said.

"Oh, for cryin' out loud." I walloped the ball. Sweep skidded out and blocked it.

"Not Missy." George smiled. "Sweep." He paused, politely looking away so I'd have a moment to take in the implications. "You've got pick of the litter if you want," and he left me alone to kick the ball to the mother of the dog I'd been waiting for all along.

Squinting up at the herd of gleaming bronze backs in the pasture, I tried to decide whether or not I ought to go say good-bye to Shannon. All along, for the last few months, I realized, I had been trying to figure out how to say good-bye. Our little shared pidgin couldn't withstand it—language is for a future together; it's for hope. Perhaps with horses, the most honest way to say good-bye is to stop talking.

Chapter Four

Kierney Talks

During an early period in their evolution, Loren Eiseley wrote, man "crossed over" from the concrete and eternally present realm of animals into a dream world, an invisible landscape of language, a dimension which lay in "his way of looking at the world around him and at the social environment he was beginning to create in his tiny human groupings." We know, however, that many of those first tiny groupings were not exclusively human, but partly canine. The human-dog relationship began in Pleistocene epoch, back when Neanderthals dodged saber-toothed tigers and hunted woolly rhinos with blades of sharpened rock. Because wolves, adept at social nuance, practiced division of labor and developed strong family ties, they were natural companions for humans—playmates, hunting partners, and guardians. We even adopted them as pups and nursed them alongside our infants at the breast. As long as 125,000 years ago wolves were part of human culture; their skulls were meaningful enough to us to set at the entrances to our dwellings. Living Bedouin-style, our ancestors followed the same herds the wolves followed, and by fifteen thousand years ago, wolf-dogs accompanied them. These canines were barely distinguishable from wolves but had shorter muzzles, smaller brain cases, and crowded teeth, all signs that humans influenced their breeding. The interdependence between humans and canines is our heritage.

Our ancestors shaped the wolf into a dog, but, I wonder, didn't the wolf shape our ancestors as well? We know the cooperation of dogs made animal husbandry possible, and therefore was crucial to the beginning of civilization itself, but what about shaping us socially, physically, neurologically? Dogs might have affected our language and the way humans look at the world. When we donned wolf pelts to hunt, had we also learned to hunt downwind, to trot for long distances, to leap into reunions, to sing harmony? Were our senses of smell and hearing stunted by over-reliance on the noses and ears of our dogs? How did it shape our ancestors to suckle pups or to suckle alongside one like a twin—only to reach adulthood as that twin aged and died? I know that parts of my character I owe to others—long-standing friends or those who were close to me at crucial junctures in my life, who either helped me or betrayed me. In the biography of mankind, doesn't the dog count as just such an influential friend?

Kierney was a border collie. She was born in 1988, when formerly just humble farm dogs, had broken out of shepherding trials and into obedience rings where they monopolized the trophies. Few outside farming and obedience circles even knew what a border collie was, and the two groups accused each other of animal cruelty and unscrupulous breeding. They did, however, agree on one thing: border collies should absolutely never ever go to "pet homes." They tried to protect border collies from being bred unscrupulously and sold to people who couldn't handle these overactive, overintelligent, overdemanding dogs.

The danger was real. It may be the border collie's particular misfortune that the very qualities that make it a difficult pet also make it a cool one. They're smart and fast, rowdy and sleek. Sadly true, many people who go out to buy themselves a jazzy dog turn out to be unwilling and unable to care for her, no matter the breed. I have this fantasy that rather than license dogs we should license people, requiring them to pass a test designed to weed out anybody with a tendency toward deadbeat dog-ownership. That'll never happen—like becoming a good parent, becoming a good master can only happen after the fact. Besides, if we licensed dog owners, I would never have had Kierney.

Because adopting a dog with a supercharged brain is an exasperating enterprise that many people have failed, George had second thoughts about offering me one of Sweep's puppies. Bad enough that for years I'd been the undeserving caretaker of a a second-level dressage horse, but now, in an unguarded moment, George had offered me pick of the litter of a breed he wasn't sure he himself deserved.

Small, snipe-nosed, cow-hocked and rough-coated, Sweep had black fur with white points on her nose, toes, chest and tail, her coat bleached brassy by the sun. Allegedly there to control the horses on the farm, from the beginning Sweep had the stakes rigged against her. Considerably larger than sheep, horses aren't inclined to take suggestions from thirty-pound border collies, especially semi-feral ones, which, because George left her alone most of every day, Sweep was. It shouldn't be omitted, either, that the animals being herded must be taught to cooperate with the dog, something shepherds call being "dog-broke." George never briefed the horses about their new canine manager.

The horses did nothing but blink at her and sigh, but Sweep tried to herd them all the same, play-acting. Along the pasture fences she ran, head down, mouth agape, lean and black and intent, wearing dirt paths in the grass from her back-and-forth trotting, freezing, staring, keeping pace, cutting them off, so relentless was the genetic urge. Although she eyed them hour after hour, day after day, she wasn't a fool. She knew they ignored her, and she'd been given an unforgettable lesson in equine etiquette—she once offended a horse who, with an easy kick, shattered her muzzle and fractured her spine. George had found her immobile in the barn. A vet arrived in time to prevent permanent paralysis, although Sweep's muzzle was permanently dented and half toothless.

Two weeks later, however, she'd fully recovered and ran loose day and night, styling her own amusement. She had her game with the wilted soccer ball, but needed a kicker for that. She discovered groundhogs, which, unlike the horses, could be overrun and killed, a sport that pleased her masters and may be one reason why she was allowed to run free. But since there are only so many hapless groundhogs on any given acre, Sweep roamed off the farm for longer and longer spells, seeking something to round up—the neighbors' cattle, their chickens, their children. Just when George was complaining that Sweep was a thick-headed menace who now cost him more in dog-catcher fees than she was worth, he decided to breed her.

That's how it came to be that around the time I befriended Sweep and lost Shannon, George had an unmanageable dog who was about to multiply herself—the vet palpated five pups. George seemed to want to live up to the standards of dog breeders, who maintain that you only breed when you have a list of worthy buyers, but he had bred Sweep without one taker, except me. Not only hadn't I cared for a dog in nearly a decade, I was a graduate student, which is to say I was a vagrant, living on unreliable, poverty-level wages in a cheap little apartment. I wasn't a worthy buyer, but what would George do if he ended up with five adolescent border collies encircling the horses and menacing the neighborhood, the Crips tormenting the Bloods—his own gang war?

So George immediately regretted his offer. "They need constant activity," he warned.

In his oversized-chalet-style house, with its cedar paneling and a window soaring two stories high, we sat at George's kitchen table, my checkbook in front of me, a pad of generic receipts in front of him. The window faced away from the barn, out over corn fields, toward the game lands.

I said, "I never know how you get anything done living behind a window like that."

Unafflicted, George firmly went on, "You can't just lock these dogs in a room. They'll tear it apart."

"I'm home all day," I said.

That was true, but I was home reading Genet and Proust, writing articles like "Cynthia Ozick's Liturgical Postmodernism," and grading hundreds of undergraduate essays like "My Big Touchdown." I had no place to keep sheep in my rented apartment. But, having lost Shannon, I needed some consolation. Just as I once decided I would make myself indispensable to Missy, just as I had once decided my parents would never regret giving me Patches, I aimed to prove to George I would do right by Sweep's pup. Never would he have a reason to say, "I'm sorry I ever let you have hat damned dog."

"I'm keepin' Sweep shut in the pen," he said, nodding toward the tiny window over the sink that faced the barn.

At first, I couldn't think what "the pen" was and besides, on my way in I'd passed the barn. I'd seen Sweep loose and stalking poor smeary-eyed Joey, the spotted pony, who was kept alone in his own corral. Then I realized what George meant by "the pen." It was a four-by-nine-foot enclosure of closely spaced planks, at least four-and-a-half feet high, used, I guessed, to restrain a horse for the vet or farrier. Or perhaps someone once kept a miserable goat there. Or a hog, to fatten for Christmas.

"But she keeps jumpin' out," George said, shaking his head.

I silently cheered to think of Sweep clearing four-and-a-half feet from a standstill. And I wondered why George kept attempting remedies he knew would fail.

"Hang on." He left the room and returned with a copy of Janet Elisabeth Larson's *The Versatile Border Collie*. "This tells you what you're getting into. Feel free to borrow it."

I was tired of borrowing. I was ready to have something of my own. "That's okay, thanks. If there's one thing I've learned in grad school, it's how to hunt down a book." And on a paper scrap I wrote out the author, title, publisher, ISBN and city—I'd phone the publisher directly. And, as long as I was writing, I made out a check and slid it across the table.

With the same worried resignation he'd worn as he said, "Sweep keeps jumpin' the fence," George took the check and wrote me a receipt for a pup.

In a couple of weeks I had Larson's book, a portrait of warm-hearted canine geniuses. I read as if this were the text of a graduate course and I was aiming for an A. I went to obedience shows and watched for myself how border collies had all the breath-taking and annoying finesse of high school whiz kids. I read Donald McCaig's *Nop's Trials* and *Eminent Dogs, Dangerous Men* and understood in my blood the glory of hot-hearted border collies working livestock crowd control. Wolfishly shrewd, border collies were the right breed for ribbons, brilliant go-getters.

I promised George I'd work the dog in obedience, just as I'd worked Patches in 4H. I'd take her to real shows and we'd earn the Companion Dog title in my dog's first year. In her second year, we'd win

Companion Dog Excellent, and right after that we'd get the Utility Dog title, which is like a dog's Ph.D. "I not working on my own Ph.D. anymore," I actually argued to George, "so I can dedicate myself to helping my dog get hers."

Maybe I'll also train her in tracking, and we'll ruin drug dealers, rescue lost children, unearth corpses, I thought, because the more I learned, the more I wanted that dog. In anything and everything from fly-ball to tracking, agility to sled dog racing, border collies are keen and joyful, and in their joy, in their radical abandon to speed and precision and diplomacy, they're God's own superstars.

One morning George called me. "I've got five pups on the ground."

I raced over, but there wasn't much to see. Down in the basement, around the corner, George opened a door to a small finished room which usually served as a combination office and sewing room. Sweep shot out, jarred me in the chest and face, gave me a pointed look, then ran upstairs, I guessed, to tear outside and stare insistently at her soccer ball.

"She probably has to piss," George sighed. He left me alone with the pile of still, black-furred pods, the mammalian answer to larvae. They lay piled on newspaper in the chilly center of a wide, shallow whelping box, about six-by-six feet with a wooden rim only about four inches high, not enough to contain even a turtle. In one corner of the box, a few damp-looking towels were jammed and layered with fur. Gingerly, I knelt and leaned forward, breathing the sweet scent of fresh puppies, urine and dog flesh, tiny paws and tiny ears. Petting them with one finger, I could barely feel their fur, as fine as the breath of sleep. It almost defied sense that they would soon transform into beasts like the one that had slammed into me at the door. They seemed designed to end here, under the nose of a raccoon or fox, a warm, compliant meal.

Sweep and George didn't come back. The pups didn't do anything except rest in their tangle of raw and impotent hope. So I went upstairs where George was putting away dishes.

"Sweep ran off," he said, crossing to that window—a glass wall—from where we could see almost the entire western expanse of the valley, Spring Creek like a wrinkle in its green face. Somewhere between Nittany and Bald Eagle Mountains Sweep ran, having recovered from whelping the way she did from every other blow to her body, supernaturally.

Soon the pups were tumbling over the low lip of the whelping box and inching over the newspaper as if blind and reading Braille with their chins. Notepad on my lap, I sketched each of their blazes—their one distinguishing white mark—and drew a nose in it. I dated it 4/27. George stood over me, his expression flickering between doubt and scorn at what would probably turn out to be some long, looping, academic road to something commonsensical, something to which other people merely took the well-worn short cut and said, "I like this pup."

"They look so much alike," I explained.

"They do," he agreed.

"And I'm afraid I won't remember them between visits." Each had a slightly different blaze—two were almost identical, but were mirror-images of each other. "These two look just like Sweep."

Warming to the idea, George held my models still for me. "These three are marked like Max, except *he's* red. These dogs will be able to have red and white offspring." He confided that he planned to keep one pup and breed it to produce red and white border collies.

"Do you know yet which one?" I asked.

He shrugged. "It doesn't matter."

Even though my experience with border collies had barely begun, I was already forming opinions, largely influenced by authors like Larson and McCaig. You don't breed border collies for coat color. You breed for good health, stable temperament, and working ability. You breed for maximum human and canine happiness, not eye candy. I bit my tongue.

"But I would like to have one I can control," George said.

Having kept mum about Sweep's lack of training this entire time, it was a relief to finally suggest, "You could go to obedience school."

"I took Sweep," he nodded, as if it had helped.

I lowered my eyes to my sketch pad. George lifted each puppy one by one and told me what he could so far. Beside each puppy portrait I wrote a few observations about the pup's character.

"This one's the runt," he said, handing me an almost solid black female with small dabs of white on the nose, toes, and tail tip, marked exactly like Sweep. "She was born last, and she's smaller, but she seems brighter than the others. She gets the best teats and nurses the longest. She's catchin' up fast."

I wrote, "Female. Thinner than others. Active, barking, holds her own. Black ruff."

Each week after that, George made a strong case for the runt. Having decided I wanted a female, I had only two to choose from, one the runt. The other female was a beauty—a wide, even blaze down her face, a full ruff like a white mink stole around her neck, the white on her legs like elbow-length opera gloves.

"Shepherds will want the white so they can see their dog in the dark," George said, suggesting it would be proper of me to leave the dog with the utilitarian markings to someone who could suitably employ them. "Besides, she's an idiot."

But the runt, one of the two marked just like Sweep, was abnormally intelligent, George said. "Instead of her mouth she uses her paws to move things—that's a sign of intelligence. Anymore she's the alpha female." The male, her mirror twin, black with small white points, was the alpha male, and the two played together, excluding the others.

"She'll make an excellent obedience dog," George said, as if he knew all about obedience. "You could really win some ribbons with her."

However, whenever I came in the room and the other pups plopped over the lip of the whelping box to greet me, the runt skulked in the other direction. In most of my photos of the litter, she sits alone with her back turned to me. The pretty female leapt on me, crawled into my lap, looked me in the eye. Everything I'd read about choosing a puppy recommended an outgoing one: "Make sure the puppy you choose is bright-eyed, friendly, and curious," Janet Elisabeth Larson advised.

I sat down on the newspapered floor. Well, I thought, now that the pups are four weeks old, George has other buyers looking them over. He knows the Shirley Temple pup will be easy to sell. I called her "Dimples." As the four friendly pups bounced their round, pink bellies against my crossed legs, I watched Dimples for signs of idiocy. Her eyes were as sharp as her teeth. She was quick after the squeak toy I pulled from my pocket. She amiably deferred to her brothers. Of her at two weeks I wrote, "Female. White ruff. Plump. Passive, whimpers, bottom of the puppy pile."

Alone in the far corner of the whelping box, the sullen female had grown as round as her siblings. At the sound of the squeak toy, she slowly turned her head, met my gaze, then lowered her eyes and squarely showed me her back, as if in some kind of protest—was she jealous? Disgusted? Afraid? Scooped into my lap with the others, she relented softly, lips pressed together and ears slicked back in worry. While I stroked her, she examined my hand like a cat who didn't trust me not to muss her fur. When she relaxed and her attention strayed from me, she pinned her twin, the alpha male, with one paw. She closed her mouth around his muzzle until he shrieked. Somehow, lying in my lap, she won the squeak toy from the others. She picked it up, trotted back to the whelping box, tumbled over the rim, and placed the toy in the far corner. The others followed her and soon had the toy to themselves again, but the little black one was now sitting just as she had been when I'd nabbed her and dragged her to my lap. She seemed satisfied simply to have gotten the squeak toy away from *me*.

I called her "Kierney" because I'd read somewhere that "Kierney" meant "little black one," (actually spelled "Kearney"). Although George said she had earned the rank of alpha female by wit, I was starting to suspect that, watching her sulk and bite, the runt got what she wanted by being so energetically disagreeable that her litter mates either ignored or humored her. She was more outcast than alpha.

"Avoid the timid, shy types, since they tend to develop into fearful or poorly adjusted adults unless given lots of attention," Larson warned. Whether on sheep or on show, Kierney would be short-tempered. She'd collapse when pressured or corrected. On farms, many sheep dogs are kept outside alone, which might suit her, but the more time this one spent alone the less likely she'd be to cooperate with her shepherd. Easily frightened, she hid and she bit. In fact, she was an untrustworthy, unlikable animal and would only worsen unless someone who understood her gave her lots of attention: someone who, for example, had once tamed nasty dogs on a paper route or won the prickly heart of a snotty second-level dressage horse.

George joined me in the basement. "Look at my walls," he fumed. The wallpaper had been ripped off the bottom three feet. The baseboards had been gnawed to splinters. "We had to move the chairs out of here."

"I noticed," I said. "Where's Sweep? I never see her."

"Neither do we. She did that," George said, pointing to gouges on the wall by the door that looked like the mark of a passing bear. "I have to hunt her down twice a day and drag her in to nurse the puppies." He frowned over the month-old vermin, who snarled, shredding the newspaper. "They're almost weaned." Folding his arms, he paused. "I'm letting them go next week. Which one you want?"

I needed more time. I started ask if five weeks wasn't too young, when George sighed. "I'm gonna haf' to completely remodel this room," he said, hiking up his pants.

Which did I want? The beautiful, outgoing but passive one? Or the plain, assertive but ill-tempered one? I sat on the edge of the whelping box. I leaned over and looked into Kierney's face. She lowered her eyes, shifted her back to me, then suddenly pounced on her favorite brother, snarling marvelously. "The little black female," I said. "She's mine."

Although he'd nudged me toward the lousy dog all along, George suddenly thought twice. "You're twenty-five," he said. "You're a newlywed. Border collies aren't good with kids, you know. Especially that one."

George sometimes seemed to make a habit of contrariness. The very book he had recommended to me, Larson's *The Versatile Border Collie*, presents border collies as excellent companions for children. But it was true that my little black puppy wouldn't take to the unpredictable grabbings of a child.

"No problem," I shrugged, half resenting his assumption that just because I was a young newlywed I'd be itching to procreate. "Joe and I decided not to have kids."

Like a lot of highly educated young couples, my husband and I decided that, given world-wide destruction of the environment and the depletion of natural resources, we couldn't in good conscience burden the planet with even one more gluttonous American child. Besides, Joe, the eldest son in a family of thirteen, felt he'd already raised about ten kids.

"No," I told George, placing Kierney firmly on my lap, "we won't be having children."

When I was a child, I used to say, "When I'm grown up, I'm not going to have babies, I'm going to have puppies."

But I loved dogs because they were *dogs*. Kierney would be my dog, not my surrogate child.

After I'd promised George that for the sake of a dog I'd go childless, I went home that evening perplexed. We lived near the farm along the crest of a steep ridge overlooking a highway. Our sun-scorched apartment was one of a dozen in a series of single-story barracks-like boxes, each with a wet basement beneath. Although in late spring the days hadn't yet gotten hot, it was already too warm in our narrow, airless, darkly-paneled rooms, where we kept the windows facing the highway closed against the din. Our finches had beeped and thumped onto their perches for the night. Joe sat in the living room grading student papers on the coffee table. In the kitchen, I began cooking tempeh and rice, a nutritious, low-fat, environmentally friendly, humane meal. This was just after the little white finch Jill drowned in the cleaning bucket, and we'd arranged to pass the heartache of caring for the birds to someone else.

Unscrewing a bottle of soy sauce, I thought, "We've loved them too much." If we had loved them less, perhaps we'd be strong enough to love them longer.

Joe had said, "I couldn't stand it if the puppy killed one of the birds."

"Joe?" I said, because our apartment was so small he could hear me no matter where he was. "If we're too sensitive to care for the birds, and we're too poor to take care of a horse, how're we going to take care of a dog?"

"A dog is just right for us," he said.

I smiled, chasing bok choy around my wok with a wooden spoon.

He said, "Lees, you're a dog person."

Finally! I was going to have a dog, not a child. If allowed, would I have made a good mother, or would I have given up, worn thin by heartache, run out of money? Having children might submerge my heart like an ancient forest rolled underground and gone to coal, and then I could burn for my little ones for twenty years or more. But childless, would I love this dog too much and burn my heart too fast, crackling and roaring into nothingness, like kindling?

With the fervor of youth, I loved animals so hard. Boycotting meat products, I cooked soy, God's "people chow," the food of nonviolent protest against an economy that sanctioned factory farming, which was the industrialized abuse of livestock. Joe and I helped bring experts to Penn State to speak about what was immoral about amusing our tastebuds with animal flesh or about scientists who padded their resumes by torturing sentient creatures. My bookshelves held *Animal Liberation, The Cruel Deception, Animal Factories, The American Hunting Myth,* and *The Power of Your Plate*. Were these just hoarse cries in the desert, heard only by we few who wouldn't even eat locusts or honey? I was equally against cruelty inflicted upon humans. Joe and I wrote letters demanding the release of Nelson Mandela, the divestiture of Penn State financial holdings in South Africa, and the boycotting of sweatshops all over the world. I cooked from *Ecological Cooking, The Complete Vegetarian Cuisine,* and *Diet for a Healthy Planet*. As far as I knew, I had nothing in our freezer, in our refrigerator, in our cupboards, or in our closets that had injured any creature or anyone—I loved life. I was a "biophile," but did I love too much?

Joe got up to set the table, his broad, strong back crowding the narrow kitchen as he reached for plates and laid out flatware.

"Biophiles burn out," I said, spooning stir fry onto our plates. Something seemed wrong—if you loved life, you devoted yourself to the broader cause, which was an abstraction—the letters and the lectures, the fundraisers—those things that were *not* alive. Things that did not love you back. That was how you burned out. We sat at our table. "George said our pup'll be dangerous around kids."

"Won't matter," Joe said. He slurped from a can of Mountain Dew.

It occurred to me, ironically, that the average American dog consumes more resources than a human of the Third World. But I was going to have a puppy. A puppy! "Joe!" I cried, because I would make the best of my lot, "We're going to have a baby dog!"

"I know, Sweetie." He squeezed my hand. "So what's the matter?" Having swiftly finished his meal, he rose to fill the sink with suds.

"I don't know." I handed him our plates. But I did know, or rather, I intuited trouble, but couldn't quite articulate it to myself: as a dog owner I would face more scorn from all quarters. Border collie people would look down on me for not keeping sheep. Animal rights activists would accuse me of self-indulgence, saying I should have adopted from the SPCA, even though they believed that breeding and dog-selling should be done the way George had (almost) done it or not at all. And then among my colleagues in the English Department, my dog would be a sign that I had divided my energies, invested in something besides publication and diluted my career with a loathsome middle-class interest.

I was a young, earnest, over-achiever who craved external validation from too many competing communities. I was a student who adored literature but wasn't quite able to sell herself among the self-absorbed *literati*, whose numbers were multiplying exponentially even as they put themselves up for auction in a dwindling market. I was a lover of purple mountain majesty and fruited plains and pledged allegiance to a nation that razed ninety-five percent of its ancient forests, turned its fertile land into dust basins, that tortured and killed millions of livestock animals every year. The planet continued breaking out in its angry neon rash—Mac Donald's, Wendy's, Wal-Mart—no, no, nothing is precious, nothing lovable in a world without miracles. Love and hope and activism weren't enough.

"Keeping a dog will be one more thing to be ashamed of," I said.

"It'll be one more thing to love," Joe said. "You can risk it."

And so I took into my arms the little pup who turned her back on the world.

The day was giddy. We had a metal crate, squeak toys, chew toys, food and water dishes, a lightweight leash and a tiny collar. As the dog care books recommended, I'd stocked up on the puppy food Kierney was already eating—I would explore the vegetarian dog food options later. A few days before Kierney turned five weeks old, I had taken an old towel to the whelping box and left it mixed in with the others. I even had film in my camera.

Saturday morning, the very day the pups turned five weeks old, we drove our little new powder blue energy-efficient Toyota hatchback car to George's. As we pulled up, Sweep tore out of the barn, raced to the middle of the overgrown yard, and dropped onto her belly, which looked strangely red and hairless. Her eyes twitched to the left, to the left, where her rucked soccer ball lay in the weeds. I gave it a swift boot for old times' sake. Sweep shot away, kicking up divots as she scrambled to block it.

George came out to meet us.

"Can a dog like that go running with me?" Joe asked. An ex-football and rugby player, a lifetime runner, mountain biker, and racquetball whiz, Joe had always imagined he'd marry a woman in running shoes, one who'd match his stride beside him. But he fell in love with me, a woman without speed or stamina, and ever since, he'd been running alone.

"This dog can run a coupla marathons a day," George shrugged. "Look at her now. We just spayed her yesterday."

Incredulous, Joe walked over to pet Sweep. When it occurred to her what Joe intended, she gave a small snarl of irritation and twisted away, swiftly repositioning herself, the better to intercept the ball should any one of us get smart enough to kick it. Joe walked back toward us, not looking nearly as chagrined as I knew he was.

"These aren't affectionate creatures," I told him, thinking that maybe I didn't like or respect that Sweep-dog after all and maybe we should've gone for a cockapoo.

Today the farm seemed torpid with green grass, mud, and flies, the glare of sun off the summer haze oppressive, the land devoured by builders, who, in a matter of weeks, had laid roads and house foundations on what had been the Belgian's pasture.

Sweep had abandoned her puppies weeks before, which seemed somehow synonymous with the developers across the street and an economy that drives people into their cars and careers and shopping malls, away from their children, away from each other and the land. Sweep was an "eighties" animal.

"Does she even see her pups anymore?" I asked, knowing the answer and turning toward the house.

"Nah," George said, following me. "It's been a week or so."

As we made our way to the basement, George quizzed, "Do you have a crate? Do you have dog food?"

"Plenty, thanks."

George entered the tattered room first, muttering, "I'm trying to paper train them." There were only two or three sheets of newspaper on the floor now, but the puppies had shredded and scattered them. He replaced them so that they covered one small corner. "Obviously," he said, deftly wiping up a turd, "they haven't quite gotten the knack."

"Hi!" I cried when we saw each other. I sat, and the mob rushed me, four tiny smooth noses bumping mine, four petal-pink tongues licking my face, four pairs of paws scrabbling at my chest. I wrapped my arms around all four little bodies, and they knocked into each other, snarling and tumbling over, pink bellies rolling. I couldn't resist rubbing those tummies, little Buddhas, pure, freckled luck.

Joe knew Kierney was the one who stayed alone on the far side of the whelping box. She sat on the pile of towels, facing me now, tail wagging, alert and solemn. As he neared her, she stood, her tail held high, as short and thinly-furred as a goat's. He stroked her head, and she sat again, ignoring him and watching me intently. The attention I'd been paying her had made her curious.

"Grab the towel," I said, and he pulled our towel out of the heap. He scooped Kierney into it and handed her to me.

"Well?" I said, grinning at George.

"Good luck," he said and held the door open.

In the car during the half-mile ride to our place, Kierney sat on my lap, calmly looking around: the dashboard, the window knob, the arm rest, the gear shift. Once, she stretched out her nose and gave one sniff to the seat belt strap. When we arrived, wrapped to her shoulders in her towel, she allowed herself to be carried to the little patch of grass by our front door. Set free, she sat down, stood up, walked a few steps, stopped, suddenly bounded a few times, stopped again, squatted, and piddled.

"Good girl!" we cried. Ears flattened, eyes wide, she cowered. "Good girl," we whispered. "It's okay." Joe and I beamed at each other. Oh, but she was a bright girl.

We placed her in the kitchen with her dishes, toys, and the crate, into which I spread the puppy-scented towel, a hasty nest. Sitting on the floor, backs against the stove, Joe and I watched. Kierney blinked at us, blinked at the rubber gorilla squeak toy, the puppy-sized Nylabone, the knotted sock, and a few other toys. I squeezed Joe's hand—her head was so broad and round, her pointed muzzle tiny and tender! Here she was, in my kitchen! She walked to the crate, leapt over the rim, turned a circle or two on the familiar towel, then sat down on it, looking out at us.

"Wow, she's cute," Joe said.

"She knows the crate's hers," I whispered. For a moment, I worried she'd never come back out, but she dropped over the rim, trotted to the gorilla, picked it up without squeaking it, and put it in the crate. One wary eye on us, she did the same with the sock, the Nylabone, and the other toys. "She knows those are hers," Joe said, astonished. All her new possessions safely stored in her den, she sampled water from her new dish and crunched one piece of dog food. Sitting on her tiny rump, she looked up at the counter, the tabletop, the walls, windows, ceiling. She yawned. Her head drooped. A moment later, curled like a tiny guard dog on the kitchen floor in front of her crate door, she was asleep.

"She's going to be fine," Joe whispered, slipping from the room.

I settled into a kitchen chair to stare at her, but the doorbell rang. Joe's brother David, his wife and their four kids had dropped by unexpectedly—the only time they'd ever done so.

"Hey!" I heard Joe say. "You're just in time to meet our new puppy!"

Kierney lifted her heavy head on her tiny neck. "Wait!" I called. "Wait outside. I'll bring her out." They all waited noisily in the front yard. I carried Kierney's tiny hot body, sat on the front step, and put her in my lap. "Don't crowd her," I said, because three little boys and a girl came at us, all of them huge, their hands plunging for her. "She's only just left her home for the first time. She's shy. One at a time, please!" I cried, feeling Kierney back against my stomach—I wished I had a pouch she could slip into. The four kids were a young and competitive bunch and none would stand idly while one of their siblings enjoyed the privilege of touching a real live puppy.

"Kids, listen to Aunt Lisa," their mother said. Michelle was a beautiful, compact and capable woman, matter-of-fact, with a ready laugh and a ready swat should a child misbehave.

"Aw, she's so cute," little Christine said, watching my face to see if I was pleased.

I wasn't. "She's frightened," I said, my pulse speeding. On the one hand, this was just the kind of conditioning this pup needed—the children were doing nothing wrong, there was no danger. But she was only five weeks old, this was her first day away from her whelping box, her first day with me, and what if her first experience with children was that they crowded her and wouldn't back off even when she cringed, even when she hid her face, even when her protector gave them firm warnings? "One at a time!" I snapped.

"Are they hurtin' her, Lisa?" Michelle asked in her Central Pennsylvania sing-song.

"No." They weren't doing anything wrong. I thought that perhaps Kierney was afraid because I was afraid for her. I empathized with her too much; I let her control the mood. Already I couldn't tell us apart.

"Which brat hurt the puppy?" David teased. "How would you like me to pull your tail like this?" He pinched his oldest son on the seat of the pants. The boy whirled and landed a well-practiced punch square on his father's stomach. And so they began one of their mock brawls.

I was left with only three cute kids crowding us like ogres, breathing and talking, six hands poking so that I could smell them and feel them and think of nothing else. For my pup, I had to act as if there was nothing to fear, the way I did when I first took Shannon into the woods. But what if Kierney felt exposed and unable to trust me?

"She's had about enough," I said. "I'm takin' her in."

Calmly, gently, I wrapped my hands around her middle so she would feel secure as I lifted her. I asked them to step back and stroke her one last time. Suddenly, her little body rumbled and before I could cry out she bit the smallest boy!

"That's what you get for not listening to Aunt Lisa," Michelle said, examining his finger while he cried. "Oh, that's nothing," she said in her perky way. "Shake it off."

I stood clutching my pup, horrified, apologizing, overwhelmed by how fast everything happened—only about two minutes total had passed.

"He's fine," she said. "Don't worry about it."

"Are you crying because of a *puppy*?!" David said. "Here, I'll give you something to cry about." He swatted the boy's buzz-cut scalp. His littlest son gladly accepted the invitation to recover his dignity and gave his dad a jab every bit as deft as his big brother's.

Seeing Christine's solemn face, I said what everybody was thinking, "Puppies and kids should be able to play together. I'm sorry. This puppy's terribly shy," I said, clinging to my bad baby dog. Any one of the other four puppies would've tumbled on the grass with these good-hearted brats. Joe and I exchanged a glance of alarm. "Maybe it's not too late to trade her for Dimples," I joked.

Perhaps I'd made a mistake in holding her firmly—maybe she felt more trapped than secure. I knew she'd had enough—maybe I should've ended the visit a moment sooner. But how much indignity must a dog withstand? If a dog doesn't wish to be "ooh-ed" and "aw-ed" over and stroked by strangers, why should she have to take it? We seem to think that most dogs are "doggies" and should enjoy nothing better than an endless troop of cooing strangers tousling their ears, and maybe most dogs do—but not all. I believed that cute dogs had as much right to be spared unwelcome touching as cute women.

Kierney relaxed in the safe height of my arms and knew that I understood her—she had given them fair warning and those kids should've backed off. And I had asked too much of her. We both would learn to do better.

That night she cried in her crate in the kitchen, a wire crate with a blanket over it like a bird cage. I fretted in the bedroom just a few yards away, feeling that it was akin to cruelty to ask a five-week-old puppy to sleep alone in a strange place. "It's okay," I called to her. "I'm right here."

She yelped back.

During the night I took her outside two or three times and stood over her in the night air, feeling the dark slide through my thin robe, sensing more than seeing her tiny black body move along the black grass.

Against my intuition, I obeyed the dog training books and conventional wisdom, keeping her crated at night. We went on like this a couple more nights, each night her cries weaker and the silences longer . . . depression . . . despair . . . learned helplessness. When I said, "Bedtime," she walked, reluctantly, into her kitchen crate.

Then one afternoon I spent hours on the bed marking student papers while Kierney slept under the dresser. That evening we had trouble.

When I said "Bedtime," she darted into the bedroom.

Although she kept slipping from my hands, I finally threw her in the crate and slammed it. When I lay down and turned out the bedroom light, she started a sharp steady bark, not a warning to an intruder or a puppy's cry for attention, but a loud, edgy, scolding bark, an annoyed bark, a self-righteous bark.

"What's that about?" Joe mumbled.

I remembered Shannon, how he'd learned to be unafraid on trail rides, and his fear returned only when he saw that extraordinary beehive. I got up, shuffled down the hall, turned on the kitchen light, and pulled the cover off the crate.

I'm five-foot-nine, and Kierney at that point was less than twelve inches. As if to say, "This had better be good," I stood looking down from my full height at her tiny round face, turned at me wide-eyed through the bars of the top of the crate. "Show me," I said, a phrase I was using for moments when she was trying to tell me something and I was going to let her explain herself. I opened the crate.

She dashed out, through the kitchen, down the hall, into the bedroom, and dove under the dresser.

Sitting down, I balanced on the edge of the waterbed frame in the dark. "Joe," I said.

"Mm?"

"Kierney's making us a proposition."

Snapping on the light and squinting, Joe sloshed to the side of the bed and peered down.

She lay stiffly on her belly, fore- and hind-legs gathered under her sphinxlike. She watched us with a side-eye.

"She can't sleep under there," Joe said.

We talked it over. Joe was afraid she might wet on the floor. I was afraid I wouldn't hear her stir in the night. Although it was lined with her towel, I relied on the clang of her body on the metal tray of the crate to wake me so I could take her out. We measured the bedroom wall, the dresser and the crate and discovered there was room for both, so we moved the dresser aside. Kierney slid along beneath it, refusing to come out.

Having once as a child been bitten by a hiding dog, I knew better than to reach under there.

We placed the crate beside the bed. "Look, Kierney," I said, snapping my fingers by the crate door. "Bedtime." She slid out from under the dresser, climbed onto the noisy metal tray, curled on her towel, and settled with obvious self-satisfaction.

"She just wanted to be near us," Joe yawned, sloshing back into the bed.

I covered the crate. She sighed. Her eyelids drooped.

The rest of the night, for the first time, she was completely quiet.

Kierney was a baby and a rather complicated one. Every night I took her out at least twice, anytime I heard her stir. By the third day I realized that she'd only had one accident, her first day with us. I talked to her constantly. "Let's go in the bedroom," I'd say as I picked her up. "C'mon," I'd call, patting my leg. "Get your ball." Within days she went to the door to ask to go out, and also went to the door if Joe and I said anything to each other about taking her out. We had trained her, yes, but she had also trained us to let her out often and at certain times, such as after a nap or a bout of play.

"Is she housebroken yet?" people would ask, and I'd have to think a moment, not just because it seemed she was never otherwise, but because the question inaccurately assumed "housebroken" was something done to her when really it was a matter of mutual attentiveness. After one piddle in the house, she understood I disapproved, and I understood that a puppy needs to urinate frequently. "We" were housebroken.

A bit of a mother hen, perhaps, I worried because she was still runty and feeble-looking and she wouldn't eat much. Noticing that she only ate when I was nearby, I lay on my belly on the kitchen floor, sat her before me, picked up a piece of kibble, and put it on her paw. Her ears perked, her tail lifted. She ate the morsel off her paw and looked at me. And so I put a piece of kibble on her tail, on each of her toys, on a low shelf, on myself. I'd say, "tail," "gorilla," "hand." Soon she looked at the spot upon hearing the word *before* the food was placed there. But the game never lasted long because she'd quickly get too full to go on.

Still only a baby, she needed a lot of sleep, but would only sleep near me or on me and I, for somebody pursuing a sedentary career, moved around a lot. She seemed to need at least one good uninterrupted nap, and so, a couple of times when she'd been extraordinarily deprived of rest by my activity, I pulled our ratty garage-sale couch cushions into the kitchen and lay on the floor with her, watching her small black nostrils flare and relax.

If I opened my eyes wide, she somehow knew even though her eyes were closed, and she'd open hers. If I held still but turned my eyes to the left or right, she looked in the same direction. If I looked directly at her, she briefly lifted one lid to see what I was going to do with her. I marveled that she seemed to have the ability to imagine herself in my place—I looked to the left, and she seemed to think that if she had looked to the left, it would be because something had caught her eye, therefore, something must have caught my eye, and so she looked to see what it was. When her mother Sweep twitched her eyes to signal the position of her soccer ball, she knew she could control others' behavior by tempting their curiosity, taking imagination to another level—she could accurately imagine I would wonder what she was looking at. And so, thrilling myself with such thoughts, I lay on cushions, on a kitchen floor, in an apartment on a hill just a mile from Shannon's hill, just a mile from backhoes and cement trucks and construction workers, watching the pattern of black hairs shift on the side of a little dog as she breathed in her sleep.

When she was four months old I took her to puppy school, basically a class in socialization. I was told, when I first called the instructor, that four months was too young, "but border collies are so smart," she added. "We'll take you."

"Good. I have to do something soon," I said in a tumble. "She's a fear biter. I've been taking her everywhere to try everything and meet everyone. She's not afraid of commotion or loud sounds or storm grates. She knows her basic commands—"

"She's a bit young for *heel*," the woman chastised. "Maybe you're asking too much too soon."

"What I'm trying to say is, she makes progress in everything *except* when it comes to her fear of people."

"Puppy class is perfect for that," the instructor said, and so Kierney was enrolled, the youngest pup and the smallest breed in her class. Most ranged from six months to a year, and most were Baby Hueys, oversized and over-muscled, like the retriever, the Dalmatian, and the Rottweiler named "Bear." We sat in a circle and played "pass the puppy." When each pup hit my lap it either mauled me with affection or tried to dash off to explore, but Kierney, as she went miserably lap to lap, religiously faced me, her Mecca. I could see how starkly different she was.

One goal of the class, apparently, was to develop the bond between master and dog. So everyone was impressed by, even envious of,

Kierney's devotion to me, which was most striking when we played "puppy recall." One class member walked off with another's dog and then, when the owner called him, let him go. Most pups eventually returned to their owners, but only after bounding around a merry while. A couple of dogs, unaffected by the rising anger in their masters' voices, had to be chased down and collared. Kierney, however, ran straight at me as if escaping gun-point abduction.

So, ironically, puppy school rewarded Kierney's most extreme characteristic, an emotional over-reliance on me. It also happened that my anti-social dog aced all her socialization exercises, mainly because the dogs weren't allowed to interact with each other, and all the people there were sweet, disarming women or men who cooed in high-pitched voices and didn't treat her brusquely, thoughtlessly, or presumptuously the way people in the real world often did. The instructor and the other students seemed to think her neurosis endearing, and they suspected that despite my protests I was secretly charmed and flattered, and maybe I was. It was nice to be strongly preferred by someone, even a puppy, but I wasn't a love-starved twelve-year-old anymore, I was a responsible, happily married woman who wanted a reliable, well-trained dog.

And so it happened that she achieved her cute puppy school diploma without making any real progress at all. She had learned the commands rapidly, tolerated everyone without mishap and displayed a strong bond with her owner. Puppy class provided some useful management tips—the words *mine* and *yours*, how to keep your dog out of your garbage cans and off your bed—but otherwise it mainly served to showcase our youngsters' various temperaments. The retriever remained rambunctious, the Dalmatian ditsy, the Rottweiler insolent, and my little black border collie remained dangerously fearful of everything except me. Puppy class taught me that her love might be less an attraction to me than a repellence for everything else.

But her love, our love, deepened, turned and sparkled, flashing its facets. In July, we took her to the Arts Festival in downtown State College, a good opportunity to socialize a dog, as it's mobbed with people and with other dogs out getting socialized. Banners snap overhead, the air rolls by greasy with the smoke of deep-fried food, and everywhere there are the sounds of shouts and children, whistles and wind chimes. Although July in Central Pennsylvania is crushingly hot and humid, water coolers are situated along the Festival route and if you aim for shade as you walk, it's tolerable. Kierney was too little to walk in the throng herself, so I held her, and every step of the way we were accosted by people asking for the honor of touching her and knowing her name.

"She's so beautiful," people cried and I'd wonder, is she? Is she beautiful? I knew she didn't fit the border collie standards of beauty, with her snipe nose and cow hocks and meagre white markings. Otherwise I could no longer see her face and body, just her needs and troubles. We were proud and relieved that our consistent discipline paid off, for she suffered people's attention, if only by going vacant-eyed and still. One night we took her an outdoor concert, and whenever the crowd applauded she barked as if joining in. People turned their heads and laughed at such an uncanny animal. "What a clever dog! What is she a mix of?" they asked, crowding us, smiling into our eyes, stooping and baby-talking. For all the world, it was as if we'd had a daughter.

Inconveniently for us, just like a little child, she was able to pick significant words out of our stream of human noise. Then words which regularly neighbored already significant words began to take on meaning, such as the word "take," which often accompanied, "out" or "car." It became vital to me not to lie to her, even unintentionally. To say to Joe in her hearing, "Before we leave at ten let's be sure to take her out," was to lie unless it was two minutes to ten. We tried spelling, but a word's spelling is really just its synonym and can be absorbed as rapidly as any other word. In a flash, I could add "o-u-t" and "c-a-r" to her vocabulary. We began paring words she knew. If she stood by the door, we would carefully say to each other, "Is she askin'?" It wasn't long before she heard that phrase and leapt up and down as if to say, "Yes! Yes, I'm askin'!"

Trainers and training manuals recommend we talk a doggy talk, which is even more rudimentary than baby talk, and say, "Duke, sit," or "Duke, no" restricting ourselves to distinct monosyllables which don't rhyme with other words in the dog's vocabulary, lest the dog mistake them—a curse it would be to name a dog something that rhymes with "no" or "bad," and so all dogs named "Bo" or "Lad" must lead lives of sheer abjection. However, in Kierney's case, it was pretty clear from the beginning that she was grasping entire strings of words, even when the sequence and some of the words varied. I could say to Joe, "Should we take her with us when we go to the woods?" in a calm, rapid, ordinary voice, giving off no other signals, and Kierney flew at the door, straight into the woods. I began searching for sequences of words that were most meaningful to her. What if I said, "Ball, get?" No matter the order of words, these were insultingly simple exercises for an animal who, since the age of five weeks, had been extricating meaning from the conversation of two graduate English students. Okay, I thought, what if the syntax changed the meaning of a word? For instance, "get" meant to fetch, to retrieve. What if I told her to get water, which could not be retrieved by her in the way she understood? A moment's pause, and she went and drank it. What if I strung several commands together? Two was easy. "Your ball's in the kitchen" is really two commands: "get ball," and "go to the kitchen."

Once I hid a chewy in the bathtub. "Get chewy in the bathroom; hop up in the tub," I said.

Sometimes when she was concentrating, her lips got stuck on her fangs, which gave her not a ferocious look, but disgusted and pursed-lipped pensiveness. So she froze with one lip up, one down, head cocked, staring at me.

"Get chewy in the bathroom; hop up in the tub."

Exhaling with a small whine, she trotted toward the bathroom, slowed down, turned around, and came back, head cocked, as if asking if she could hear the command one more time.

"Your chewy's in the bath tub. Go hop up and get it. Go look in the tub."

She sat down, which was her way to tell us she could not do what we were asking, something we'd learned from having made commands out of her bodily functions, "poop," and "tinkle." If she couldn't oblige, she'd sit. We'd respond, "You don't have to?" and she'd jump up and run back in the house.

I had reached her limit. "Go find chewy," I said, heart sinking.

Ah, she seemed to say, that's what I thought you meant. She dashed off, only to turn around and come back. Wait, she seemed to say, I know there was more to it than that. One front paw raised, ears pointed fixedly at me, lips stuck and bunched over dry fangs, eyes blank, she listened, trembling. Say it all again?

"Go find chewy," I said, defeated. "I think it's in the bathroom."

She ran to the bathroom. I heard her snuffle. I heard her nails strike the porcelain inside the tub. I heard them hit the linoleum again and trot back to me. Instead of giving me the chewy, she glanced at me with a little flicker of contempt and settled down at my feet for a well-earned gnaw.

Friends, stunned by how conversable she was, often exclaimed, "It's like living with a chimpanzee!" She was "freaky," and "weirded people out." Our friends and we lounged in the living room talking or at the kitchen table eating or playing a board game, and amidst the steady stream of words and laughter Joe'd say casually, "Should I take her?" and I'd say, "Sure."

From where she hid curled behind a chair near one of her secret stashes of rawhide chewies, Kierney got up and walked to the front door.

Someone would note, "Hey, she understood, and you never said the word 'out!'"

When she came back inside, everybody watched. Head lowered and to one side, she stood, ape-like eyes showing their whites, black irises sliding away, then back, checking to see whether we were still watching her, wondering what to make of our attention. Her sides suddenly collapsed a little, revealing that she'd been holding her breath.

Someone said something high-pitched and reassuring, "It's okay, girl." Her tail swung. She moistened her nose with her tongue, her breathing picked up, her ears moved forward, her eyes darted, from us to one direction after another, which, I knew, meant she was considering whether or not to take this opportunity to play with various toys in various locations, all the while weighing the vulnerability of her stash of rawhide.

"Kierney," I said.

Her gaze snapped to mine.

"Why don'cha get your gorilla?"

Kierney cocked her head, glanced at our appreciative guests—happily at the women, warily at the men—decided to risk her rawhide, then sped away. A moment later, she skidded into my knees and placed the gorilla in my lap.

The conversation or the board game forgotten, our guests laughed, remarked on the comparative stupidity of the dogs they knew, then laughed all the more uproariously to see Kierney's reaction to their attention rapidly cross her elastic face: annoyance, fear, happiness.

"Where's your ball?" I said, hoping to distract her with a game our guests would like. "Go find your ball."

She exhaled sharply, looked at me, at the gorilla she'd just delivered, at the guests, back at the gorilla, then stood firmly. She'd gone to all the trouble getting the gorilla, let's play with *that*.

"No," I said, putting the gorilla beside me on my chair. My guests would tense at what seemed an unreasonable demand. Although she challenged my authority more and more frequently, I'd explain, it upset her too much to outrank me even for a moment, so for her sake I sometimes had to stand by my decisions even if it caused otherwise needless trouble. "Go get the ball."

She cocked her head at the word "ball" and froze, looking up and away with the expression of someone doing long division.

"Just go get the ball," Joe scolded.

As if smacked, she cringed, then dashed around the apartment and came back distressed.

"It's in the bedroom," I said.

At that our guests either fell rapt and murmured, "She's amazing," or doubted me, "Aw, c'mon. No way."

She ran to the bedroom. We heard a decisive thump as she pounced. Head and tail held high, Kierney came back in the room with her tennis ball soundly between her jaws.

"Holy shit," the doubters said.

I kept records of the words she knew, about a hundred and thirty of them. "Dish." "Chewy." "Bad guy." "Joe." "Basement." I observed that most were nouns, the names of places and objects. The rest were not nouns in English, but for her tended to serve as nouns which referred to activities or events or movements. "Off." "Look." "Run." "Here." Just as it does for many Americans, the word "car" referred not to the object but to the exhilaration of trembling in a car flying headlong into God knows what dimension. In fact, the boundaries between nouns and verbs began to shimmer and disappear. Every word referred to the entirety of an experience, all the objects and activities intertwined. Say "thirsty" and I conjured up for her "water," "dish," and "drink."

However amazing the results, my early experiments with language may have contributed to her insecurity. Unable to bear making an error, she listened too hard to every command, hesitated, got into the habit of needing everything repeated.

Obedience instructors would later remark that she "thinks too much," a serious weakness under the impatient eyes of judges who reward snappy military responses to orders. I'd turned her into an egghead with a Liberal Arts sensibility. Obedience work is Law Enforcement.

Beginning our training for the Companion Dog title, our "Bachelor's degree," we had more against us in her brooding-poet temperament than I had anticipated. She couldn't get through an exercise without wincing, cringing and rolling her eyes. She was a "soft" dog, given to maddening over-compensation, swamping her own mind with self-reproach. And during obedience maneuvers, handler and dog aren't supposed to touch each other, but, like an anxiety-ridden toddler, Kierney could do nothing without pressing her head or side or rump against her "Mommy." However endearing such behavior was in a puppy, she was reaching adulthood with the demeanor of a high school kid still sucking her thumb.

When one technique after another failed, I had to be careful about changing my training approaches too frequently. For a sensitive dog, one instructor recommended no corrections at all and frequent treats and exuberant praise—jump up and down and shriek, "Oooh! Good girl!" But Kierney was alarmed if I suddenly acted like the host of a kiddie show. She was more confused than motivated by the introduction of food into our training sessions, and actually refused it. Straightforward, low-key exercises, spare, lukewarm correction, and little, if any, praise seemed most effective. I had to go easy on the repetitive exercises, because the challenge of daily life often seemed more than she could bear. It was as if her mind was full of some kind of clamor only she could hear.

I loved her, and conversation with Kierney fascinated me, but I had goals.

I knew people who entered dogs and horses in shows, and who, when it came clear the animal just wasn't going to make the cut, replaced that animal. They either back-shelved the old one or sold it. I couldn't afford two dogs. And Kierney wouldn't easily adjust to sharing her home and humans with another dog. She also would have a great deal of trouble adjusting to a new home and family. In fact, things might go very badly for her in a new home. Gradually, I stopped dreaming of trophies as high as my shoulder. Instead, I worked for something probably unattainable and maybe a little weird—my dog's peace of mind.

My aunt fell and broke her ribs and punctured a lung. Without question, Joe and I canceled our classes, put the dog in the car, and, early in the morning, drove to New Jersey. There was a kennel around the corner from my aunt's house, and so we left Kierney there just for the day. We planned to drive back to Pennsylvania after dark.

When we dropped her off, I was calm, matter-of-fact. Kierney seemed no more nervous than an ordinary dog might be when left behind in a strange setting. However, when we picked her up, she was frantic. Trying to set a temperate mood, I greeted her warmly, not solicitously or profusely, but she behaved as if she'd been nailed to a table and tortured.

She alternately cringed in terror of us and then threw herself at me, wild for reassurance. I had friends who had a dachshund like that and, because of her, they never traveled. They arranged their lives so the dog was rarely alone. Any relationship is a balance of deciding how much you each can tolerate without resentment. I like to think I'm adaptable. I'd been tolerant, compassionate, imaginative, resourceful, persistent, disciplined, good-humored, and hard-working. I had trained a bratty terrier and won Shannon's cooperation—neither of those exactly docile and agreeable animals. After the kennel stay, however, Kierney seemed to have slipped into a state of perpetual red-alert from which I could not recover her.

Now I felt powerless and guilty. What had I done wrong? Maybe my coddling had caused it. Maybe I was too stupid to fix it.

Before I was married, when I lived alone in a studio apartment, the friend of a friend had a yowling, strawberry-blond nightmare of a cat named Jasmine. The woman was about to marry a man allergic to cats. Unable to find anyone crazy enough to take this animal, she was on the verge of euthanizing the cat when I volunteered to take her. The lease said no cats, but the windows of the apartment building were full of basking felines. Yowling and growling whenever I moved, Jasmine hid behind my bookshelves by day and crept out to eat and use the litter box by night. It crossed my mind to sleep with my arm over my throat, just in case. But because I ignored her, she soon purred in my lap as long as I didn't pet her. She made a game of hunting me—not a strand of my long hair or my shoelace, but *all* of me, bodily, as if I were Chief Inspector Clouseau and she my own manservant Kato. She landed on me as I exercised innocently on the floor, lolled in the tub, sat myself on the toilet—and never once did tooth or nail make a mark on my skin. She would not *be* touched, but she would touch in force, a silent, playful saboteur. After a couple of months, the day my landlord expelled my cat along with all the others in my building, uncannily, my aunt told me of a woman whose cat had died the very same day—a difficult strawberry blond female named . . . Jasmine. Joe and I drove my Jasmine three hundred miles. In the car, she crawled up inside my sweater, inched down my arm, and rode the entire trip bulging my sleeve like a pig in a python. Last I'd heard, Jasmine, well-loved and untouched, had become a virtuoso rabbit-killer.

So I knew of myself that I didn't need to cuddle an animal to feel we had a satisfying relationship. I knew I'd once been good enough at putting fearful or distrustful animals at ease—cats and horses as well as dogs—that they became more peaceful, cooperative and trainable, not just with me, but also with other people. However, after months of toil and many hours of consultation with trainers, I had barely come close to realizing my smallest hopes for Kierney. Now, in less than a day, I'd made a small and reasonable request of her—that she pass a few hours in a kennel—and I'd undone the little peace so painfully gained.

I appealed to the medical profession. "She'd have been worse off if she didn't have you," our vet said. "You've given her comfort and stability. " He recommended letting her come into heat once before spaying so that she would reach full maturity, and perhaps she'd "calm down."

For Kierney at nine months old, heat was a long, messy and distressing experience, and when it was over I scheduled her spaying, a procedure otherwise known as a radical hysterectomy. For me, an animal rights sympathizer, the surgery presented some conflicts. On the one hand, the pet overpopulation problem necessitated widespread sterilization, much more acceptable than the slaughter in so-called "shelters" and "humane" societies. But pet overpopulation was caused by irresponsible humans. There had to be a better solution than performing drastic invasive surgery on thousands of otherwise healthy animals. Why weren't there birth control pills? Why wouldn't the vet just tie her tubes? Couldn't we just skip it? It wasn't as if Kierney, who feared and loathed other dogs, would ever get near enough to mate. But of course, I couldn't take even a remote chance on reproducing this animal.

The bigger problem was this: the surgery required an overnight stay. After her brief stay in a kennel, where she endured no invasive procedures of any kind, she'd had a drastic emotional set-back. What was this experience going to do to my desperately neurotic dog?

When I'd left her there, she had screamed for me. The nurse whisked me away, her reassurances belied by the alarm on her face.

I went home and sat on my couch, thinking about Kierney, alone in a strange place for the second time in her life, about to be drugged senseless and have her belly slit open. What did I have in store when I brought that dog home? As the refrigerator hummed, the baseboard heat ticked, the windows rattled in the January blast, I sat hunched with my knees together and my arms wrapped around my smooth, whole belly, but through the bars of a cage I saw bright light and white-sneakered feet, smelled strange smells, heard busy voices and the scratching, snuffling and yelping of strange animals. Curled in the back of my cage, I tumbled in the pounding surf of terror. Rocking myself like a little girl, I let myself cry and knew how I loved Kierney despite everything, maybe because of everything. I knew how powerless I was. I could not help her. And I thought too much, I felt too much, I knew too much—Kierney's fears awoke in me a more vivid awareness of the animals in laboratories, enduring not just the abominable Draize eye test and the Lethal Dose 50, but thousands of creative variations on torture that had "significance" only in the most shameful academic sense. "The question is not," wrote Jeremey Bentham, "Can they *reason*? nor Can they *talk*? but, Can they *suffer*?" Kierney could do all that, exceedingly.

At end of the day when I called to check on her, the vet said she was awake, on her feet. "It's amazing," the vet said. "It's as if we did the surgery days ago. You might as well come get her."

The anesthesia had been a blessing. She didn't seem to recall screaming when I'd left her, but acted like an ordinary dog recovering from a minor ailment. Maybe the vet was right, and sterilization was a miraculous behavioral cure-all. Having inherited her mother's supernatural healing abilities, that very evening she wanted to play catch and "go nuts," a game she played at dusk in the front yard, a joyous racing in wide, random, elliptical orbits around me and Joe— her nucleus—faster and faster, crazier and crazier, our black electron rhythmically snorting, actually flying as she passed us without touching the ground, sailing an easy eight or ten feet in a stride. She was ready to run, but I kept her on lead for a sober and mercenary outing.

But as soon as she was allowed, we let her run again in the night, and as always part of me followed her—just as once Patches pulled me on my Raleigh Chopper bike right out of church and Shannon cantered me upon the language of flesh—I followed her, whether brave or reckless, I don't know, but all the same, I set sail upon a roil of wonderment.

There's a tale a priest I know tells, about five angels watching God create the universe. One, an engineer, asks how is it done? The second, a philosopher, asks, why is it done? The third, a CEO, asks, when will be it done? And the fourth, a real estate agent, asks, how much is it worth? But the fifth angel just cheers in amazement. "Wonder," the pastor said, "is the spirit's response to Creation."

In a not-altogether different mood at all, Paul West used to tell his students that gorgeous prose occurred when "the microcosm fights back against the always victorious and uncaring macrocosm, whose relative immortality we cannot forgive." But he was always exhilarated, headlong in love with the pageantry of the mind and the universe. "A novelist's proper response to the abundance of Creation," he would tell us, "is to add to it."

As I've said, I'm impressionable, I'm susceptible to emotional contagion, and so, no matter how much trouble my dog was, her amazement amazed me. For instance, upon her first sight of someone rolling by on skates, she did a bona fide double-take and sat down to study this affront to physics. When she crested her first sand dune, presented all at once with the Atlantic Ocean, she sat herself down in perfect awe. What amazed me was the profundity, the immediacy, the intricacy, the obligation, the implications that arose as she crossed into my dream world and I into her concrete and eternally present realm. Our tiny family grouping was now one-third canine. Interlaced, secret and unexpected, heretical, we were a song across the valley between human and canine, a song fifteen thousand years old. She talked to me, talked to me as if she'd always been alive, triumphantly taking on the yoke of her name upon her, Kierney, Kierney, yes, you exist, you are here and I see you.

So I watched and she ran as if the blackness of her body merged weightless with the dark, as if she could swim in the black like a whale pumping past continents in its sleep, as if she were her own planet hurtling without friction or destination round and round and out and out across the universe that spreads like water spilled upon silence, ever beyond the reach of human thought.

Chapter Five

God's Take-Home Exam

When I remember Kierney, I remember her evading my touch, a gyroscope that balances and floats out of reach, her body more blur than matter. So I've been surprised that on videotape we're in constant contact. If she's carrying a twelve-foot log, she's knocking me in the shins with it; if I'm sitting, she's spinning between my knees. Never did she have enough time to catch the ball, shred the paper towel tube, or appease my anger. When she slept, she dropped like a sack of wooden blocks onto the hardwood floor and exhaled herself in one steamy breath.

As she grew, Kierney was awake for longer stretches that had to be filled. The language exercises absorbed her, but they couldn't hold my interest long enough to suit her. I had classes to teach, classes to take, and a novel to write for my Master of Fine Arts degree. Hoping to lose her in a maze of thought, I gave her longer sequences of commands, but was obliged to repeat them often. And then, as soon as she solved the verbal puzzle, she wanted another. We played a variation of hide and seek, in which I hid her toys and told her to find them one by one. At best, I could hope it'd take her ten minutes to find them all, but she was usually faster than that, and whenever she got stumped, she'd stare at me and whistle in her throat until I gave her clues. I invented physical puzzles—a treat in a paper towel stuffed in a toilet paper tube under a laundry basket. I found ways to join two toys—tie her Nylabone inside her sock or stuff a squeak toy into her Kong—and she'd whip her tail to and fro as she took the toys to a private place where she could concentrate on separating them.

However, the best activities backfired because it was hard for me not to watch her work. I loved to see her track the scent of a hidden toy, pull the cushions from the couch, lift the rim of a basket, reach into a jar with her paw, stop and study the kitchen chair I'd placed by the sink. Finally the only way I could get my work done was this: while I typed, I let her drop a ball near my foot, and I'd scoop it up and toss it. It got to be part of the rhythm of typing: type-type-type, period, space bar, scoop, toss, *catch*! Type-type-type, period, space bar, scoop, toss, *catch*! The game of catch thrilled her indefinitely and I could do it

71

absent-mindedly. I tried not to be annoyed that I'd thrown the racquetball over two hundred times in the last hour.

Some would have locked her in her crate. But Kierney spent the entire night in her crate, in addition to several hours every day while I was on campus or out running errands. To crate her while I worked at home would have meant adding another six hours or so to her confinement, which would be neither kind nor fair, although it's common—at the time I knew of two young German Shepherds kept in side-by-side crates all but two hours of every day. I knew of a miniature poodle who passed his entire life in a tiny, lightless laundry room on a bit a newspaper. To inflict such boredom on Kierney would be cruel both to her and to me—how could I comfortably inhabit my own mind if I were someone who shirked my responsibility to her? In such cases the only moral thing to do is to find the animal a better home.

As a youngster, she depended upon my watchful eye for her physical well-being, and for her emotional well-being she depended on my company—I provided her comfort, activity, new experiences, and social interaction. I wouldn't give up on her. In order to ensure that she grew out of her fear, I took her to construction sites and ball games, and I walked her over various surfaces—logs and lawn chairs—so that she'd develop confidence in many different settings. I also took her into people's homes, into stores, offices, and Penn State's Pattee library, safely betting that her cute cleverness would override the fact that, as a non-human, she was a violation of public health.

Yet I was no closer to trusting her. Her moods changed according to variables that escaped my understanding—she'd randomly flicker between confident or fearful, submissive or defiant, grateful or surly, joyful or despairing, needy or independent, faithful or menacing. It was as if she were three dogs, one a revved-up, can-do athlete, the other a tender, brooding poet, the last, a nasty piece of work.

The animal rights movement was big on what our duties were to animals, but to a lot of those people, animals apparently owed us nothing. To expect anything at all was to oppress them. Although I could happily join the activists in boycotting meat and products connected to animal experimentation, I couldn't help disagreeing with the assumption that humans were wrong to want or expect anything from other animals. I believed that interaction with other animals was a frank necessity of life on Earth. To deny us those interactions would be to do us emotional harm and to increase the likelihood that we would behave toward them in cruelty and ignorance. To make demands of my dog was no anthropomorphic fantasy, nor was it a power trip. Anybody who knew and respected Kierney could see that, as a fellow language-bearer, *she* had certain moral obligations—and she wasn't meeting them.

Kierney stayed a criminal, a sinner. The problems weren't just the predictable ones, such as boredom turning to vandalism, over-eager greetings or maniacal careening about the house. Our problems were more than personality conflicts. Kierney bit people.

For a dog, biting is a capital offense. In three separate incidents at the vet's, she cowered under my chair. Two different children and one stupid adult reached under to pet her. They did it despite my admonitions and got bitten.

"Biting is a response to incoherent authority," Vicki Hearne wrote.

What more could I do to make myself coherent to her? And was I really *that* incoherent? Surely I was not less coherent than I had been as a teenager, but neither Patches nor the mean dogs on my paper route bit me. Shannon the crabby horse bit other people and kicked them, but he was gentle with me, even when I annoyed him. The menacing cat named Jasmine had bitten and scratched other people but she eventually let me stroke her and carry her against my chest. What was I doing wrong with Kierney?

With her, there was incoherence, yes. Something was not sticking together, not cleaving, something was ill-suited, not adapted, but where and why? The evidence seemed to suggest that I generally possessed coherence. I had a calm and stable relationships with my college writing students. I enjoyed long-term friendships and a peaceful marriage. I seemed to be consistent, articulate, and intelligible to every other person and every other animal, and most of the time with Kierney too. But there were moments when something like a dark insect with many legs and many feelers and many eyes thrashed within her, and she couldn't see me anymore—we didn't know each other. Something kept interrupting, unraveling, erasing.

More than most dogs, Kierney was given to free-association or transference: a command she learned in the house she immediately could obey outdoors or in the water, and she could easily vary or adapt the use of a word or skill. In other words, she was gifted at coherence, at making connections and associations between things. Perhaps she was too gifted: some people suggested that Kierney was a genius, which in humans can coincide with neuroses and foul temper. I also considered that the incoherence might exist in her victims, people who did not understand her body language as readily as I did—Shannon was most aggravated with me when I rode incoherently. Was it possible that Kierney was simply uncompromising, unforgiving? Was she, like Shannon, a snob?

I found myself absorbing her attitude. During our obedience walks I irritably warned strangers away from her, not just for their own safety, but to insist upon their manners: we were working on our *heel* and *stay* and it was rude to interrupt.

"I remember she was haughty," Joe said. "When we were out working or running or playing Frisbee, she'd openly ignore people."

Despite the fact that she obviously didn't welcome attention, some people forced it on her anyway. It drove me wild with fear—if *they* *made* her bite, *she* would be the one to pay, maybe with her life.

"She bites," I snapped, and they looked at me as if I was crazy—how could such a pretty dog sitting precisely at my heel be wicked? Looking me up and down, they seemed to wonder whether or not I was refusing to share her or if I were the sort who enjoyed a dangerous dog, the way Wendy had relished Shannon's seventeen-hundred-pound temper tantrums. Besides, I appeared to be too a nice girl to have a nasty dog.

One afternoon I sat at the Creamery enjoying an ice cream while Kierney rested under my chair. Suddenly a man behind us whipped his hand out from under my chair with a shocked look on his face.

"You should always ask first," I said. "Shame on you. Don't you know any better?"

I was getting crotchety. I wished I could just wear a sign, "Beware of Dog," but I knew no one would believe it. I wasn't sure I myself believed what I had on my hands. Indeed, how could my sweet, needy pup so ungratefully disobey *me*, the one she depended on for her very life? She was unlike any animal I'd ever known.

And that life! So riotously happy when my women friends came to visit, she rocketed from the floor, aiming her nose right at their faces, nearly knocking their eyeballs down their throats. At the time, stores carried novelty spectacles with screen in place of lenses, and Joe and I joked we needed them for our guests. We took her for romps in Alan Seeger park, a wooded mountainside nature preserve, where she ran heartfelt circles around us, charged through the brush, leapt fallen tree trunks four feet high, and plunged face-first into streams, barking and burbling as she pulled sodden nine-foot branches from the water. We took her for a spellbinding week at the ocean. A spindly black bolt of pure energy, an elusive, supercharged particle of antimatter, she blasted through the surf, a speeding hole in space-time set against the great heaving glare of the sea. No matter how far or fast it flew, she caught every Frisbee-toss, unaffected by the complaint of displaced gulls. Winning her own Preakness, she snatched the Frisbee from the sky, then spun in the glinting tide pools and pranced back, her toes mincing upon her reflection in the glossy sand, tossing the Frisbee overhead and catching it between her teeth, loping along, alive, alive, alive, alive, cantering back to me, to me, where I stood, as ever, on the shore, all stillness and introspection.

Paul West was coming to dinner. Rigged with a pace-maker, he suffered several chronic illnesses—"I'm my own chemistry experiment," he'd say, when he took us out to eat, lining pills beside his plate. He rarely went anywhere and didn't drive. Having recently published *The Place in Flowers Where Pollen Rests*, he made ready with Hopi lore and laughed and fretted over the complaints that a Hopi chieftain, offended by the novel, had made. Paul kept a a kachina doll of the Hopi sky god Sotuqnangu on his television set in place of an antenna, like a stocky, primitive robot guarding him from disturbing satellite images. Paul and the Hopi god had much in common. Both were known for splitting people in two with lightning.

It was one thing to invite Paul West to our bird room where he sat on our couch tapping his knee to our finches' faint trumpet and percussion score. But what worlds would collide when Sotuqnangu met our Cerberus? At the very least, Kierney, at only thirty pounds, could, I knew, knock "the finest living stylist in the English language" right off his sneakers and out our screen door. It wasn't so much the impropriety as the danger—a man with a pacemaker mustn't be "bumped." Plus, Paul wasn't just any man with a pacemaker, he was a man who'd written *A Stroke of Genius*, in which he said his "heart was cuddling a tiny propeller forever," and that he housed "a silver interloper where the sun had never shone and where there was never rest." If we crated her, she'd wail and interrupt conversation. Whatever we did, she was going to impose herself on us with her many mute requests.

So we decided to keep her locked in the kitchen, where she'd have both freedom and attention but no access to Paul. But the kitchen had no door. Joe found a large piece of particle board and mounted it with hinges and a clasp to the doorjamb, a solid, four-foot-high baby gate, and we were set.

When Joe brought Paul into our house, we saw it had been wise to restrain her. The front door was directly opposite her particle board barrier. As soon as she heard Paul's voice, she clawed, shrieked, and scrambled at the board, splintering it. Paul backed against the door, his broad-cheeked, thick-nosed face widened with alarm. He spoke as I'd never heard him, with an almost childlike ingenuousness, "She won't get me, will she?"

"No," I said, resting my hand on his arm and watching her face as it rhythmically breached the rough edge of the particle board, lips twisted over razory teeth, eyes rolling white in the visage of the frantic and insane. I wasn't at all sure she wouldn't get him. "She just wants to say 'hi.'"

"Hello, there," he said, recovering his good nature and taking off his jacket to reveal one of the three velour sweat suits that composed his limited wardrobe. He was, like many great artists, too much the lord of another world to submit his body to our fickle fashions or to the pinch of our tailored jackets, our wing-tips or hiking boots, our linen or wool. Invited to a banquet in his honor, he would approach the podium, as always, zipped handsomely into his stretch velour.

As Kierney raged and I led him to the couch, my heart sank with the certainty that he'd never come to our house again. "My God, Leeza," he said in his Americanized British, "What's she doing in there? Slaughtering an antelope for our dinner?"

Joe hung up Paul's jacket and marched toward her. Sudden silence. Reaching over the divider, he swung her back and forth, soft and heavy, thumping against the oven door and skittering across the linoleum. I cringed. We heard snarls. "No!" Joe thundered. A squeak of submission. Joe looked up brightly. "It'll be okay now," he said to Paul. "It's probably best if you come greet her now."

"You're joking." Paul turned to me and searched my face.

"This'll help," I said and handed him a racquetball.

"Ah. Thank you. A rubber grenade." Squeezing the racquetball in his palm, he got up, walked his bionic body halfway to the divider, and looked back. Joe was telling him a story about Kierney, and he was listening. Ever since Joe had throttled her, she lay still, waiting, silent and hidden on the other side of the particle board. "She's dematerialized," Paul laughed hopefully. "You've shaken the She-Wolf back to the lip of Dante's Hell." He stood in the middle of the living room, then tossed the racquetball. It arced up near the ceiling, then came down cleanly and disappeared over the divider with a soft *chuck*. Two pairs of claws gripped the top of the board, a nose, fangs, and racquetball slid over the splintered edge, a pink tongue gave the ball a push, and it fell. It bounced, twice, thrice, and bumped to a stop.

While I got dinner together (bluefish, in his honor), he continued tossing the ball, asked questions about her, and trusted me to pass in and out of the kitchen without releasing her. Finally, as I cooked, he came right up to the divider. The four-legged lunatic and the novelist looked each other in the face. "Why, she's beautiful," he told me, as if her beauty were the very kind of overwrought incongruity that gave his art its force.

I looked down at her. She stood splay-legged, bat-eared, hunched and intensely troubled that two humans looked at her now—we might both throw balls at the same time. "Everybody says that," I said, passing the bluefish over the barrier, "but I'm blind to it. She looks to me like something sprung from the mind of Jim Henson. During the *Dark Crystal* days."

We told Paul about my father's visit to the house. My father had once cared for a friend's miniature poodle and, tirelessly mischievous man that he is, he figured out that if he threw the ball just right, the dog would chase it and smash headfirst into the wall, repeatedly. So, when he was visiting us he spent a fair amount of time trying to play the same prank on Kierney. As he worked on timing his pitch, I heard him laugh and talk to her, "Ah, you're too quick," "So you're wise to that one." He finally gave up, impressed, but as he left he took me aside and said, "I don't know why you choose to keep that wild animal."

For a good ten minutes, Paul had stood leaning his elbow on the divider, studying her, tossing her ball, nodding and marveling as we told him her stories. We spoke of language, how there was no correspondence between the sound of the word "horse" and Kierney's horse-shaped squeak toy other than the one she and I agreed to impose on it, and wasn't it amazing that two such disparate creatures as a human and a dog could agree, especially when the dog cannot *say* "horse" at all? He spoke to her as my father had, not condescending baby-talk but as if translating for her, "Oh, you don't want it thrown in the sink again? You want me to throw the rope now? Well, bring it to where I can reach it." And she answered him in her way, lips bunched over her fangs, her gaze swift and direct, her reactions immediate.

Although she sighed loudly and occasionally moaned while we ate, we managed to speak of other things. However, by the time I drove Paul home I was more than tired of talking about her, but Paul had me alone and said, pointedly, "So, you're rid of your birds? I liked *them*." I felt obliged to defend not so much Joe's decision to give them away ("Joe works too hard," Paul agreed, "You should take him to Florida"), but to defend my decision to live with a wild animal. "I grew up traveling all over the world, but now I can't afford to go anywhere, Paul, not even to Florida. Kierney's another culture, another way of being. With her, I feel as if I'm on a long trip."

We talked about how I'd given away the birds and missed them the way I used to miss the swimming pool and the swinging vines and the monkeys and the broad leaves of Djakarta and the wide, dark, fragrant expanse of my Ghanaian nanny's upper arm. We agreed that a place, a culture can linger inside you. And now guests didn't visit Joe and me so much as they toured our life with Kierney, carrying their own places into our very different one, bringing with them, say, a place where food dropped must be cleaned up, where a woman may brush her teeth without meeting a beggar for toothpaste, where dogs are little more than animated houseplants, or a home that can be left for weeks because there's no life in it to sustain. Joe and I had become tour guides, telling stories, defending, explaining, leading others to understand and appreciate the fact that here, in a small apartment, two adults share a history with one adolescent border collie and live ensnarled in habit and obligation and a most mysterious joy, a euphoric absurdity.

"The entire universe is made of nothing but constant, arbitrary juxtapositions," Paul said. "And it's the job of the novelist to recreate the universe. All a novelist has is a mind which reports on minds to minds."

"Each of us is always alone with the universe and alone with our own mind," I said. "The visitor tours your little corner and then leaves you in it. If you're a writer, it's worse. Prose is just a variation of graffiti. The reader sees your scribble only after you've already walked away," I said, but I was thinking, Paul has visited, met my dog, and now he will walk away and leave me alone with her.

I drew the car up to his apartment building.

"You're a brave girl." He patted my knee and kissed my cheek. "Take care, Leeza."

Surd. From Latin, *surdus*, meaning deaf, unhearing, unheard, meaningless, irrational, voiceless. A writer, Paul taught me, "must admit no distractions from the existential surd." I was his brave girl. I must face the surd.

I'd be typing or reading, and Kierney would drift slowly into the room, staring. She'd stop. "What is it?" I asked, but instead of fixing me with her quick eyes or charging to the door to protect our house with her cannon-fire bark—her usual response to that question—she just stood there as if I hadn't spoken. Sometimes, outside, she crossed the yard as if bidden by a vision of Our Lady of Sorrows. Lately, she'd entered the living room as if she'd just overheard me and Joe say something unforgivable. Puffed with self-righteous fury, she walked back and forth, glaring at us as if she just didn't know *what* she was going to do with us *now*.

Sexual maturity and spaying had done no good. She was worse. A few times she went skulking along the wall, snarling as if we'd cornered her and meant to kill. Once, to break through, I said, "At ease," the obedience release command, and her eyes went blank and her head tipped as if she were playing the lead in a canine remake of *The Three Faces of Eve*. Suddenly we had our little black pup back, tail wagging, head low and apologetic, bounding upon my lap as if long absent.

The surd welled in her, arbitrary, voiceless, deaf. The incoherence was *hers*. Naturally, irrationally, we searched for a reason. Had we ignored her or scolded her—was it a pout? Was she taken from her mother too soon? Neurotically, she kept chewing off the white tip of her plumed tail, as a human does fingernails. A zombie, she walked until her chin slid onto the couch cushion, her chest bumped the frame and she stopped. Was she moping because permission to jump onto the couch was denied? But she didn't hear me when I asked, "Do you want to hop up?" and didn't hear me when I finally caved, "Okay, hop up."

I had the vet check her vision and her hearing—she was fine.

Our obedience instructor, who owned English Springer spaniels, had never experienced anything like this behavior, but chalked it up to Kierney's adolescence, her extraordinary intelligence, her sensitivity, her subtlety, the notorious neuroses of her breed—all part of the sufferings of our young Werther, melodramatic, mysterious, poetical— as if it were widely understood that the border collie is a small but enigmatic city, a Venice worthy of contemplation.

Then one night I was lying on my back on the couch reading Proust, "The Sweet Cheat Gone," aloud to Joe. Joe was in the armchair going through the mail. Kierney marched slowly in, head up, eyes vacant.

"Hiya, Drifty," I said, and went back to my book: "And when all is said, even in the case of a single dead person, can we be sure that the joy we should feel in learning that she knows certain things would compensate for our alarm at the thought that she knows them *all*; and however agonizing the sacrifice, would we not sometimes forbear to keep those we have loved as friends after their death, for fear of having them also as judges?"

Nodding, Joe opened another envelope.

There came a low rumble, thunder in the room. When I looked, Kierney was barely a foot away, aiming her fangs at me as if they were hollow and dripped poison.

"No!" I boomed, and started, but she leapt on my chest, knocking from my hands *Remembrance of Things Past*. The next thing I knew two fistfuls of flesh and fur had replaced the book in my hands. She forced herself forward as I held her back, the strength in my arms shuddering against the strength in her thighs. So close to my eyes I couldn't focus on them, her teeth flickered against the black night of her throat. When I tried to throw her off my chest, she roared and surged toward me with such force that I knew that if she decided to slice up my face, she could do it. She was holding back, hesitating; she was deciding.

In my periphery I could see Joe standing over her, huge but helpless. I was her hostage. When I spoke, when he spoke, she snarled louder. I saw her as if all my body could see, a sphinx on my chest, piercing claws, trembling flanks, the terrible fan of her hackles.

"Do it!" I cried. "Get her off me!"

Suddenly, *deus ex machina*, she flew up and away. Joe threw her down and grabbed her by the skin of her throat and bellowed at her. When he let her go, she ran and hid.

Joe and I looked at each other. Whatever we were doing to help her, it wasn't enough.

Once again, I consulted several local dog training experts. "She's testing you," they said. "You're going to have to be consistent with her. Maintain your dominance."

"We do that. We've *been* doing that."

Each conversation was the same. I heard no new advice. After hearing our story and meeting her themselves, they were as stumped as we were.

"Work her fifteen minutes in the morning and fifteen minutes at night," they said. *Take two aspirin . . .* "Call me and let me know how it works out."

Finally, I took her to see another vet, and he had an answer.

"She's in marvelous health," he said. "She's well-muscled. Her heart is powerful."

He and I stood on either side of a surgical steel examination table in a small room boasting a framed diploma, and in the air lingered the stink of rubbing alcohol and the oily coat of the previous patient.

"Could it be her diet? I'm feeding her vegetarian dog food," I confessed guiltily.

He shook his head and ran his hands over her rippled flank. "Whatever you're feeding her is fine. Diet's not the problem."

I had my arms crooked around Kierney's neck and around her middle to restrain her. Her claws slid and clacked against the metal.

He stroked her long, silky back. He sighed sadly. "She's insane."

"What?!"

"You'll never be able to trust her. You'll never have any peace."

"What do you mean?" I could feel the heat of her body and the thrust of her panting side through my sweater. I closed my arms more tightly around her, until I felt my own breathing bump against hers.

"Dogs sometimes suffer personality disorders." As he pet her, her nibbled-off tail swished and she leaned her weight into my arm as best she could on the slippery table. She was asking to be let down.

"Just like humans? Should I take her to a psychiatrist and tell him how her mother was an inattentive workaholic? That the breeder sold her when she was only five weeks old?"

"Sure. Or it's temperament, an innate instability."

I closed my eyes. I'd known better all along. I'd been a fool: *Avoid the timid, shy types, since they tend to develop into fearful or poorly adjusted adults.*

"Usually, when I see such severe . . ." He made a broad, absent gesture with one hand. He tried again, "When this kind of unpredictable behavior occurs in a dog, most people choose to put it to sleep."

"No," I said. "It hasn't come to that."

"It's a lot to ask a person to care for such an animal."

"It's not a lot," I said, choking up. "It's not." I hid my face in her fur. I felt like begging her for help.

"Well, there's always Bob Martin," the vet said.

I'd heard of Martin. He was notorious in town. Several of my unsuspecting friends had taken their boisterous dogs to his class and every one of their dogs had suffered some extreme correction at his hands that drove my friends out of the room, tearful and stunned by their own sudden rage.

"I'd sooner kill her myself," I said.

One day I was looking at the calendar. I checked and checked again. I was pregnant.

"Joe!" I cried, instantly overjoyed. My period was about only three days late, but I was *never* late. There had been other signs. I was coming home ravenous and making dinner at three in the afternoon. I'd crawled out of a hot tub nearly fainting. Strangely, Kierney had been greeting me when I came home by thrusting her muzzle in my crotch as if I had a brand-new body chemistry.

The next morning a doctor's test declared me officially pregnant.

The most luxurious elation I've ever known lasted about a week, when it occurred to me that I had been trying *not* to get pregnant. Part of me felt that God, in the persons of the Pope and our Natural Family Planning coach, had promised that assiduous practice of God's chosen birth control would work. We'd studied NFP thoroughly, trusted, and disciplined ourselves. We'd been assiduous. We obeyed. Now what were we going to do? We couldn't afford a crib and jars of pureed green beans, let alone one of those black-and-white mobiles to stimulate our baby's intellect. I didn't know how to take care of a baby—I didn't even *know* any babies. What, if anything, was God thinking? Just as I was praying for Kierney, just as I'd realized I might be her last and only hope, God made me singularly unsuited to care for her. How could we keep her? Every day she was more articulate, subtler, stronger.

Even so, none of these anxieties could quell my happiness; my former life looked like a dingy of toothpicks; devotion to my writing, to the Church, even to my dog, all was falling apart and had to be rebuilt. Joe too, was testing our new ship, only without the gale of joy I had at my back. Suddenly Joe proved himself to be more than a feminist. What if the baby was a *boy*? Would he be forced to abandon Kierney, his running partner, in order to raise a gun-loving baseball fanatic?

"There's nobody like that on either side of our family," I said reassuringly. But I was hoping for a girl too.

Joe took Kierney running several times a week. She'd polish off five miles and come home only to dive on her Frisbee and flip it between her teeth and paws. "She's better if she's gotten some exercise," Joe'd pant brightly. "Don't you think?"

Pinching my nose against the cold, sweaty vapor coming off them, I looked up from *What to Expect When You're Expecting*, which had just informed me that I had a parasitic tadpole smaller than a grain of rice embedded in my abdomen. "I don't know *what* to think." Kierney was too glorious to be insane. She was too intelligent. Too talkative. Prancing in place, her knobby, ductile face studying mine, she had no idea that her crazed fear had proved self-fulfilling.

If I couldn't find another suitable home for her, we might be forced to put her in the pound, where she'd be killed. Or we'd put her in a situation like our own, in which case she might bite and then be killed. No farmer wanted such a dog, no matter how fit and brilliant. Besides, change of family could do her irreparable damage—just that one day in the kennel had her plunged into an insecurity that only my steady patience could remedy. My hope was in some person who would welcome the opportunity to show pity, a person with a generous heart. George wouldn't take Kierney back—he had mounting fines to pay the dog law officer. He'd been letting an entire pack of dogs run loose:

Sweep, her son Toss, and his new, wheezing and dysplastic French bulldog, which he now planned to breed. I tried all my obedience, farm, and animal rights connections, but they yielded no possibilities. It seemed there were hundreds of healthy, brilliant but *sane* dogs in need of homes, and there were few people with hearts that big.

One night I had to drop something off at Paul West's apartment. I knocked on his door, and he answered, wearing only boxer shorts and an undershirt.

"Well!" I said, "I've been *wondering* if you ever wore anything besides a velour sweat suit."

"Diane buys me those to make me presentable. Come in, hurry, Leeza."

He sped away from me in a living room lighted only by a television. He was writing a novel about Hopi Indians, and a statuette of the god called Sotuqnangu stood on the top of the television. Lit by the screen below him, he appeared strangely faceless.

Paul settled himself on the couch. "You've been watching Voyager Two, of course? My God!"

Dropping beside him, I saw on the screen a vivid bluish orb. "Neptune! Voyager's arrived at Neptune!" Paul was a father figure to me, so I wanted to tell him about my pregnancy, but also wanted it to be the right moment. I wouldn't let my baby be eclipsed by Neptune, so I could wait, but it wasn't easy. I was bursting to tell him. As I often do on such occasions, I had to contain my excitement—my voice gets too loud and my long, thin body becomes ungainly, coltish and too strong, and before I know it, I've interrupted someone, made him wince, knocked into him, or my wild hair has lashed him across the eyeballs or whipped a fountain pen from his hand. "Wasn't Neptune that loser of a god who couldn't get anything right? Except the horse! He created the horse!" I was filled with happiness that Neptune created the horse.

"Look," Paul said, pointing, "What they thought were arcs are rings." He sat silent until the commercials, when he said Voyager had found a third moon, six moonlets, a streak of white which must be an atmospheric jet stream. "And see? That's the Great Dark Spot, akin to Jupiter's Great Red Spot."

I said, "I'm pregnant."

Paul did not look at me. "How does Joe feel?"

"He's worried. He's stringing together three part-time jobs as it is. And, like you, he wants me to write."

"Among many curious findings," said the hushed announcer, "is that Voyager's picking up a magnetic field that's tilted fifty degrees from the axis of rotation and it's mysteriously off-center."

Looking down at his big round hands, Paul joined them into a moon, at crescent phase in the television light. Quietly, he said,

"You've got a big decision to make."

Had I discussed our birth control practices with Paul? I guessed I must have. Or maybe Joe did? Paul often questioned my Catholicism. To him, it was an irritant and an intellectual curiosity. Now, clearly, he somehow guessed that Joe and I had been agonizing for the past week over how the sperm could have lived so long and how we ever could have taken such a foolish risk as trusting God and self-discipline over synthetics. What to do when I'm fertile again? What kind of Catholics were we going to be now that the sympto-thermal rules had failed us? And how to answer Paul's implied and highly personal question?

I said, "I'm thinking we'll use some combination of Natural Family Planning and the diaphragm. I don't know."

"That's not what I meant." The image of Neptune flickered, great squares of it disappearing and reappearing as if a child struggled to assemble the simplest of computerized jigsaw puzzles.

"We apologize," the announcer said. "Mission commander Stone informs us that the transmission from Voyager arrives at one twenty-billionth the power required to run a digital watch. Voyager's voice is easily lost in the electromagnetic noise of space."

He said, "So you're going to have the baby?"

"Yes." My legs stiffened as his meaning dawned on me. I felt myself leaning as Kierney had when she yearned to jump off the examination table. "There's never been any question. A baby's . . . not too much." My mind whirled up and away as if leaving Paul down below on his couch with his galaxy, as if I were looking down on him as he constructed the model of the Milky Way on his basement floor many years before—had I ever told Paul how much I loved him? This professor had a hand in creating me, had said, "You're a novelist," and it was so—he was one of my gods, my Prince of the Peacocks, Lord of the Written Sky. How many times, before my very eyes, had he taken the universe in his hand and polished it up for me like an apple? Who was he now, suggesting what he was suggesting? Didn't he know me better? Did Paul West love me too?

"We . . . we're in difficulties," I stammered. "I'm overwhelmed, no doubt, but, there's never—" I'm not Paul's daughter, I reminded myself, nor his niece, nor his lover—I'm simply one of the teacher's pets. "Joe and I agree I'll keep writing."

"Of course," he said, as the television station showed us immaculate pictures of Triton, Neptune's trophy moon.

"Triton appears to have a methane atmosphere," one announcer reverently purred, "And its surface is covered with puddles of liquid nitrogen."

"That's right, Tom," said a more exuberant partner. "You can see here some steep Alpine mountains. Looks like Earth, doesn't it?"

Beside me, Paul jeered, "Except for the pink ice."

"However, Triton is decidedly unlike Earth," the sober announcer concurred with Paul. "Thanks to Voyager Two, we now know that

Triton has pools of a dark, oozing material, oceans of slush, and volcanoes of molten nitrogen. It's the coldest known object in the solar system."

Abruptly, the picture of Neptune itself was restored, revealing the jerky image of long stony objects floating over a shifting white storm pattern. As I watched, awe drove through me like a freight train, for Neptune, for Triton, for Voyager II and for satellite television, for Paul and for my baby. I *would* write. "What's that?" I asked. "Must be one of the rings over a cloud of frozen methane."

"Either that or sausage links above a twirling glob of pizza dough," Paul said.

"I *will* keep writing," I declared, and began to prattle, compulsively, defensively, naively, untruthfully, about how we did not regret our religious faith and we would valiantly pursue our goals. I could feel Paul's interest in me escape like oxygen from my little life-support capsule. Already, my life as a writer was hissing away. He seemed to think I'd floated off to a dark, chilly, cobwebbed corner where minds die and dour creatures breed and believe in God.

I would not lose Paul. He liked me in part because I was one of the few who wasn't afraid of him—or rather, I was someone in the habit of disobeying her fear. I dared, carefully, to argue with him. I dared to make him laugh.

"What would the others think," I scolded, poking him with my elbow, "if they saw us sitting alone in the dark in your apartment at night, watching TV together, and *you* in your boxer shorts?"

Gripping his broad, bare knees, he threw back his head and let fly his wicked laugh, a hot, raucous, bawdy bray, as if from some far-sighted jester on high, and I was with the real Rat Man, the real Byron, the real Sickert, a gargoyle in the flesh.

"Did I tell you?" I teased. "There's a rumor about us." And there was.

"Yes," he snickered. "They're afraid of you, Leeza. They're small. For years they've been out to subvert me and mine. They're afraid of success. Art terrifies them."

"Well," I said, resting my hand on my middle like a knocked-up gal, "what *will* they say about the baby?"

Lowering his face, he chuckled into his wide-fingered fist, big shoulders and stomach shaking.

"They're calling this 'the last picture show,'" an announcer said.

Paul and I fell silent.

"Due to Pluto's bizarre orbit, Neptune is the most distant planet in the solar system. Voyager Two now drifts toward the heliopause, the point where solar wind dies down and interstellar space begins. Voyager's Chief Scientist Edward Stone announced, 'This has been the journey of a lifetime,' and he quoted T.S. Eliot, 'Not fare well, But fare forward, voyagers.'"

Paul patted my leg. "You'll be all right, Leeza," he said.

If God is testing me, the answer's probably right in front of me; that's the way God works, I told myself, groping for hope in Central Pennsylvania. Right in front of me were Appalachian forests, farms, and cities, where a lot of people feel that a front yard just isn't complete without a blue gazing ball on a white pedestal, a pair of kissing gnomes, and a life-sized particle-board black bear rising out of the ground like a nightmarish piece from a giant jigsaw puzzle. Likewise, the back yard just isn't a back yard without a ramshackle dog house and a barking dog attached to it. Around here, highway restaurants and warehouses have big dogs chained out to yelp their lives away in the weeds. From trailer parks to bumptious aluminum-sided split-level developments, at the rear edge of plot after plot, dogs are chained out, regardless of their owners' social rank, relegated to a patch of dead lawn and a shanty-town-style dog house.

So I shouldn't have been baffled when, one afternoon while I was wondering what to do with my mad dog now that I was going to have a baby, I overheard a man tell his friend about his new border collie and say, "He's an outdoor dog, so he'll be fine living in the garage." But baffled I was. How is a garage "outdoors," what is an "outdoor dog," and why hadn't I thought of building my border collie a dog house, tying her outside, thereby solving all my problems? Beneath our apartment we had a basement room and a garage, both of which opened onto a small grass and cement area with a pinwheeling laundry rack like a shabby antenna. We could tie her to the pole of it. Kierney could be an outdoor dog.

A few minutes later, driving home and away from the stranger with the new outdoor border collie, I wondered why such a simple, familiar, seemingly self-evident resolution confused and upset me. A lifetime dog lover, when I heard people say they were going to get an "outdoor dog," I *always* wondered what they meant. Alien, ringing like silver Chinese exercise balls in the palm of my hand, the two words rolled around and against each other, their meaning sliding out of my grasp.

Like many lifetime dog-lovers, well before I'd learned to appreciate the debt Western civilization owed the steam engine, I knew that in the Oligocene epoch, *Miacis* evolved, gifting us with hyenas, weasels, cats, bears, and dogs. Well before I'd ever sat down to a column of numbers and successfully carried a "1", I had imagined golden lupine eyes floating in the shadows of a caveman's fire. The way some people can discern almost molecular distinctions between different makes of cars, I could tell an English Cocker from an English springer spaniel and a Cardigan from a Pembroke Welsh corgi; at a glance I could identify the Lurcher, the Belgian Tervuren, the Bullmastiff and the Beardie. While I might not've recognized by name a movie actress I'd seen a dozen times, if a dog raced across the screen, I yelled out the breed.

Given my knack for canine nomenclature, I felt I should know the general appearance, head and skull, neck, forequarters, hindquarters, coat, color, gait, and temperament of the "outdoor dog," which probably numbered in the millions in Central Pennsylvania. So when I got home, I shoved past Kierney, who leapt right up to my ears, and headed straight for my bookshelves, which were stacked with copies of *Dog Fancy* and *Dog World* and over two dozen dog books. For all the completeness of my library, "outdoor dogs" appeared in no index, no table of contents. If I could only cure this peculiar semantic blindness of mine, perhaps I'd find the answer which would save Kierney's life.

As a girl, I'd read *White Fang* over and over. Surely, I thought, White Fang was the quintessential outdoor dog. While I searched the bindings on my bookshelves for *White Fang*, Kierney watched me as if I were about to pull a squirrel off the shelf and dangle it over her head. Having found the book, I stumbled over Kierney on my way to my chair. Here, in this of all dog books, I thought, I would find outdoor dogs. I remembered Jack London's dogs and wolves as lone spirits, adventurers, creatures who ran miles through the day and through the night, "running over the surface of a world frozen and dead," where "they alone were alive," seeking "for other things that were alive in order that they might devour them and continue to live." For an hour I turned those pages I'd turned so many times long ago. For about an hour Kierney dropped her slimy racquetball onto the pages, and I threw the ball for her and wiped away the spittle-smears, uncovering profound canine yearning and conflict. I chased through the text, coursing for answers to a tumble of questions. What's all this about lords and the Wild? Do dogs hearken to the Wild?

It wasn't long before I determined that the Wild is not a synonym for wilderness, which serves as nothing but a setting. The Wild refers to a culture of canine making, with its own laws, its own "indoors"— dens and caves—and its own four-legged lords. And dogs don't long for the Wild, unless they were originally raised by wolves, in which case the longing resembles homesickness. In the world of Jack London, dogs raised exclusively in a human culture with human lords tend to fear a dog of the Wild, rather the same way natives of Appalachia who've never left their mountain might fear an Arab, an African, or a Californian. Adopted by Indians in his puppyhood, White Fang had the heart of a dog, and "the lordship of man was a need of his nature." *White Fang* is not about a wild dog reveling in the elements or in his freedom, nor about a dog who dreams of one day being chained alone to a patch of backyard dirt, but about how an abused wolf-dog, caught between two cultures, finds his "love-master," Weedon Scott. When he finds Scott, he lives alongside him, indoors and out.

I remained blind. So I took from my book shelf Elizabeth Marshall Thomas' nonfiction study, *The Hidden Life of Dogs*, in which Thomas observes a Siberian husky named Misha, the canine Odysseus, while he explores the city of Cambridge, Massachusetts, as if it were "the wine-dark sea." Having recently read this book, which both chronicled and glorified the life of a wayfaring dog, I quickly remembered that it wouldn't help me to understand what people usually meant when they called a dog "outdoor." Thomas climbs on her bike, pedals off, and tails Misha in search of "what ordinary dogs want." She discovers that Misha, as Everydog, essentially wants to trot around seeking the company of other dogs. When he's finished visiting, he goes home to his "wife," a Siberian husky named Maria, and scratches on the door to come in. By Thomas' observations, rather than an "outdoor dog," Misha might be most accurately called a "tireless socialite." None of my books were going to help me.

Personally, I didn't know many dogs tied or penned outdoors myself. I did know a few, but only a few, who ran free. Less than a mile away through farms and forests ran Sweep and Ross, and across the state ran my old roommate Mary's dog Bingo. Whether Lassie, Benji, the Tramp, or Pete the Pup, an affable free-roaming dog is a romantic figure indeed, but as the automobile has encroached further into our lives and its roads have further crisscrossed our lands, the numbers of such neighborhood characters have drastically dwindled. Few of us have grown up under the spell of a dog who adventured in forests, fields and garbage dumps, accompanied bands of kids, won the affection of households scattered all over town and answered to many different names. Nowadays, when wandering dogs like Sweep and Toss pop up, they're nuisances arrested by the Dog Law Enforcement Officer and their owners have to pay bail. As a type, free-roaming outdoor dogs are endangered if not extinct, and, living right on a highway in a town with strict leash laws, I couldn't turn Kierney into an outdoor dog simply by throwing her out the door to run with Sweep and Toss. She would have to be tied.

Turning to my computer, I logged onto the Internet to send a query to a border collie chat group—"What is an outdoor dog?" One person, both an electronic and non-virtual friend of mine who owned three border collies, responded by telling me about Grover, the border collie he'd rescued from abuse, who hadn't been well socialized and therefore was slow to grow attached to him or his wife. "Grover is what I consider an outdoor dog," my friend wrote. "Weather permitting, he would stay outside almost all the time if given the choice. He does ask to come in sometimes, but he's soon back by the door. I think he just prefers to bask in the sun on the hillside or roam the property looking for rabbits, groundhogs, and whatever." At last, I had a definition I could understand: an outdoor dog is one who enjoys being outside alone. Why, during my childhood, my own fox terrier Patches was an outdoor dog, a scent-junkie snorting invisible lines— squirrel/cat/sneaker/lawn mower. Whenever she got loose, she actually ran until she collapsed. Patches happily spent hours tied in the yard, stock-still, nose alive and eyes flat, tripping on the wind.

However, the few times we'd ever tied Kierney out, she'd ki-yied like a puppy. Looking back, I saw she was exactly like every border collie I ever owned since. Once, a few years later, I went off for a bike ride at the same time Joe left the house. When I pedaled back home two hours later, I found our border collie Pip on the back step frozen in an obedience-ring *sit*, his head raised as though he imagined me standing formally beside him. When I opened the door for him, he burst into the house as if he'd been holding his breath. Yet this was the dog who'd spent his first and most formative months of life tied out on a sheep farm.

Another time, friends of ours arrived for a visit and rang the doorbell. When I opened the door, my border collie Casey Jane stood merrily among them. Stunned, I asked simply, "Why's my dog with you?" My friends said, "She was curled up sleeping under that window." I saw the screen had come loose. Having jumped out, perhaps after a squirrel or a passing dog, Casey Jane had wanted to come right back in, found that she couldn't, and, forsaking dogs and squirrels and cats and garbage cans and recycling bins and ball fields and wooded parks and all the friendly college students passing on the sidewalk just a few feet away, she chose to sleep, to shut down until rescued, right at the spot where she'd last been near me.

Although the border collies in my life have all been purebred, born out of actively working stock, all of them lean, muscled and well exercised, designed to spend twelve hours a day tearing after sheep over the craggy Scottish hills, they shunned freedom as if it were illness. They bond deeply and crave not just constant action, but constant interaction. My dogs enjoy being outdoors, especially if there's a Frisbee or another dog around, but they don't prefer it to being cut off from one of us human pack members—like a child lost in a shopping mall, a soldier separated from his unit. For a lone pack animal, life can be purposeless, dangerous, and dull.

The more I thought about my friend's definition, the more I realized that "outdoor dog" was not, as he used it, like "outdoorsman," "seafood lover," "doll collector," or "Dionne Warwick fan." My friend was a sensitive, responsible, articulate dog handler, solicitous of his dogs and of his friends, but he was the only person I'd ever heard use the phrase to indicate an individual dog's taste. "Outdoor dog," as he used it, neither applied to Kierney nor illuminated for me what *other* people meant when they used it.

I talked to people about it. I noticed most of the people I heard use the phrase "outdoor dog" seemed to be using it as a general breed category. They said, "My dog's an outdoor dog," as if they'd bought the dog from a knowledgeable salesperson at a lawn and garden shop. It's a descriptive phrase—the dog stays outside by virtue of breed. On one categorical level you have your Toys, your Hounds, your Working

Dogs, and then on an even more general level, your Indoor and your Outdoor. Toys, of course, usually—but not always—fall under Indoor, many of the others, Outdoor.

The determination seemed to be size only in part. To some people, anything as big as or bigger than a beagle was an outdoor dog. Along with size, another general characteristic, one that I found strange considering the northeastern winters, was that an outdoor dog was often short-haired—Doberman Pinschers, Rottweilers, Pointers, Weimaraners, Bullmastiffs, and of course a variety of crosses of these breeds. Many tended to be of breeds originally developed for ferocious outdoor activities, such as dog fighting, bull baiting, guarding game lands from poachers, hunting mountain lion, and warfare. Although the present day specimens of outdoor dogs might never even have chased a cat or bitten a paper boy, people behaved as if letting them inside would be like letting in a live chain saw. Around the region I did see quite a few large, heavily-coated dogs like German shepherds and shepherd mixes tied or penned out, as well as an occasional Great Pyrenees or chow, but generally the large, well-upholstered dog seemed to belong indoors, like a couch. Although more logically suited to the Pennsylvania elements, Golden Retrievers, Old English sheepdogs, collies, and Labradors fell under the category of Hearth Dogs, the kind of dog that poses well in family-portraits, a jolly pal who helps the baby learn to walk by letting her cling to the fur on his rump. In one suburban block in the middle of winter, while snowblowers blasted sidewalks clear, I once spied the mystical, smoky face of a Siberian husky contemplating the blue-white expanse from behind a double-paned window, while a couple of doors down, a boxer stood virtually naked in a snow-filled pen.

People argued that an outdoor dog develops a thicker coat, but it seemed to me that a coat could only grow as thick as DNA allows. I had to admit, though, that a rough-coated border collie such as Kierney, who billowed like milkweed when she shed, could grow insulation sufficient for twenty-degree days and ten-degree nights in a thoughtfully constructed dog house. Kierney and her thick coat came out of stock traditionally kept outdoors, sleeping in barns and running on wind-swept Scottish hillsides. As far as physicality was concerned, Kierney qualified as an outdoor dog, even if she'd mope about it.

However, people often used the term "outdoor dog" to prescribe an individual dog's lifestyle regardless of its breed or its coat density, in order to fit the owner's convenience. One woman said to me, "We're getting a German Shepherd. He's going to be an outdoor dog." Another said, "I hate fleas," which was meant to explain to me why her beagle was chained twenty-four hours a day to his dog house. In these cases, I had to assume other possibilities were open to the dog before it came to live with them—the dog might have gone to someone else who might've prescribed a different fate—the flea-killing pill Proban, for instance. These dogs became outdoor dogs much the same way some children became pianists despite, perhaps, a preference for swimming or chemistry. The young pianists had pianos; outdoor dogs had chains. Decisions were made on their behalf, and if anyone originally questioned the wisdom of these decisions—to insist on piano lessons, to keep a dog outside, even to have a dog or a child in the first place—they held their tongues. To people who used the term "outdoor dog" in this way, the dog did not necessarily belong to some category of outdoor beasts, like goats and elephants. The phrase indicated a choice made for her, usually well before any of the dog's own preferences could have manifested themselves.

Such was not the way I'd make a decision for Kierney, as I was too much of a non-speciesist, I suppose. But I had to admit, my circumstances had changed and just as the one woman didn't like fleas, I didn't like raising a baby alongside a criminally insane dog.

There was a third usage which did describe a dog's individual character, yet not in the way my friend, Grover's owner, used it. A family has brought the dog into their home and into their hearts, yet somehow the dog has proven itself unworthy. It's then banished, blacklisted, "in the dog house"—it's an "outdoor dog." The label in this case resembles "convict." A list of crimes reveals that the dog jumped on guests when it should have been clear to her that she had grown rather large for that, she failed to housebreak herself, she nipped in play and showed no remorse when her victims cried out. Left alone, her chief recreation was vandalism. For her repeat offenses, an array of misdemeanors and felonies, she received a life sentence, chained, caged or penned outside. In this the way, my sister's Kelpie/McNab mix became an outdoor dog, isolated from the family she had overwhelmed and confined alternately to the fenced yard and to the garage—albeit temporarily—until my sister found her a more suitable home, where she received, I assume, the alternative sentence of rehabilitation. This spiral of human lassitude and canine crime also seems to be the same way many dogs become "pound dogs." No one would say I had neglected Kierney, and I had long attempted rehabilitation. Certainly Kierney, with biting humans on her record, could be given the maximum sentence, even if most of her victims were fools whose skin she hadn't broken.

The truth was I knew a great deal about outdoor dogs. The man who runs our local SPCA and investigates abuse against dogs told me that the average lifespan of a dog kept tied out is five years. I knew all this, and still I remained blind to the meaning of the phrase, rather in the way I find certain activities incomprehensible, such as sky diving. The fact was that I had so rarely heard the term "outdoor dog" used the thoughtful way Grover's owner defined it that I bristled at the very sound of it. The phrase called to mind outrages I'd witnessed, dogs who were helpless against attacks from stray dogs, raccoons, or cruel children, dogs with water dishes empty or thick with ice, dogs standing in their own worm-filigreed shit.

Such was the life of the two Weimaraners tied to trees on short ropes in an upscale backyard, faces scabbed and running pus because they'd become food for deer flies. I was a kid at the time, about twelve years old. Every once in a while, I'd go over when the humans weren't home and untangle the dogs, clean up the crap, rub insect repellent on their faces. One day contractors came to build a high wooden privacy fence on the property, and I was relieved to think that the dogs would soon be running loose in a fenced yard. But then the contractors got near the end of the yard, where the dogs were tied, and built the fence shy of the dogs—rather than contain them, the fence shielded the people in the house from the sight of them. Puzzled, I waited several weeks after the fence was finished, but the dogs stayed tied, tangled, fly-bitten. Finally, heart pounding, I called the SPCA myself, and a day later, the dogs were gone.

I heard of an otherwise sensible and respectable man who kept three miniature dachshunds chained out, one for each of his children. Oddly, each little dog was attached to a chain, which was held fast by a cinderblock laid on it. The man kept them this way even though their first outdoor dachshund died savagely under the snout of a raccoon and another was crushed to death by the little girl who loved him when she, trying to free a tangled chain, dropped the cinderblock on him.

People who owned outdoor dogs seemed to lose one after another to cars. The story usually went like this: one sunny Saturday, roused to pity perhaps out of boredom, the dog's owners unhook the chain to give the dog a little exercise and then, oh unholy horror, the dog rips around willy-nilly right out into the road! It doesn't even seem to know its own name! "The children saw everything," they say, and, knowing I'm a dog lover, pause to share with me a look of pained confusion. "Sheppy didn't die right away," they say, and give me the look again. And so to spare the children nightmares, they do what they see as the right and responsible thing: as soon as possible they get another hale and hearty beast to take up the fallen chain.

These same people often had several such tales to tell, all of them almost identical, including the pained confusion—something hurt, something was wrong, and they just couldn't quite tell what. They hope I will tell them and forgive them. Their children were nine, seven, maybe only five years old, and already had watched more than one big dog die on the side of the road. Or, their dogs were stolen. Or poisoned by a neighbor to silence the barking in which outdoor dogs tend to indulge, hour after hour, day after day, sending out the sound like a beacon light, a smoke signal, a note in a bottle.

My favorite outdoor dog was Jack, an oversized, fawn-colored beagle who belonged to a relative of mine, but Jack's gone now. Jack was chained behind the shed where he couldn't be seen from the house, thereby presenting no aesthetic blight to the landscaping. "Gosh, if you can't see him how do you remember to feed him?" I asked. "That's a problem," my sister-in-law admitted, "sometimes I don't." Although the responsibility fell on her, the family beagle technically belonged to her husband, who came from a family of hunters whose tradition it was to enter the woods with guns and a beagle. Mainly the beagle bayed behind the shed, perhaps so that his three sons could be exposed to the sound and have the opportunity to touch and even play with a real hunting dog, as he did growing up. The beagle stood behind the shed in the way that, in many hunters' homes, black velvet paintings of deer hang on the walls, turkey-hunting videos are stacked beside the VCR, and assorted "outdoor" species stand here and there inside the home, taxidermied.

During my first visit to their home, I walked outside and around the shed to meet Jack, a polite, thin-coated dog. Blessed as he was with a long chain, he kept his semi-circle of packed dirt fairly clean, choosing to eliminate only at the very end of the chain in an out-of-the-way grassy spot. Exposure to the elements had aged Jack to a look of long-suffering wisdom—or to a look of stupidity brought on by prolonged lack of stimuli—hard to say which. I heard he had come to them like that, having spent his first four years chained in somebody else's yard. After nearly a year behind my brother-in-law's shed, hunting season came around, and—the way I heard the story—Jack found himself awakened in the night, snapped to a leash, led to a truck, and driven into the autumn woods.

As the night sky above the scraggled canopy slowly lightened to a navy blue, Jack waited, chained now to the porch rail of a cabin built on a stream bed. He stood in the wet darkness, he trembled, he whirled at sounds, he lowered his tail and bristled, he lifted his tail high and raised his nose to the wind. After a half an hour or so, he felt more at ease, turned circles and lay himself gingerly in the damp leaves. Inside, the men oiled and loaded their rifles, put on their coats, stomped into their boots, and pocketed their flasks. There was laughter, yawning, the smell of coffee. Finally they came outside, spoke to him, and bent down to thump him on the chest. One man threw him the heel of a sandwich. Dawn came late to the shadows of the forest. In the clinging darkness, they opened and slammed the doors of their trucks. The familiar man, the one behind whose shed he had spent three full seasons, bent and spoke to him excitedly. Then the man did something that he'd only done once before, a few hours earlier, behind the shed. He released the clasp at Jack's neck.

And Jack ran. He ran and ran. He did not bay. Behind him at first the voices of the men laughed and then yelled, "Jack! Jack!", and the sound of the word faded, faded away to nothing, as the dog ran.

It's been years since Jack ran. The family quickly filled his space behind the shed with another beagle. As for Jack, since his story is one that can be conveniently told to children, I know it may not be true—Jack may simply have been run over. A fawn-colored dog in the woods during deer season might easily have been shot. It could be that Jack just dropped dead behind the shed, and my brother-in-law didn't drive to the woods to hunt with him, but to bury him. Yet, somehow, I won't believe any other version, perhaps because I can still hear the triumph in my mother-in-law's voice when she called to tell me Jack ran away, as if she and I had shared in some unspoken conspiracy to free him. I think of him running still, through a forest of pine and rhododendron, over a world wet and rocky, where he alone is alive and seeks other things that are alive. In my mind, Jack runs, the forest filling his senses: a rotten log, a patch of carrion, a bramble, a pile of exotic dung, the blundering rump of a scuttling possum. Run, Jack, run!

In troubled sleep I turned, my belly hard, round and heavy, stomach muscles splitting down the middle, my very sternum separating in my chest. When I slept, I had vivid, recurrent dreams that I looked down to see my dog nursing at my breast. I woke in the night, disturbed and embarrassed by my own dreams. Thick-coated convict or not, Kierney would not be banished from the house by me, a student, a teacher, and a new mother whose lifestyle allowed little time to visit with an outdoor dog. I would not leave her chained to unrelieved boredom, danger, and loneliness, her mind atrophying and her neuroses multiplying unchecked by my discipline and affection. Spine and feet aching, I turned in my bed. If I gave her to someone else, the lunatic would probably bite and be killed for it. Oh, I had to sleep! Maybe I'd drive her to that cabin by the stream and tell her to run, tell her to go find Jack. She wouldn't run. She wouldn't even take her eyes off me, I knew—I was her sun, and she orbited me. Neither of us could defy the pull of gravity between us. Curled foxlike in her crate, nose tucked in her brush, she slept, an orb of darkness in the black box of our night. I couldn't betray her. I was so troubled and self-pitying that I even heard myself think, maybe I'd have to give my own baby up for adoption, anything that might cut through what had grown to be a mountainous, tangled ball of emotional, ethical and theological yarn. I lay in my bed, frowning in the dark, and prayed, "My God, please help me now. There's no way for me to pass your test. I'm out of acceptable solutions."

Bob Martin was not a tall man, but his German Shepherds, imported from Germany out of police dog stock, were oversized, lean, and sound. Before the class of about fifteen people and as many dogs, the award-winning police dog trainer strutted in his basement rink, chain-smoking to classical music. Not one dog in the room was without awe of him, not one person without respect, except, perhaps, his dotty wife, who disrupted the class by frolicking in and handing out clipped coupons for dried onion soup mix and Honey Nut Cheerios. Once moved by the music, she twirled ballerina-style across the training arena shaking her white hair, so that Martin had to halt class, apologize to us, and lead her away. I felt a little sorry for him until I learned that his star student and assistant, a large-breasted, narrow-hipped, warm and exuberant young woman with dark eyes and dark curls actually lived in the house with them.

I didn't join the class at first. Urged by Kierney's breeder, George, I called Martin, told him my troubles, and he offered a private lesson.

"I dog must never bite a human unless you tell it to," he said. "Keep a choke chain with a bit of rope on her neck at all times."

I'd long been taught that it was unsafe to leave a choke chain on a dog, but I was listening.

"This is how you stop a vicious dog," he said, and demonstrated with one of his own shepherds—you take the choke collar and lift, disabling the dog by pulling its front paws off the floor. You hold the dog that way until it struggles, and you don't stop until the dog whimpers in submission.

His dog withstood the demonstration sleepily.

"Never lift its hind legs off the floor," Martin warned me. "Wait until you hear the high-pitched squeal of submission," he said. "Remember, the punishment comes from the choke chain, not from you," he added.

I strongly doubted dogs were that stupid. They knew darn well who held the end of the choke chain. From what I could tell of Bob Martin so far, even if he was a monster, he did have some dog sense. I needed a new way to convey clear and honest disapproval for egregious behavior. Willing to at least try it, I put a choke chain around her neck—without the little rope, which seemed too unsafe—and enrolled in his class.

At our very first session, as usual, Kierney hid beneath my chair.

"See," Martin said. "This is trouble. Get her out in the open." I pulled, but she resisted. Impatiently, all in a flash, he reached under, she snarled, and the next thing I knew, he pulled her out by her leash and she hung before my eyes, *all four paws off the ground*. She twisted and clawed the air, choking and hacking, screeching in submission, spinning, eyes bulging, shuddering—I just sat there, looking right into her terrified eye. I was immobile. My integrity shattered. Martin dropped her at my feet like a sack of garbage.

She shuffled back under my chair.

"No!" he hollered, more at me than at her.

Beginning to breathe again, awkwardly I bent over my pregnant belly and reached under the seat, stroking her. I gathered her into my hands and slid her into the light, propping her against my legs. The room had fallen silent. Looking down the row of people and dogs, I saw the people turn away in awkward but sympathetic denial. The dogs cringed and shivered, licking their noses, watching Martin as if, when he strangled Kierney, he'd simultaneously strangled every one of them.

In a flash, I marveled at their ability to empathize—then I was outraged by the proof that he had indirectly tortured a whole room full of innocent dogs.

He went on with his lesson as if nothing had happened.

And, as if forsaken by God and having no one to turn to except the Devil, I stayed put.

"Never speak in anger. Never touch them in anger," he said, taking this opportunity to repeat the lesson for everyone. "Always use the lead. Never strike with your hand. If your dog does something off lead or in the house, correct them with the choke chain, hit them with a magazine or throw something at them, like a paperback book, but never let the punishment come from you. If punishment always comes from an object, the dog never knows it comes from you. Only love comes from you." To illustrate, he graciously bent and stroked Kierney's head while she skulked and shuddered and wagged her tail.

"If only love comes from you, Bob, why do they fear you?" I wanted to ask. "Do you think they're that stupid?" Paralyzed, I asked myself why I hadn't tried to save my dog. What kind of mother was I going to be? Where were my protective instincts? It wasn't faith in him that had frozen me there—was it shock?

In our private lesson, he told me "Never lift its hind legs off the floor." The man had lied!

He was an experienced dog handler—he *knew* that she'd growl if he reached beneath the seat—she had been set up by him, framed! How had she and I arrived at this Hell? I should've held her more accountable all along, shouldn't have been so understanding, and when she showed me her soul, I shouldn't have looked.

I sat, bloated with pregnancy, picturing myself walk out. Over and over. And still, I sat.

I stayed the rest of the class. When he called me for my turn, I got up, did the little left-turn, right-turn, and halt routine, and Kierney performed for me with the same abjection as the other dogs.

When I got home and told Joe what had happened, he ranted and threatened to ruin the man—Martin didn't know who he was dealing with, people well-connected to hardcore animal rights activists like us.

I left the choke around her neck all the time. A few nights later, hearing Kierney clanging in her crate, I rose heavily from the waterbed to let her outside, even though she hadn't needed to go out at night for many months. We shuffled into the night air. I heard her drizzle into the grass, then pad into the neighbor's yard.

"In," I said, but she didn't turn around. "Let's go *in*!" I hissed, and she returned. As we went back into the bedroom, I ordered her, "Crate," but heard the click of her nails pass the crate—the stinker was going to try to sleep on the floor! I swiftly caught her around the middle to guide her into the crate, but what should I hear but a snarl and what should I feel but her teeth bruise my hand!

The biting had to end and end now.

With some kind of intuitive sight I found the ring of her choke collar in one sweep and lifted her off the floor in the dark of my bedroom. How heavy she was, and how dark it was! How she fought me, both of us blind, both fighting for the same life—the irony of what I was doing made the moment dense, sluggish, muffled. She hung twisting from the hand that loved her most, making terrible hacking and gurgling noises, her claws running on my body, searching for purchase, and I kept knocking her free, back to hang on the chain that closed her throat. I sobbed—oh, God, have I never loved anyone?—she will not die she will not leave me she will *not die*! Cry, Kierney, cry so I can release you! She didn't cry but strangled in rapidly escalating hysteria, and I began to notice that all along there'd been a dull, rapid thumping on the hand that held her, like someone doing a drum roll on my hand with padded sticks.

Waiting for her to whimper as Martin had taught me, I braced that drumming hand with my other, she was so heavy, and I grew calmer, grimmer.

"What's going on?" Joe's said.

That strange tattooing on my hand persisted. Evenly, I said, "Turn on the light."

And I saw her. Her eyes were wild and her lips drawn back, and she was using her blade-like back teeth to scissor my hand. For Martin she had squealed "uncle" immediately, but me she looked right in the eye, not pleading for help, but damning me to Hell.

I noticed, dispassionately, that on the skin of my hand, where her teeth hammered, black marks weirdly multiplied, their appearance strangely separate from the movements of her teeth, as if inked by a poltergeist. It was only by way of dream logic that I made a cause-effect connection.

I noticed too, her gasps became about a half-tone higher, not puppyish, not submissive, but good enough for me. I let her down. She catapulted into her crate. With my injured hand, I slammed the crate shut and locked it.

Then I noticed I was sobbing and may have been all along, "Poor Kierney, poor Kierney." Three seconds, thirty minutes, I had no idea how much time had passed.

Joe led me into the bathroom where we saw my hand—it was bluish white and covered with small, deep gouges, not bleeding—the hand of someone dead. "I betrayed her," I whimpered while Joe ran warm water over the broken skin. I flexed my hand, the color returned, and the blood ran.

"You're gonna need stitches," Joe said.

"No, they're puncture wounds," I sniffled. "It doesn't hurt." I was shivering and sweating at the same time.

"It's two a.m." he said. "C'mon."

The emergency room technician asked, "Can you describe the dog that bit you?"

"No," I laughed, "I can't describe her at all."

Joe laughed too, and the technician looked up.

"It was my own dog."

The technician nodded. "Most people I see with dog bites were bitten by their own dogs."

The punctures didn't require stitches, but I had no record of a tetanus shot. Because I was pregnant, he gave me one, bound my hand, and sent me home, a pregnant woman capable of strangling a loved one, but immune to tetanus. The light was still on in the bedroom. As I passed the crate, Kierney watched me in fear and awe, the way the dogs did Der Fuehrer Martin.

The next morning I called him.

He laughed. "Never grab a dog in the dark. They don't see any better than we do."

So, it was my own fault. "Now wait a minute—" I was thinking, how could night blindness have been the explanation? She was no idiot—she wasn't with strangers in an unfamiliar place. She knew exactly who'd grabbed her and why. She had no reason to bite me—it wasn't like my sweet, needy, and submissive dog to defy me for the simple privilege of sleeping on the floor. Either she didn't recognize me, which confirmed she was crazy, or she was arbitrarily and excessively defying me for the sake of defiance, which again confirmed she was crazy. Why couldn't we approach Kierney as "not guilty by reason of insanity"? Why weren't there insane asylums for dogs? But I never got say any this because Martin interrupted me. Kierney's reasons or anti-reasons for biting me didn't matter to him.

"You should see the scars on *my* hands," he chuckled. In his world, all dogs, crazy or not, craved power. It was the handler's job to convince the dogs they would never have it. "Next time grab the little rope, not the ring; get some distance from the teeth. But you did good. Things'll be better from now on."

Over the next few days we concluded that Martin was right, strangling Kierney turned out to have been the best thing for her. Now what terrified her most was our disapproval. When someone scary approached her, instead of hiding and snarling, she ran to me for advice. Each night, as the sun went down, she grew nervous, and when we went to bed, we were heartbroken to find her already in the back of her crate.

"All we taught her to do was sleep in her crate," I said, but no.

Until this night, I was her master, but only when she was sane. Now, indoors or out, night or day, dark or light, I was master of her madness too.

Chapter Six

Brain Lightning

Hands clasped, chin up, smug, I'd been walking the solemn Communion line for five years, still one step away from heresy. Weekly I professed a belief in the Holy Spirit, the being who, when I knelt in the college chapel and prayed, "God, teach me to love," had lit within my chest, in my diaphragm, the site once considered the seat of the soul. Five years had passed, and only now, thanks to Kierney, was I wondering: if there were a Holy Spirit or a life force, was there an unholy spirit or a death force? I believed my black dog had a soul, and she had a conscience, and she had the capacity for language and confusion and discord and even insanity. Like the gorilla Koko, Kierney lacked only opposable thumbs and the lingual-laryngeal equipment for speech. The many meanings of the words "lunatic" and "moonstruck" tagged her like perfectly thrown darts. With a skull wide enough to admit evil, she seemed in thrall to some sort of demonic weather system—but what sort? Are there forces in the universe that, like the radio waves permeating our planet, suffuse the atmosphere of the brain? What if some portion of the cerebral cortex can tune in Satan's station—or God's—depending on how we twist our cranial dials? Do some of us experience drift and static? Is it easier for some to capture one broadcast over another? And how close are the bands?

We lived next door to two Christian fundamentalists, a newlywed couple, Cindy and Fred. I'd bump into them when I took Kierney for a walk, or when I checked the mail, or took out the recycling, and the next thing I knew I'd be in their living room, listening to them tell me they believed—without much awe, I noticed—that God was literally "in us all."

"Doesn't that stagger you?" I'd say. "How can you keep from throwing yourself on the rug and kicking and screaming? How can you get up and drive off in that Subaru every morning? How can you pick your nose? Why aren't you studying astronomy or growing orchids or spoon-feeding lepers or chanting in a monastery? Tell me again, what exactly is it you do?"

They had office jobs—the monolithically boring duties of which I was helpless to comprehend—and they worshiped God, all right. Praise the Lord, through constant prayer they injected the power of Jesus into every FAX they sent and miracles unfolded before their eyes. "Prayer is a practical power," they explained. "Something you carry with you and use in your work."

"Sort of a telekinetic tool belt?"

They puffed and denied it, but that's exactly what it was. Prayer for a pay raise *caused* a pay raise. Cindy and Fred were obliged to pray for sick persons, because prayer would cure them; therefore, *not* to pray was akin to murder. Their voluminous memory for Bible verses and anecdotes of uncannily-answered prayers might nearly have won me over, except for the exceptions, which sent a plague of locusts into my mind, a black cloud of buzzing insects blotting out the laser beam of truth they labored to fix on me.

Cross-legged on their couch, I sipped Breathe Easy Tea, an herbal remedy Cindy had prepared for me because when I walked into her apartment I had sneezed. I was saying something about having seen good, young, sick people die despite the pleas of entire religious communities.

"God must have loved them so much He wanted them with Him," Fred announced from his armchair. A tall, handsome, expressionless man, Fred considered me fallen from grace, not so much because of my irreverent conversation but because I went to Catholic Mass. For some reason, my Catholicism became more and more problematic to him the more my pregnancy showed.

"My grandfather was foul-tempered, and he smoked and drank whiskey and kept setting fire to the couch when he passed out on it with a lit cigarette," I said, smiling sweetly over my tea cup. Delighted, I noticed that Fred winced every time I, in the glow of motherhood, pronounced indelicate words like "whiskey," "cigarette" and "couch." Mischievously, I went on, "My grandfather would have a stroke and lie dying in his own vomit, unloved and cursed by the weary Christians who took care him. And then you know what? He'd get better."

"God must have had a reason to cure him," Cindy replied, fresh-faced, voluptuous in her tailored suit. "Perhaps He planned to convert him and use that conversion to glorify His Name."

"But that means you have no evidence that God rewards people according to how many prayers they receive. I'm glad," I said scandalously, before they could tell me that they prayed because they had faith and not because they had evidence. "I want to believe God is fair. What about the lonely and the destitute who suffer in obscurity, un-prayed-for?"

They replied that God even took care of those people Christians inadvertently overlooked.

"Well, then if God chooses whom to cure regardless of your prayers, when you pray for someone you're doing no more than a child who's allowed to pretend he's helping to cook dinner, when actually the adult is making all the decisions and doing all the work. Honestly," I laughed, "don't you ever wonder if you're just getting in the way?"

Years before my own spiritual awakening, people like Cindy were why I wouldn't dare look twice at religion. I was afraid if Jesus got ahold of me I'd lose my God-given faculty of reason. I discovered I could enjoy Cindy's conversations provided I took her frequent interruptions—"Praise Jesus!" or "Give it to God!"—as a kind of speech disorder, a reverse Tourette's syndrome.

One afternoon Cindy and I left our husbands home and she took me to the outlet malls in Reading, Pennsylvania, to shop for my impending baby. During our shopping expedition, God, through his Holy Hotline, helped Cindy make several wardrobe decisions—including whether or not to buy the red nylon dress with a plunging neckline. "Yes," she cooed, "God says He wants me to enjoy my body."

Indeed, God had blessed Cindy with a flat stomach, firm hips, fair and flawless skin, luxurious dark curly hair, and breasts orbed like twin moons. Slowly oscillating her elysian cleavage before the fitting room mirror, she modeled the dress for me, her white breasts in the red fabric waxing and waning and waxing again.

"If beauty be truth," I told her, "then it would be a lie for you not to wear that dress. It'd be a sin."

After she paid for the dress, we strolled through the mall, and I confided my spiritual conflict with Kierney. Ever since I'd shown that dog that I could take her life with my bare hands, she was terrified of me and obeyed me in fear. Now I was her Hitler—when I said, "Collar," she had sat with her eyes closed and ears folded back, head extended so that I could slip around her neck the choke chain with a bit of new rope dangling from it, a ready noose—she wore it the rest of her life.

Month after month, nightfall made her fling herself into her crate. She wouldn't come out or be consoled until dawn, so much did she fear I would kill her at dark. Each morning I'd greet her with a cheery, "Good morning!" which she took as a stay of execution and happily twirled in her crate until I let her out. She bounced at my face, gratefully bathing it with her tongue. She had always been tormented by vague fears and random anxieties, but now all her dread focused on me, her comforter and her protector.

"I returned her sin with my own," I said, as Cindy paused at a bath oil boutique.

"You've got to be cruel to be kind," she replied.

My I.Q. plummeted. I stumbled from the vertigo. I think I managed to blurt, "Yeah." Sometimes I had to remind myself that Cindy had completed a double major with honors and now held a steady grown-up job.

"God gave you Kierney," she said, pausing at a shoe store to lift a red spike heeled number, "because He knew you would care enough to do what was necessary to keep her alive."

But there were millions more dogs in neglectful and malicious homes, in so-called shelters, and in laboratories. In East Asia, millions of dogs were bludgeoned to death for their tender meat. "Why did God single out this one troubled dog for a good home and forsake millions of others?"

Exasperated, she said, "God doesn't forsake them. *People* do."

The intellectual elevator had suddenly gone up, losing me between floors.

"God tells me you are responding to His Word, and very few people do that, Lisa." She put down the spike heel and picked up a comparatively modest red pump. "But you go ahead and believe what you want," she said, giving me a worried look that told me she thought I was making my own trouble.

Maybe I was. "I want to believe what's true."

"Jesus says He is the Truth." She clutched the bag that held her new red dress.

Stultified, I lost all inclination to analyze and, although we looked at hundreds of baby items, I didn't buy anything. "God hasn't sold my novel yet," I said gloomily. "But when He does, now I know where the outlet malls are."

I half-listened to her dismal complaints about Fred, problems easily fixed by a little pixie dust, so I figured she didn't need my ear or advice and took her tales of domestic misery as the babble of a worldly child playing house. Following her through stores, I thought, surely, she's right. God brought Kierney and me together. God must've brought me to Cindy and Fred, to comfort me and set me straight. Why resist? I had to admit, I found their anecdotes about uncannily answered prayers exhilarating, and even repeated some myself. Such stories seemed to satisfy a bodily need, the way hugs and laughter do. Whatever their marital problems, for Cindy confided plenty in me, she and Fred would be fine—they were tuned into God's broadcasting frequency.

Still, the dial was delicate, the band narrow. It seemed to me that their reception was getting little interference compared to mine, which came and went with the solar winds. How I wished to be locked into God's station too! How blissful to pray and to know that our little family would be in His care, effortlessly fine! But it couldn't be ignored—no matter how I tried, I just couldn't tune in on the same kilocycles Fred and Cindy did.

On the way home after dark, on the side of the road of a lonely stretch of turnpike, our headlights flashed on a tractor-trailer, the cab crushed against a tree, the driver lying inert across the hood in a shimmering spray of glass. Just as suddenly, the spectacle was gone.

"Pull over!" I cried.

"No," she said as we flew on. "Someone else will stop."

But no one before us had stopped, and, shifting in my seat to face the dozens of headlights out the back window, I saw no one else pull over. This was in the days before cellular phones, so there was no chance people were dialing for help from their cars, and the turnpike exits were more than twenty miles apart. "We're *all* thinking someone else will stop!" I had studied this phenomenon in Intro to Psychology—why hadn't Cindy? Luckily, we passed a sign that announced an exit approaching in seven miles. "Get off here, and I'll phone for help at a gas station."

She drove past the exit.

"Why didn't you stop?!" I cried.

"Shh!" she said. "I'm praying for him."

She was dialing 911 on her Holy Hotline. Of course.

Her car felt like a small box trap. I held my breath and closed my eyes, trying not to burst into a helpless rage. Every moment it seemed we might crash and lie broken on the roadside, choking on the exhaust of passing cars. I kept seeing the truck driver's body spread-eagle, face-down in the glass on the hood—I can see him still. Fifteen minutes passed. Fifteen miles. I had failed to note the mile-marker, but I could give the police a proximity . . .

"My brother's on trial for manslaughter," Cindy said.

"What?"

"He and his best friend were in an accident." Her teenage brother had been driving, both were drinking, the car crashed into the side of a bridge, throwing both boys from the vehicle. Her brother was unharmed, the other boy killed. Burning with sibling loyalty, she complained about the unfairness of the judicial system—after all, the dead friend had been drunk too. "He hadn't buckled his seat belt and that was *his* to do."

"If somebody had stopped to help he might've lived—"

"Oh, he died instantly," she spat, waving her hand. "My brother could get *five years*. It could ruin his chances at college!"

Thirty miles. By now the State Police had surely happened upon the trucker. I told myself I was lucky—maybe the trucker had been a decoy to lure knee-jerk Good Samaritans into an ambush. Or when we saw him he was already dead. Anyway, what good could I have done had I stopped? I was with child and with Cindy, a woman who had a vendetta against people who die on the roadside? My brain felt cramped; I couldn't think.

I kept remembering the doe I'd once seen at dusk struggling in the road at rush hour. Car after speeding car hit her again and again and she kicked and convulsed. Standing on the roadside trying to think of a way to help her, I could hear the thump of her body, the clatter of her hooves, her thin screams. Finally I leapt right out onto the road to try to stop the cars, but it was twilight and hard for the speeding and tailgating drivers to see me. One after another, they swerved toward the opposite lane or screeched around me only to hit the deer anyway. I didn't know how could I keep from getting myself killed, how I could get the doe and her slicing hooves off the road, how I could restrain her and transport her in my Toyota to a veterinary hospital—but somehow I'd manage it all. Then, overcome by the dark, by the endless stream of cars and the doe's interminable agony, I threw myself onto the grassy embankment, holding my ears. Suddenly, a pick-up truck pulled over and a big mountain man in got out. "You okay?" he asked.

"There's an injured doe in the road!"

Surprised, he turned and saw her, paused, then launched into the road between cars, grabbed her by a leg and hauled her onto the grass beside me. Relieved, I looked at her and we lay there a moment, side-by-side, both of us quiet and safe. The man stood over us, and I lifted my face to tell him thank you.

"Good eatin'," he grinned.

She was dead.

Hurtling along in Cindy's car, I pressed my hands on my great belly and felt my baby hiccup. Now I had less and less room inside my body for air and food and, perhaps, also less room for thought. Un-Cindy-like, I prayed, wordless and painful, as if fanning twigs on a fire. What good was I in the world? Scraps of church prayers drifted past, took flame, and disappeared: *I have sinned through my own fault, in my thoughts and in my words, in what I have done, and in what I have failed to do . . . I believe in the maker of heaven and earth, of all that is seen and unseen.*

Elusive sparks of hope and understanding rose in the night air, bright but fleeting against the cool black sky.

When I brought my baby home from the hospital, Kierney ignored her, whether because we had trained her well or because she never would have hurt my baby in the first place, I didn't know or care. I was so tired that I craved death, just for the rest. One good thing was that the demands of my newborn gave me ample excuse to avoid Cindy and Fred, whose conversation pained me after we'd left that man on the roadside.

Then, while my baby was still quite tiny, Cindy and Fred separated and moved out. I sat exhausted on my couch, fighting the thought that, had Cindy helped that trucker, her marriage would've been saved.

After weeks of broken sleep, I put my baby on my back and took Kierney for hikes in the woods and on campus hoping the exercise would knock me out. Set free, off lead, Kierney loped gorgeous rings around me, a feathered horse on an invisible tether. For her, those were the best times, running, her legs drawing underneath her great stretches of earth as easily as breath. Having me at home around the clock satisfied her, too, as if my constant companionship were all she'd ever wanted, despite the way she'd started her life, an ill-tempered pup who once turned her back on me.

So that I could talk to her when the baby was sleeping, I taught her a sign language, "hush," "down," "c'mere," "wait," "let's go." Like the patois of twins or the conspiracy of thwarted lovers, our secret, silent speech gave us an intimate harmony, the unheard harmony of synchronous minds. Many nights when I desperately needed sleep and was denied it, I sat in the living room trying to suppress my raging frustration and to coax myself to sleep by reading a book. She came to me, black forehead wrinkled, and pressed her face to mine, brow to brow, so that the bridge of her muzzle slid parallel to the bridge of my nose. Eye to eye we gazed. Her nose was dry from sleep, and I kissed it. Clenching her ruff in my fists, rolling my forehead against hers, I'd whimper, "I can't *believe* I'm not sleeping!" I could feel her mind but a fraction of an inch away from my mind, separated only by thin fur, skin, blood and bone. "Kier," I'd say, "Kier, Kier." I'd feel a breeze on my shins, the puff of her plumed tail. "Help," I'd whisper, and she'd skid across the room and snatch up her ball. Smiling, I'd sign to her, *No, drop it, come hug,* and she'd be in my arms again, soft and fragrant, my best friend and my waking dream.

Yet our peace could be bitter. Joe and I couldn't speak crossly at Kierney or in front of her. Now that I'd betrayed her with a choke chain, she over-reacted to any sign I was displeased. Even to curse so much as a household appliance meant the dog would spend the next half hour recovering. If I cried—and with a colicky baby plus insomnia, I cried a lot—she'd relive that horrible night, because I had cried then too. Trembling, she stood with her front paws on my lap, clawed at me and stared imploringly. If I covered my face, she pried my hands free, licked my cheeks and eyes, bumped my nose with hers. "Go away," I'd groan, burying my face in a pillow, but "go away" was the one thing she couldn't do. She shoved her face between mine and the pillow, insisted that I gaze into her eyes. In fact, she'd flip into an almost superstitious frenzy, as if, should I break our gaze, something might happen to separate us forever—I might be possessed by a demon again. She'd harass me so much I'd forget what I'd been crying about.

Those days I didn't think much beyond the raw infant in my arms, my tiny tyrant, torturing me with sleep deprivation, nursing until my breasts cracked and bled. My vampire baby threw up milk and blood. And I loved her ferociously, as if I were curled around her in a hole in the ground, nostrils full of dirt, eyes near blind in the dim light that barely shifted day to night. While we denned in our little bubble in the earth, time rushed its banks and flooded, a rising tide, consuming continents, centuries. I knew, clearly and emphatically, exactly what good I was in the world. I was my daughter's wraith, a servile ghost whose purpose was to provide food, warmth, cleanliness, and safety. For the first time in my life, I felt that my flat teeth, my flimsy arms, and my brittle fingernails were enough to kill a man, lion, or bear. I no longer remembered whom I once had been, but had visions of a funeral pyre in which the woman I once was burned and stirred, day after day, changing in the flames.

Guardedly, I was now a believer in Bob Martin's dominance theory— overwrought as Kierney was in all things, her fear-biting had been her attempt at a coup, a bid for alpha. We had quashed the revolution. Unable to deny that the man had saved my dog's life, late summer and early fall I took Kierney weekly to Bob Martin's, new baby on my back. "When her position in the family pack is clear," Martin said, "she'll calm down. Dogs like to know where they stand." Every time we took the long drive over the mountain to Bob Martin's Dog Training School, Kierney proved him right by singing her high-pitched, muffled howl of happiness, a throaty whine that I could imitate, "mmmMM! mmmMM!" We sang together all the way there.

At Bob Martin's, as others worked their dogs each in turn, Kierney sat, pressed trembling against my leg but looking across my knee, focused, observing the other dogs as if learning from their subtle errors and successes. The other people grew fond of Kierney's sensitivity. While it delighted me to know she was well-liked, it bothered me that in Martin's presence she lost her baroque individuality and became nearly identical in demeanor, if not in form, to the dozen or so German Shepherds whose handsome faces watched Martin teach, transfixed by the one who'd been merciful enough to let them go on living.

After Martin's class, she'd sleep all the next day. It was the only activity that had ever exhausted her.

So it came to pass that by the time the baby was just a few months old and Kierney had quickly mastered Companion Dog work, I dared hope to compete in dog shows. Registered with an Indefinite Listing Privilege number, because at that time border collies weren't an A.K.C.-recognized breed, Kierney and I entered a local obedience competition as a trial run and earned a Qualifying Score.

Perhaps during the past turbulent year, I thought, my only spiritual problem had been that I lacked patience. If I could see through God's eyes, perhaps I'd see the whole of space-time, each living creature but a particle rising and falling in the biosphere, one displacing the other, a kind of convection. Now my dog and I had risen, had been lifted up, I a good mother and Kierney a good dog, on her feet, in charge of her mind and body.

One night about six months after Delaney was born, I woke to a new sound, a hard, fast, rhythmic bang, like Hollywood thunder. It resembled Kierney scratching an ear with her hind foot and pounding the metal tray in her crate, only it was too loud and fast for an itch. I had never heard such a sound before, but I knew right away what it was. "Kierney's having a seizure," I said to Joe. "Turn on the light."

Kierney's legs seemed to be multiplying, machine-made, spilling into the crate and filling it. Her head thrashed as if she were a toy powered by a monstrous rubber band.

"What should we do?" I said.

"I don't know. Pull her out so she doesn't hurt herself on the bars."

So that's what we did. We stood over her as she foamed and thrashed and her wild legs churned.

Until that moment, her beautiful body had always done exactly what she told it to. Her wild and clever brain, which she had fought so hard to tame, had abandoned her. Her soul was gone, stolen, no sign of it anywhere, as if some thief had picked it from the pocket of her body. We waited for her.

"I saw a man have a seizure once," Joe said.

"What did you do?"

"Nothing. But we weren't supposed to watch so that when he came out of the seizure he wouldn't be as embarrassed."

"How could you *not* watch? I've never seen anything like this," I said. "It's going to give me nightmares." It went on, long and empty seconds, and there was nothing for us to do.

Finally, face pressed against Joe's shoulder, I heard a silence drop upon the room. I turned and saw Kierney lying unusually flat—maybe her skeleton had been pulverized.

Then, panting hard, lifting her head and trailing a sticky white strand, she stumbled blindly to her feet and began to walk, fast. My breasts heavy with night milk, I wanted to stroke her, clean her face, soothe her.

"Kierney, good girl, it's okay, it's Lisa," I said, words which usually brought her to me with her head and tail low, rump swinging, but she marched right past me and hit the wall as if her skull were a rock tossed by a careless hand. She veered into the hallway and disappeared. We heard a crash and found her tangled in the legs of a kitchen chair. Blind and deaf, she walked compulsively. Joe had to work early in the morning, so I stayed up with her and steered her away from end tables and waste baskets. Slowly, she became more alert and responsive, but she could not stop walking. Finally, I shut her in our room, and we lay awake to the sound of her clicking toenails. In the dark, she'd thump into the wall and shuffle there, legs going, a battery-powered toy with no "off" switch.

In the morning, Joe went to work and I took Kierney to the animal health clinic, where the on-duty vet, a young man fresh out of veterinary school, explained that this disorder would most likely prove to be idiopathic epilepsy, meaning, it had no known cause. Kierney stood on the examination table between us, still panting as if spent.

"Has she had any petit mals?"

I'd never heard the phrase.

"Tiny seizures. Does she ever drift or stare at nothing?"

"Yes. Often. And sometimes when she comes out of it she's aggressive. She's bitten me. I brought her in here, and you guys told me she was insane."

"Well, I wouldn't have told you that. Some epileptics have seizures which manifest as aggressive or destructive behavior. After petit mals some don't recognize their surroundings and get hostile because they're frightened."

"Well, that explains everything. That's exactly what she's been like," I said. "Why is this the first mention of epilepsy then? Why did other vets here determine that she had a personality disorder?"

Stroking her, he shrugged. "Probably because she's a border collie."

"But isn't *epilepsy* more prevalent in the breed than insanity?"

He laughed, nodding. "That's hard to say. Both are hard to diagnose." Distracted now, he was pressed for time. "Still, last night's seizure may have been an isolated incident," he said, slipping a biscuit into Kierney's mouth. "So for now, just watch her."

Although I welcomed a reasonable explanation for her hostility and her eerie moods, the news had thrown me—we had the hang of her insanity; our experience and our knowledge and our discipline—our sanity—had incorporated her insanity and made it sane, with great expense of time, money and pain. Had we wasted it all? Were we going to lose more time, money and comfort?

This young man was the first vet at this clinic to have spent any time explaining anything to me, so I tried to commit his name to memory and to keep him talking a moment longer. "What could have caused it?" I said. I wanted to *do* something. I was thinking, I made a promise to this dog, something like a wedding vow, for better or worse, in sickness and in health. I had already gone beyond what I'd thought myself capable to save her life once. It was the vet's job to help me keep my promise. He was telling me she'd had frequent petit mals and that this was a progressive disease. "What do I do when it comes back? How do I stop it?"

"It may never happen again."

"Can a seizure kill her?"

"Not unless she has one in front of a moving bus." He was jotting for a long time in her file and he needed to think carefully. I waited. Finishing up, he closed the folder and laid his hand on the doorknob. "What you saw last night was a grand mal, and it's unusual in a dog as young as two years, but she's all right now. Look around your house for antifreeze and clean it up." He opened the door.

To keep Kierney from bolting through it, I put my arm around her. "I'm sorry," I said, straining to keep Kierney on the table. "Are you in a hurry?"

"No, it's not you," he said, shaking her folder to straighten the papers. "You can let her down."

Kierney sprang lightly to the floor. "If she has another grand mal, what should I do?" He just stood there lost in thought, so I prodded him with detail. "Will she bite her tongue? Should we restrain her?"

"Tongues heal fast. If she has another seizure, keep her cooled off, because an epileptic dog can die of heat prostration, and call *me*," he said, hooking a thumb at himself. "Unless chronic epilepsy is treated by medication," he said, pausing with the door opened a crack, "seizure activity grows more frequent and severe. Seizures draw a map in the brain and follow it further each time. Anti-seizure drugs halt the pattern and over time erase the map. Then medication can be withdrawn."

"So it *is* likely to happen again. And if we had stopped the seizures at petit mals . . ."

"It's hard to say," he said, and left the room.

Not until three months later did the next seizure strike, a neuronic tornado, and then every few weeks another felled her, and we began treatment. It was no good blaming the clinic for not diagnosing her epilepsy sooner. Now all that mattered was that they stop it. I asked for the young new vet each time, but he was rarely available, and finally he left to practice elsewhere. In defiance of the neural pathway theory, Kierney's dendritic arsonists weren't systematically burning a path through her brain. Each seizure set fire to new ground, random as lightning. Medication had no effect. The vets were confused—epilepsy didn't get this bad this fast.

I searched for the devil in our den. Maybe it was the herbicide our landlord soaked into the ground to make it easy for him whip around the yards on his ride-on mower. Tank of toxin on his back, he sprayed herbicide everywhere, making a foot-wide berth of dead grass around the apartment building, around fence posts and trees, poisoning his tenants' vegetable and flower gardens. He even saturated the ill-conceived, loose stone "retaining wall" that he'd built on the hillside out front of our apartment—the stony dirt slope had surprised him by opulently sprouting weeds. Although the weeds would've done a better job of retaining the hillside than the loose round stones, which tumbled onto the lawn, he preferred his vegetation dead, and so every other week he juiced them and left them a messy brown scribble of straw despite complaints from gardeners, bird lovers, pet owners, and young parents.

"I wouldn't be able to say that your landlord caused her seizures," the vet-of-the-day stammered, blinking. "Without knowing the exact chemical components . . . perhaps a chemist at the university could help you put together a case."

"It's okay. Her seizures don't coincide with the ground-poisonings anyway." I had alternative possibilities to try on him. It could have been that when Bob Martin and I used her choke collar as a garrote, her brain was deprived of oxygen.

"No," the vet said quickly, as if familiar with complaints about Bob Martin. "Actually, a dog's neck's solid and well-muscled. That doesn't have the same effect as it would on a human."

I wondered how chained dogs who jump fences manage to strangle to death.

"Bob Martin's corrections can't do a dog lasting harm."

You haven't seen Martin correct a dog, I thought. When distraught dog owners come to you complaining of him, you think in their sentimental ignorance they're overreacting. Can you see a bruised neck through fur?

But there were other possible causes. God help us, maybe it was the vegetarian dog food. Or the little tastes of toothpaste I gave her twice a day. The vet said no and no again. Or it was Joe's rough-housing. Joe had a game of slapping Kierney's face until she growled deliriously and fell on her side while he thumped her head against the hardwood floor. Their game was too violent for me to watch.

"She loves it!" Joe would say, and she *did* seem to.

"Naw," the vet said, "that wouldn't do it. You'd know if she had a concussion."

"Well, you haven't seen them play," I said.

Later, sitting on the couch, clenching my teeth against tears, I watched my dog. My proud and able friend, who could soar over a five-foot fence with no more effort than a sigh, blithered on the floor as if ten thousand amperes were ripping through her. It amazed me that smoke didn't drift from her fur. Once I again I'd let myself dream—Utility Dog work, sheep herding trials—and now here I was again whittling back. A year before all I dared wish was that I might trust her not to bite my child.

Now, I'd just be happy if she didn't explode.

As I'd once told Paul West, getting to know an animal was like traveling to another country—a body unlike mine, habits and wisdom with strange logic, the surprising landscape of another brain, its alien weather systems, a new sky. In Kierney's case I'd been a reckless explorer and acculturated myself too deeply, never expecting that she was a portal into the realm of epilepsy, cosmic wormholes in the mind.

I tumbled in.

"She's had three in a row!" I cried into the phone. "I'm holding ice on her belly right now."

"Let's up the phenobarb," the vet said. "What are you giving her?"

"I'd have to go look at the bottle," I said. "What's it say in her folder?"

He put me on hold. So, he hadn't been writing things down, and now I was going to have to repeat everything. He came back. "Okay, I have the chart."

To the sound of him breathing and turning pages I added, "One side of her face is swollen, and she's been throwing up." Having no idea which of the six or eight vets from this clinic I had on the phone, I pictured him flapping a blank piece of paper just to appease me. "It was worse this time," I said, my voice rising. We needed this man's help, whoever he was, and he was too busy, just like the rest of them. "She was terrified. She *knows* when it's coming. She's in my lap now and—"

"You needn't worry. Carney—"

"*Kierney.*"

"Kierney's an epileptic. Epileptics, human or otherwise, aren't conscious during seizure activity. They don't suffer. It's a blessing, really."

Epilepsy, a blessing? "I've been *told* she's not conscious, but what I'm *observing*—"

"They have no memory of the event, therefore they have nothing to fear. It's more upsetting to those watching, and it'll be less so when you accept that."

I suspected that the possibility that an epileptic is conscious is simply too terrible for anyone, even a doctor, to face.

Kierney lay still and reeked of urine. Her eyes met mine, her pupils the passages of underwater caves.

"Ah, here. Increase the dosage by a half-pill twice daily. Wait—" he turned more pages. "I mean, up it a quarter-pill. You can cut it with a knife."

Sitting on the floor with Kierney in my lap, I hung up the phone furious. My sweet athlete was too exhausted to walk. Heat rising from her bloated side, she labored to pant, and I held an ice pack on her belly. Her face was drawn in a wide, red grimace, her hot tongue draped across my leg. True to the maddening irony of medicine, the phenobarbital had caused side effects which tortured her more than the intermittent seizures it was intended to curb. It gave her a ravenous appetite that day and night did not relent. Guiltily, she ate whatever she could mash between her teeth: grass, straw, mud, wood, cardboard, carpet, Styrofoam, cement chips. She was gaining about two pounds of weight a week. The medication also made her incontinent and therefore anxious and humiliated.

I could count only one blessing to this illness. She had always lived as if she'd been secretly receiving threats in snipped newsprint, I KNOW WHERE YOU LIVE. I'M GOING TO KILL YOU. Now that the grand mals assaulted her, she finally seemed to trust me and Joe and even other people, as if she finally knew who'd been sending those threats. When a seizure was coming, she could run to me and whimper like a puppy, searching my face, *help me.*

Her epilepsy confirmed my hunch that she'd had the best of reasons for the worst of her behavior. Poor Kierney had known all along that she was handicapped. Maybe she'd expected to be killed by us, her pack. That wasn't at all far-fetched. Some vets warn people who own more than one dog to isolate their epileptic when it's seizing because the other dogs may attack him. Humans, too, have shunned or even killed their own epileptics. In the Middle Ages, people with epilepsy were chained in prison-like "hospitals" for their entire lives, and, as recently as 1939, Nazis began euthanizing the sick and disabled, including epileptics.

One night after a fit, my dog paced the dark as if trying to put psychic distance between herself and her unseen predator, and I lay awake wondering how to help her. Her suffering was beyond the scope of the vets. It was beyond my mothering and imagination. What powers had I left?

"You're a prophet," a priest had told me a year before.

I'd gone to confess that I was writing a novel. I'd studied the Marquis de Sade and created a depraved pedophilic character. "When I'm writing this character, I feel like I *am* him. So I must be sinning in my heart."

The priest had laughed gently. In the dark confessional, through the screen, I could see his profile tilt up and down, amusedly nodding. He told me, "What you're doing is not a sin. There're different manifestations of faith for different personality types. Yours is the prophet mentality. You confront sin. You study it so that you can cry out against it. Yours is the most difficult path of all."

"Prophets are the ones who get killed, aren't they?"

"Yes," the priest had chuckled.

After several unsuccessful months trying to control her seizures with phenobarbital, we had made our star sprinter obese. Periodically, her legs whipped out from under her, beating as if to break themselves. She wheezed, dribbled urine, and stumbled. People mistook her for a geriatric dog.

One bright afternoon, hungry but otherwise purposeless, Kierney meandered in the yard, not sniffing anything, not listening, not playing, not even suffering a petit mal. Uncomfortable and hopeless, she drifted near one of the people she used to consider most loathsome, a neighbor's rambunctious four-year-old boy. Joe and I watched the boy approach her. Built like a big, square hassock, she stopped, panting hard from her walk across the yard. The boy spoke to her. She let him pat her head.

"She's dying," Joe said.

We packed her right in the car and took her to see the next available vet.

"Lethargy, incontinence, and depression are all signs of irreversible brain damage," he said soberly. He flipped through her file. The number and order of the pages always seemed to confuse the vets.

"Carney's epilepsy is severe and uncontrollable," he announced, and looked up at us expectantly.

Joe and I silently returned his gaze, we on one side of the examination table, he on the other.

"That's out of the question," Joe said.

"She's only two years old," I snapped, my arms around her broad, soft back. I had a powerful urge to bite down on something, to feel one of those tongue depressors in his pocket shatter between my teeth or to feel my molars crunch through the gristle of his index finger.

"She's only two," the vet mumbled to himself, as if the detail was surprising but inconsequential. "Okay then," he said, clicking his fountain pen and adding something to her chart. "We go on as we are." And he left the room with another little shrug, as if to say, "You asked for it."

"Epilepsy" comes from the Indo-European root *slagw*, meaning "to seize," so the dog I had waited nearly a decade for, the young mortal I raised and coddled and punished more passionately than I thought myself capable, was not so much seizuring as being seized, stolen, ravished by someone unseen. The grand mal, the great ill, can be unnerving for those who witness it, because it's more visible and violent than most ailments, and its fury seems to lack cause or agent. The face you have kissed empties of charm and sense, and fills again, a monstrosity. The lips yank themselves into an agonized laugh, and, although you've been warned not to entertain such feelings, you'll be unable to resist your compassion and fear. The eyebrows lift as if the eyes beneath them gaze into a pit that belches forth unholy swarms. Millions upon millions of winged scorpions stab and clamber over what they have won from you—why else do the teeth chatter and the body thrash? Why else does froth pour from the mouth you have lovingly fed? Science reveals something of the neurology involved, but when you love the one who usually inhabits this body, fallen from you choking on the floor, you may, standing in your lonely distress, sense the presence of a demon.

Religion aside, I wondered if I'd summoned it. The tendency to consider such a thing is a fiction writer's occupational hazard. When the sphinx of epilepsy put her paw upon my dog, my Master of Fine Arts degree had been earned and my novel—a ghost story exploring the relationship between an other-worldly child prostitute and a pedophile—was finished. Although my manuscript was far, far away with my agent, the novel and the research I'd done remained within me as if I'd dwelled two years in a malevolently haunted town, where a girl's murder filled the high school corridors like a snake, its fluid ribs bunching and extending. I had based the pedophile on the portrait of necrophiles in Eric Fromm's *The Anatomy of Human Destructiveness*. For the sake of my novel, I'd read *Naked Lunch* twice and taken notes.

The snake slithered inside me, bunching and extending with my every breath.

Now, for my next novel, I was method acting, *becoming* a new set of characters so that I could write credibly about them. With the help of a friend and Upton Sinclair's handbook, *Mental Radio*, I was teaching myself telepathy. Like a gymnast her body, I was contorting my mind to the form of my books. But a brand-new mother who's just quit a job and finished writing an emotionally wrenching novel is a vulnerable person, *without* an epileptic dog and a hobby in telepathic communication.

Six months after the first seizure, early in the morning, she had one attack immediately followed by another, and another—a medical emergency. The primary danger was that her body had no time to cool itself, and she could die of heat exhaustion, the body's own China Syndrome. We put her into the bathtub, ran cold water over her and called the veterinary clinic's answering service. A smooth and convenient place for her to thrash and stumble, the bathtub kept her from cutting or scraping herself and the curved slippery bottom prevented her from getting up between seizures and tangling herself in the kitchen chairs.

Many times in the last year, we'd taken her to Alan Seeger Park. There was one spot in the forest where, thanks to the intervention of a chainsaw, the walking path went right through the middle of a fallen tree trunk, five feet in diameter. Kierney loved to leap upon the trunk, which bridged a creek, and to race the length of it and back. As Joe and I passed between the two ringed walls, she'd stand above us laughing and yapping. Her sharp voice rang through the forest, creating an aural picture of the leaf-occluded landscape: a cliff face, a gully—the area always sounding much smaller than it really was, as if her voice condensed it. Up there on the fallen tree, she was a sight: rangy and black, deep rib cage arched sharply up to her spine greyhound-style, her waist narrow enough to close my hands around, her legs leaner than kindling, all of her poised, clawed, and fanged—fit enough to shrink the mountain to a morsel and swallow it whole.

But this early morning, a bathtub five feet long and two feet deep contained her, the white porcelain box a stark display case for the four black legs which kicked and spasmed, went rigid and limp. She didn't even try to stand on them. When the vet on call arrived at the clinic, Joe made his move between seizures and carried her to our hatchback while I woke the baby and put her coat on over her pajamas. As we drove we heard Kierney snuffle and whimper and claw at the rug. Shut in a small car out on a public road, the sounds she made were shockingly intimate—as if she were masturbating to orgasm over and over.

She was caught in a mental hurricane, thunder and hail, tree-snapping winds, tornadoes migrating through her mind in droves. Swiftly at the clinic Joe and the vet swung her onto the operating table, and the vet thrust a prepared needle into her shoulder, sinking her into a phenobarbital stupor, submerging her into the fathomless deep of coma. The surface went still. But what swam with her below, where no light penetrated?

"Leave her here. We'll bring her out of it every few hours to see if the seizures've stopped."

Empty-handed, we went home.

Part of me thought it unconscionable to plunge Kierney and her monster out of sight rather than keep them thrashing on the surface where you could watch the fight. Just below my awareness, just beyond the vision of common sense, the scaled ribs shifted. We drove off, and the beast was in me, cold and coiling. I burst into tears. Joe pulled to the side of the road.

"She's unconscious," Joe said, holding me. "She doesn't know where she is or what's happening."

As the person who knew her best, I had trouble believing she was unaware of her seizures. True, she didn't respond during them, and of course at that moment Kierney had been erased by a chemical stupor, but generally the way she acted before and after an attack suggested that she recalled *something*. "That's not possible," the vets said. Even my friends told me, "You're causing her anxiety yourself. And you'd better watch it—stress can bring seizures on. The more you worry about them, the more likely they are to happen."

When she ran to me and leaned against my leg, trembling with fright, staring at a fixed point as her eyes went blank and tiny yelps of fear rose in her throat, I dropped what I was doing and against all medical wisdom, common sense and convention, trusting only that Kierney and I were honest with each other, I helplessly took her in my arms and told her, "I love Kierney, my good dog." I could feel strange rumblings in her muscles, an alien catch in her breath, the press of her head on my arm as if to beg me to keep her, my Persephone, from going underground. No matter what anybody said at any other time, *this* is what I knew. So I held her, at least until her head yanked away from me, her side slammed the floor, and her soul whipped out of her. With less heart, I kept talking—just in case she could hear me—"It's okay. Lisa loves her good girl." And if my baby daughter was asleep at the time, and if Joe was out, I'd be left alone, alone in my cheap, ugly, poisoned apartment, alone with the terrible suspicion that Kierney knew her agony full well.

As I write this, I have before me a book I didn't have then, a book published a few months after a long needle freed Kierney from her demons forever—*Brainstorms: Epilepsy in Our Words*, subtitled, *Personal Accounts of Living with Seizures*. Voices in the book speak the words I knew but never heard because Kierney couldn't use words to tell me. The book reveals that it's common for epileptics to suffer in the moments preceding a seizure. The experience is given the graceful term "aura," the "cold breeze" some epileptics feel blowing along their limbs. One epileptic described the aura as "an abject sense of impending doom," another reported "feelings of panic and suffocation," another said, "the general feeling is of being in front of an oncoming train with no way to escape," and yet another said, "I'm being sucked into a constantly narrowing tunnel." It cannot be said that epileptics don't suffer at all.

More, just as I feared, I turn pages of this book and I'm suddenly inside my worst nightmare, the great scaly flanks of the sea monster heave under my hands, flashing colors like an angry squid, electric tentacles, a neon eye, a beak more terrible and more powerful than death itself. It seems, after all has been said and all, sadly, all has been done, that some epileptics *are* conscious during seizures—"One side of my mind was racing from scene to scene while the other was whirling and gnashing in dark chaotic colors moving in total clear blackness making weird shapes and movements; [I thought], this must be what purgatory was as far as blackness and mashing of colors," and "[I was] fearful that I would be like this forever." One writes, "while my seizures occur I am very aware of what is going on [and of] my muscles contorting all over my body." The voices rise, "sounds are too loud, lights are too bright, touch is too heavy. . . I have a strong, almost uncontrollable need to flee," "it felt like I was dying," "[there was] a strong pulsing feeling through the whole body," "hearing voices . . . get scared. . . . say to myself why me."

But back then, when Kierney was alive and snared by tentacles flashing pink and orange in a sea of total clear blackness, the day the vet submerged her in a phenobarbital sea and sent me inland, away from the shore, I tried to believe what everyone was telling me—epilepsy is a pain-free, self-anesthetizing disease. Without Kierney beside me, I had nothing to do. I couldn't go into my paramedic mode, and become frank love and efficiency—grab the towels, ice packs, phenobarb and rectal thermometer. However, as her adoptive mother, intuiting that she was trapped in front of an oncoming train over and over and then gnashed in chaotic blackness again and again, I grieved. I feared my oversensitive and emotionally dependent dog would wake from her Purgatory and find herself trapped in her hospital cage and alone, in Hell. How could I have left her? But I had. Several times that day I phoned and was told she was sleeping, they were busy, they would call me if anything changed. The day passed, the clinic closed, night fell. How could I lay me down to sleep?

All day long I'd tried to relax, busy myself, but then I'd hear again what the vet had said, "Sometimes they don't come out of this," and I would writhe. Down deep inside, a little voice, the part of me that was both myself and my dog, would whimper, *We are fearful that we will be like this forever.*

Tired and reassuringly pragmatic, setting a good example, Joe rolled over, slept hard, and left me alone to pinch my pillow and weep. How dare God torture my dog after I had loved and obeyed Him? I had fought for compassionate dominion of His creatures. I followed the laws of His Church. If He loves us and we return His love, why doesn't He protect us, treat us gratefully? He had betrayed me, broken my heart, and mocked my hope. He led me to protect animals from abuse, and here He Himself was abusing the animal I loved most.

No, I told myself, there's got to be a way to preserve my faith. I'm going to need it, whatever it is. What would Cindy and Fred say? "God never gives you anything you can't handle." I liked such notions, spiritual bubble baths, although I knew they didn't make sense—if I were weaker, then would I have a healthy dog? Conversely, I could hear Cindy and Fred say that God gave Kierney epilepsy in order to test me, the way He tested Job, on a whim, on a dare from Satan. But why pick on a poor dog—why not go directly after me? "That's how Satan really gets to you," Cindy and Fred would have said, "by attacking those you love."

Oh. Did that mean my daughter was next? What kind of God would punish me for daring to love? How could I kneel and thank Him for my dear little girl if I thought that doing so might give Him an opportunity to torment me?

That night as Kierney lay dying in the hospital, I was too angry to count my blessings. I mused that all mortals had an implicit Declaration of Independence from the Creator, one that granted them the rights to temporary life, liberty and the pursuit of happiness—the *pursuit*, not happiness itself. I tried to snap my situation into perspective by recalling all I'd read about epic suffering in the world: Nagasaki, Dachau, the Bubonic Plague. I imagined having been scorched by an atomic bomb, wilting from cholera in a concentration camp, finding a festering bubo in my armpit. I remembered that Paul West's wife, the poetess and aviatrix Diane Ackerman, when her life got rough, used to quip, "At least it's better than being sucked out of a plane at thirty-five thousand feet." Losing Kierney to *status epilepticus* was better than being caught in Shaanxi in 1556, when an earthquake snuffed 830,000 souls. It was better than having Jack the Ripper lop my innards. I tried, but knowing that innocents had been flayed alive by napalm gave me no comfort. The immediacy of the night had taken me, a night during which someone I loved lay dying, dying young, dying unjustly, inexplicably, in agony.

I had nothing left to do but pray, but to whom and why? All prayer did was draw me into the dark of my own heart, to walk the beating caverns, to feel my way along slick walls and through slamming valves, to breathe blood, to stumble into the vault of the demon of Job. *Who can open the doors of his face? his teeth are terrible round about. . . . Out of his mouth go burning lamps, and sparks of fire leap out. Out of his nostrils goeth smoke, as out of a seething pot or cauldron. . . . When he raiseth up himself, the mighty are afraid.* My fingertips tingled, my blood crystallized, my breath sped, the veins in my brain whispered—*I have uttered that I understood not; things too wonderful for me, which I knew not.* Leviathan, "Wriggly One," Great Serpent Nehushtan, unholy indeed, the fountain of all unholiness. I fell, unable to say the one thing I had come to say.

So my night advanced, slouching toward dawn. I got up, ate a snack, read a magazine, nursed the baby when she called, then tried once more to lie down for sleep, but sleep is too near telepathy. After having spooked myself with my little mind-reading exercises, I was half afraid I'd see Kierney in her hospital kennel—and half afraid I wouldn't. Sometime during those grueling hours I must have slept, for I forgot myself and a prayer escaped me, a telegraphic directive, *live!* Then in a lucid, Technicolor dream, I swam inside her sea storm, splashing on the surface. Near me she breached and her mouth turned and slashed, bloodying my breast. She hauled me below the breaking white mountains of water into darkness as keen and piercing as sunlight. Deeper and deeper, she swam me past clawing shapes, querulous colors. She bit, spun, and ripped. She and sea serpent were one. *Canst thou draw out Leviathan with an hook?*

"There might be nothing to fight," the doctor had said.

I burst upon my bed straight awake, as if someone had shaken me with the news, "Wake up! Kierney's dead!"

A large, fragrant shadow, Joe moved only to take breath, and I was alone and quaking with the possibility that I'd had a vision, that I'd received news from the nether world, that I'd finally tuned in radio station WGOD, only to find out that I couldn't handle it. If Kierney was dead, I didn't want to know yet. And if I *hadn't* had access to God, I didn't want to know that either. I didn't wake Joe.

I tried to calm myself, unwilling to fall asleep again, half-heartedly telling myself that, if Kierney were dead, her ghost would've appeared to me, the way my murdered friend's ghost did several times when I was writing the novel dedicated to her. I told myself this even though I usually figured that I'd dreamed those visions of my murdered friend sitting dead and cross-legged on the end of my bed. Now I had to admit, anything was possible.

Morning came, and no ghost. I got on the phone. "How's my dog? She's the epileptic in your back room?"

"May I have the animal's name, please."

I was pissin' sick of this routine. "Come *on!*" I wailed, too tired and distraught to be polite. "She's the one convulsing in your back room. I'm the same woman who phoned you eight times yesterday."

"Then may I have *your* name, Ma'am?"

With a sigh, I gave her all the data she needed to investigate the situation, and after about ten minutes, a vet got on the phone. "Carney's sleeping. Why don't you call back later?"

She was alive, I thought happily, hanging up the phone. Maybe Cindy and Fred were right! They'd say that Kierney had been dying and my prayers had called her back. Alleluia! But then maybe in my grief and fatigue I simply imagined whatever spiritual vein I thought I'd tapped. Maybe there's no difference between delusions and revelations. Maybe there's no radio band of universal good to which we can attune ourselves. I'm overwrought, I said to myself, and I'm vacillating between skepticism and superstition.

I was determined to maintain at center a solid, practical faith. Several times during the day I called the vet, obediently repeating my dog's full name. They kept her all that day, and I spent another night kicking and sweating and sinking through a sea of prehistoric predators. I slipped in and out of half-sleep, in which my overworked eyes compulsively strained to see Kierney, and did. There were moments I swore our minds had run full-tilt into each other, and we frantically clung together.

Although for two full days I, the heartbroken owner of the epileptic border collie, had been phoning every couple of hours, never was I treated with any recognition or gentleness. What had happened to this veterinary clinic? Years before we'd brought our finches here because one vet specialized in avian medicine, but now we were without an individual contact, and the place had grown and mechanized. I might as well have been calling an auto repair shop to inquire about the status of my car.

The morning of the third day, my call was directed to a new voice, a young voice, maybe yet another new vet. He opened Kierney file. "Um . . . wait. Yeah, we were just talking about this dog, as a matter of fact. It looks like last night she was accidentally given three times the lethal dose of phenobarb for a dog twice her size, and yet she's up on her feet. She's a remarkable case," he said, as if he expected me to swell with pride. "This dog just won't stay sedated. Her chart says she's been whining non-stop. A couple of us took turns coming in last night and she kept getting up and pacing around, so we each just dosed her again. That's how she OD-ed."

When angry, I get cool and sarcastic. "I've noticed you people aren't in the habit of checking the charts."

"Man! She's got a *really* high tolerance."

I didn't say anything.

He went on, "Here's the bad news. You ready? Okay, unfortunately, the post-seizure activity isn't passing, her anal tone is bad, she's incontinent—"

"She's had the bad anal tone and incontinence for months from the phenobarb—"

"—she shows no recognition of her surroundings. We've determined that she's brain blind and we think it's time to euthanize her. Why don't you come on out? Take her for a last walk if you like."

"Brain blind?"

"You know. Her eyes aren't visual? The brain doesn't accept input? Brain blind."

As soon as we called her, our favorite babysitter rushed out to watch Delaney, and we raced to the veterinary clinic, where someone led us toward the back rooms. One of the older vets stopped us in the hallway to prepare us for the worst, but as soon as I spoke, a shriek rang from a behind a door. "Is that her?" I cried.

"Can't be," he said, looking doubtfully over his shoulder. "There's a puppy back there."

But I knew my dog. "She hears me!" I called to her, pushing the vet aside as the cries escalated. "She recognizes our voices!" I opened the door and faced a wall of kennels, floor to ceiling, cubbies with cage doors, most containing a cat or dog, one a rabbit. Operating tables gleamed in full view of the kennels. In a bottom cage, Kierney stumbled, wagging her tail and shrilling joyously. "Let her out!" I said, opening the cage myself. Reeking of urine and antiseptic, she clumped into my arms.

"See how she falls?" the vet said, piteously. "That's brain damage. She can't see or hear. She doesn't look at any of us or respond when we test her hearing."

A tear welling in the corner of his eye, Joe knelt and stroked her, and Kierney licked his chin. "*How* do you test her hearing?" Joe said, his lips white with anger.

"We say her name."

"And she doesn't respond to *you*?"

"No."

Joe nodded, snapping on her leash. "We're going to take her for that last walk now."

The vet let us out a back door and propped it open. "They can't even *pronounce* her name," I muttered, loud enough for the vet to hear me as we crunched across a gravel parking lot. "We can get a second opinion."

Behind the clinic was a small wood, and a broad, hardened path slapped through it, lined with paper soda cups and cigarette butts. Fatter than I'd ever seen her, rump wet, Kierney walked alongside us into the woods, dragging her feet in a scritch-scritch rhythm, another side effect, either from phenobarb or brain damage. I told her "heel," and, weaving, she did, but when we stopped, she overshot, skidding onto her chin. When we came to a turn in the path, she broadsided a tree. "You okay?" I asked her, and she flashed me a reassuring grin.

"She hears us," Joe scowled. "Drop her leash." I did, and Joe threw a stick. As if from the depths of a dream she launched herself, the syrup of a three-day sleep clinging to her flanks. Falling forward but not down, she crashed over the stick, skidded around wobbling, scooped it up and tottered back to us, unable to run but enraptured by the chance to try. "She can see," Joe said. "Kierney, *heel*." She dropped her stick, stood still a moment, swaying, then tried to move sideways toward Joe's left leg, but the effort toppled her. Panting and confounded, she pulled herself to a sit and waited, the way she did when we asked her to relieve herself in the yard and she had no need.

"Don't have to?" I asked her jokingly.

Her tail shuffled a few leaves and cigarette butts.

Joe knelt beside her, and motioned for me to join him. Hidden in the briar, I hadn't crouched in such a shabby wooded lot since I was a teenager coughing on my first rolled joint.

Joe glanced toward the open door of the clinic, where an assistant waited for us. "Did we leave anything inside?" he said, hushed. It was the only time I'd ever seen him in the urgent and secretive attitude of an adolescent.

"I don't think so."

In one swoop, he tucked Kierney's bloated body under his arm and we scrambled for the car like bandits.

Chapter Seven

Flirting With the Riptide

Frequent traffic lights hobbled the busiest street in our town. Strip malls and construction sites scarred it. Rising out of a sudden swamp of red dirt, a Wal-Mart mushroomed, interrupting the bucolic view of a large stone and wood-plank barn on a hillside pasture. The horses were gone. It occurred to me that I would never be able to walk that store's vast floor without sensing the ghost of the field beneath it. Everywhere I looked, I saw finality; in the midst of the perpetual flux that is life on earth, there really are endings without beginnings anew. There are irretrievable losses, ruins, extinctions. Dodo birds and Pompeii have second lives in lore, but that life doesn't belong to the clumsy, trusting birds themselves nor to the people who got buried running for air. Lives end, lives are forgotten, stories are never told. I thought of the empty lots, empty houses, and empty stores in Joe's hometown, washed out in the flood of 1972 and never rebuilt, windows sucked hollow like the eyes in animals dead on the roadside. One way or another, gone from me were my grandparents, my parents, my little sister, my childhood home, my dog Patches, my finches, my boyfriend Gavin, my horse friend Shannon. Somehow the finality of loss seemed never to have occurred to me before, maybe because I'd been so young and optimistic, a fighter, a survivor, a believer.

"I don't want her to die, Joe."

"Isn't Nudie epileptic? Doesn't Steph take her to Michelotti?" Joe said. "He's a mile from here." We had a good sitter with our daughter, time on our hands and an allegedly dying dog tumbling off the back seat. The stink of her crowded the car. We called Dr. Michelotti from a pay phone.

"Bring her right over," he said.

In his waiting room, his assistants, young women in white lab coats, knelt in a small crowd around Kierney, tsk-tsking to her story. One woman took Kierney's long black face in her hands and said, "You poor, sweet sweetie." To my gratitude, they magically already knew her name. They slipped treats from their pockets, and Kierney, barely able to sit up on the slippery tile, swayed and leered happily in the midst of them.

A tall, handsome man with close-cropped blond hair called to us from an examination room. We went in, and Joe lifted Kierney's heavy, unsteady body onto the surgical steel plinth. With my arms locked around her wrestling-style, her heavy breathing rocked against my chest.

Pale-eyed and efficient, Dr. Michelotti palpated her neck quietly.

"To determine whether this is primary or secondary epilepsy I'll need the results of her baseline serum chemistry profile, complete blood count and urinalysis. I'll send for her file."

Instantly alert, Joe and I both listened hard. We'd never heard some of these terms, but they were most welcome.

"Let's help her stand," Michelotti said.

Together we guided her to her feet on the slick surface, the moment reminiscent of visits to the pediatrician, a doctor examining my baby, her body an extension of my own. I needn't look to know and to feel under my hands that Kierney stood crouched, nose up, ears flat, watching him calmly, but the snipped tip of her tail wagged nervously. Pushing steadily against my shoulder, she panted a hot, unfamiliar steam into my face.

"It's unknown what initially causes the brain cells in the cerebral cortex to release a turbulent discharge of neurons," he said, running his hand down her side, then slipping it between her thighs. She clamped her tail down shyly and held her breath. Gently, he palpated her abdomen. "She's constipated," he observed.

Joe and I exchanged surprised looks. New students in his impromptu seminar, we nodded respectfully as he addressed the matter of epilepsy.

"Some studies implicate abnormal levels of neurotransmitters and the enzymes that control them, but almost any change in the neuron's environment can cause an anomalous discharge." Unlike most men, who spoke only to Joe, Michelotti addressed us both.

"Each individual has a unique seizure threshold," I replied.

Michelotti looked me in the eye. "The problem lies in the extremely low level at which some dogs seize with no detectable stimulus; their low threshold is probably genetically determined." He walked to a shelf, turning his back, and Kierney thumped into a clumsy sit, relaxing against me. Then he came back, folded her ear inside out, and flashed a pen light into it. Timidly, she lifted her nose to his face, and he let her lick his chin. "If it's idiopathic epilepsy, there'll be no positive diagnostic findings."

"You'll have to rule out every other possibility," I said.

Joe was quietly sizing the man up.

Kierney leaned into me, not so much out of fright, but for balance. Her body didn't feel as tense as it usually did on an examination table, where she worried about getting a shot or having medicine squirted into her nose. Maybe she just liked this man's gentle drone, but then again, maybe she was too brain damaged to care what happened to her. Maybe she was retarded now.

"Her age suggests that her epilepsy is idiopathic," he went on, speaking more thoroughly and rapidly now that he sensed his erudition appreciated. "But you say she's had petit mals since adolescence. You may have been observing the postictus, unaware that she had been seizing out of your sight."

We hadn't thought of that.

"In dogs less than one year of age, the cause of seizures could be anything from hydrocephalus, strychnine poisoning, chlorinated hydrocarbons . . ." He lifted Kierney's lips in a grisly mock snarl and peered at her teeth and gums. When he let go, she lowered her head submissively, as though to reassure him that her ferocious look had been unintentional. "Tetanus, distemper, hypoglycemia, dietary deficiency," Michelotti rattled, "liver or kidney failure, parasitism, or head trauma."

I winced, thinking of Joe's rough games. But this was the vet we'd been waiting for, one willing to go gumshoe on the mystery of Kierney's disease. I glanced at Joe to share with him a hopeful smile, but he was frowning at Kierney. "She's never been sick or injured," he said, a catch of grief in his throat as he lay his hand on her thick rump. She looked up at him, and for a moment I saw again the tireless dog who sang and spun in circles just because Joe had put on sweats and bent to touch his toes. "She's the best athlete I've ever known," Joe said.

"She's overweight from the phenobarbital," Michelotti told him. Running his hands over her padded ribs and flanks, he turned his pale, scary-blue eyes aside, seeing with his fingers. "Beneath she's well-muscled." My sister had eyes like that—when we lived in Ghana the people used to ask if she was blind. Searching Kierney's body with his hands, Michelotti nodded to himself, as if deducing that he could easily recover the able body buried in gamy fur and fat. He flashed his light into her pupils, and said, "There's no brain damage."

We were stunned. The news was too good, too simple, too abrupt to be true. "What about the stumbling?" Joe said.

"This dog is intoxicated."

We gaped at him.

Michelotti clicked his pen light off. "It's not epilepsy; it's a barbiturate overdose." Then he added, without any trace of humor, "Although it *is* hard to tell the difference between brain damage and drunkenness. We'll wean her off the phenobarb for two weeks, then run her blood and start over from scratch. Tell me, is there a history of epilepsy in her pedigree, or was there any pre-natal trauma?"

"I can ask her breeder about the pedigree," I said. "And I know she was the runt."

"It may be she suffered inadequate fetal oxygen supply, or asphyxiation during the birthing process," he said, hooking his stethoscope into his ears. Familiar with this routine, Kierney slumped onto her belly and elbows while he slid the silver disk over her fur. Joe and I stood silently, holding our breath as if it would help the good doctor hear better. "She has a strong heart," he reported. "Border collies are tremendous athletes. My concern now is that the epilepsy has progressed unchecked." He started to tell us how epileptic neurons in the brain recruit normal neurons into the original "seizure focus," enlarging the area of the brain that produces seizures, but I interrupted.

"The old vets said plenty about repetitive and progressive seizuring, but we're pretty sure we've seen no pattern."

"Each hemisphere of the brain is a mirror image of the other." More news for us. A seizure focus on one side of the brain shows an abnormal EEG, he explained. Within weeks, the normal side will show similar EEG abnormalities. In time, the mirror focus can cause tonic-clonic activity on its own. "Uncontrolled seizures not only lower the threshold in any given animal," he concluded, "but also multiply the kinds of seizuring possible."

I lit up. Captivated by the phrase "any given animal," I asked, "Do other animals have seizures too, horses and elephants?"

"If it has a brain, it can have a seizure."

Did he have a sense of humor? "Imagine Jumbo!" I said.

He smiled.

"An ostrich? A seahorse?"

He raised one eyebrow. "A whale," he said, giving me a how-do-you-like-that? nod, then abruptly went on with his business, leaving me lingering in his wake, awed by a convulsing polar bear, eagle, octopus, sloth.

"I'd like you to bring me her seizure log," he was saying as he ruffled Kierney's ears. She grinned under his hand, head flat, nose narrow, mouth hanging impossibly wide. "And I'll send for her veterinary file. I'll need to see the results of her physical and neurological exams and her serum profile."

"She had nothing like that, did she, Lees?" Joe said.

"No, I'm sure of it," I said bitterly. "And I know there's no seizure log. Obviously, the other vets barely kept track of anything or they wouldn't have overdosed her last night." I watched Michelotti's face for some sign of censure against the veterinary clinic, but got nothing.

"I tell anyone who has an epileptic animal to keep a special diary detailing the time, duration, and severity, the preictus and postictus, as well as behavioral abnormalities or any possible contributing factors."

How sensible! How reassuring! If nothing else, at least I'd feel less helpless with a pen in my hand.

Kierney allowed Michelotti to gather her into his arms and lower her to the floor. "We'll rule out mimics," he said, "cardiac and pulmonary diseases, narcolepsy, cataplexy, myasthenia gravis, and metabolic disturbances."

He opened the examining room door and led us toward a high

counter, where one of the lab-coated women who'd been kind to Kierney when we arrived stood typing at a computer terminal. Although he spoke rapidly and there were people waiting, Michelotti remained attentive to us. "I'm going to compile a record, patient's profile, history, results of complete physical and neurological examinations," he said, "vaccinations, potential exposure to toxins such as flea preventives and vegetation sprays—"

"Vegetation sprays?!" I cried. And I told him about our landlord's herbicide dependency.

Shoulders slumped, hands in his lab jacket pockets, Michelotti looked beaten. "I can't prove anything, but I swear I see more seizuring dogs the morning after the county dusts for gypsy moths and Dutch elm disease. Dogs that have never seized before."

The woman typing at the computer lifted her head. "Where's Rachel Carson when you need her?" she said. Her name tag read "Shelly."

"I've been saying for a long time, somebody should do a study," he said. "We'll look at the herbicide, at injuries, behavioral changes, and diet."

"She's a vegan," I said.

Eyes the color of a hazy summer sky, he turned them on me, blank.

"We're strict vegetarians," I stammered, noticing that he was really rather tall. "We feed her a special dog food that has no animal products in it."

He shrugged. "Meat isn't precisely the dog's natural food."

"If you look at the labels, commercial dog food is largely corn meal," Shelly added.

"In the wild," Michelotti said, "a large part of the canine diet is predigested plant material."

Relieved, I smiled. Here were people who weren't afraid to face the repugnant fact that man's best friend was born to eat shit. And both of them had let Kierney lick their faces. "Kierney can't get enough cow flop," I said. I liked to imagine that wild canids were closet vegans, subsisting innocently on what dropped from ungulates' back ends.

But Michelotti wouldn't let me forget that dogs kill. "When prey is plentiful wild dogs will eat the stomachs, intestines, and fatty organs, and leave the muscle tissue."

I thought of how some children will scrape the cream out of Oreos and leave a pile of bare chocolate cookies behind. "Yes," I said, "I've read that. That's why we dared take the chance with this dog food. And border collies are bred to be fuel-efficient."

"I'd say from having examined Kierney that she's well-fed. Bring me the nutrition label and we'll make sure it provides enough fats and proteins." Still careful not to exclude us, he turned to Shelly, "Schedule Kierney for a CBC, urinalysis, BUN, ALT, ALP, calcium, fasting blood glucose level, serum glucose level, serum lead level, and a fecal. Depending on what we get and how much you can spend, we might later do a CT scan or an MRI."

I looked at Joe, knowing we couldn't pay for any of this, but I could see Joe was certain we'd find a way.

Michelotti looked down at Kierney, who had wedged herself between my standing legs and ignored everyone, as she always did, especially the friendly golden retriever who tried to greet her by scrabbling and whimpering on the end of his leash. "Kierney has been developing a tolerance for phenobarbital for months," Michelotti said. "It's no wonder she metabolized enough in one night to kill two Saint Bernards."

He prescribed diazepam on an as-needed basis to prevent status epilepticus. "We have to wean her carefully from the phenobarb," he said, gave us instructions, then shook our hands and left us to Shelly to schedule future appointments.

"What is it that we expected from our shamans, millennia ago," Lewis Thomas wrote of doctors, "and still require from the contemporary masters of the profession? To *do* something, that's what." We had found our doctor.

Over the next year, Kierney had frequent grand mal seizures. Once, she kicked off an emergency with thirteen grand mal seizures in thirty minutes, which landed her in Michelotti's overnight. We found no cause. A glance at the vegetarian dog food nutrition label had amazed Michelotti; "This is the best diet I've ever seen!" All her tests showed her organs healthy, and her liver enzyme abnormalities were compatible for barbiturate use. "Her blood work proves her diet is superior," he said.

God alone was to blame for her seizures.

Over the months, we adjusted conservative doses of potassium bromide, phenobarbital, diazepam and Karo syrup, experimenting with the recipe for Kierney's brain, and slowly the seizures tapered off. Finally, at three years old, Kierney was once again lean, dynamic, sharp-eyed and razor-witted. To our surprise, as the phenobarb had ebbed, her mood remained stable, much less neurotic. She let the tuft of white on her tail grow in. I could take her to the playground with Delaney, and she'd pant in her down-stay, unafraid of the people who stopped to pat her while I pushed Delaney on the swing. Comically, head low and shoulders hunched, she rode the merry-go-round and went down the roller slide. I still warned parents and children away from her, but the warnings were less urgent and more effective. People listened, maybe because in her heavy adult coat she looked less inviting and her endearing fearfulness had grown to haughtiness; she could turn a very chilly shoulder. But when people didn't listen to warnings, she tolerated them better.

By the time Kierney was three, we had rented a four-bedroom house just a block from the campus where Joe and I worked, in an old, shady neighborhood of stone houses, narrow streets and sidewalks with front porches that offered their friendly steps to passers-by. We had an attic and a basement, a huge kitchen, a dining room, a living room and a fireplace—but the windows were pure salvation. Each room had at least two, starting at about level to my knees and reaching above my head. In heavy casings, drafty and single-paned, each was made of eighteen squares of glass set in wood frames like tic-tac-toe boards. The wide ledges were pocked and rotten from being left open to the rain. Writing long chapters, I sat before them, gazing at the branches that crowded each view, trees that were probably the same age I was but which seemed ancient. Maple, elm, and hemlock made free-form brown strokes and green and gold splashes against the timeless gray of the neighbor's slate roof. With her nose, Kierney left her own silvery hieroglyphics on the panes.

One Saturday afternoon in our wide new living room, Joe and I sprawled on the couch, cooled in the play of summer shadows. We watched as Delaney, twenty months old, closed her fist around Kierney's collar. "Be gentle with the dog," I said.

She pulled, and Kierney looked at us pleadingly.

"Delaney, careful," Joe said, but the dog seemed okay.

Delaney pulled, "C'mon, Kierney," she said, and walked the dog in a narrow circle, just turning her around and around on the hardwood floor, spinning. Suddenly, Delaney sang out, "Kierney is my friend!"

"I never thought I'd see that," Joe said.

"I never thought I'd see it without having to rush to a pediatric plastic surgeon," I said.

"Well," Joe said heavily, "There was a time when I didn't think the dog would live."

We watched our little girl dance with a dog that had bitten three children, round and round, the dog wagging her tail, no more annoyed than any other adult dog would be to have her neck yanked and to be forced to stumble in purposeless circles.

"Kierney's a new dog. It's as if she's had shock treatment," Joe yawned. "Her brain's back, without the baggage."

"Kierney is my friend," Delaney sang, and around they went again.

For the first summer, fall, and spring in our new house, we soared at cruise altitude, all sunshine above and a fluffy bright bed of clouds far below. In the last year or so, I'd gotten an article and a couple short stories published, then Rutgers University Press agreed to publish my novel, *Body Sharers*. My book placed nicely in some competitions. Agents courted me. Joe had won the Bobst Award for emerging writers and New York University Press published his collection, *Indentation and Other Stories*. The Dean of Earth and Mineral Sciences made Joe's part-time tutoring position full-time, and we were confident and settled, preened on our nest.

Meanwhile, our little girl grew more beautiful and sweet with each passing week. Everywhere we went, people stopped me and told me she looked like the Gerber baby, the Campbell soup kids, or a Hummel figurine. Some said I should get an agent and a portfolio and get my kid on TV. It horrified me to think of capitalizing on her little face, dragging her to photo shoots, inviting agents and photographers and editors into our peaceful little world of kitty cats and Playmobil. Her beauty had one purpose—to enthrall Joe and me. I couldn't take her in my arms without swooning, couldn't look at her plump pink cheeks and long eyelashes without delirium, couldn't hear her cry without my heart breaking like a wave on rocks, fluid and mutable, the power of life on earth.

And, at three years old going on four, with her invisible assassin under a chemical restraining order, Kierney became almost sane. At least, she became confident enough to stay in a room by herself for the first time.

Her biggest problem was our new cat, a mama nursing two kittens. The cat's SPCA file said her name was "Spooky," an unimaginative homage paid her scrawny black Halloween body and eyes like two runic gold coins. After examining her, Michelotti said Spooky was still an adolescent herself, malnourished and badly stressed. Hardship notwithstanding, she was clumsy and, compared to most cats I've known, dull-witted. But suckling those teensy kitties gave her a supernatural ferocity directed full-blast at Kierney, who somehow threatened the kittens merely by being a live dog. Kierney could not so much as click her toenails on the kitchen floor, and that cat arched, puffed, spat and pinned the dog—six times her size—under the kitchen table. It took the cat weeks to acknowledge Kierney's exaggerated displays of submission—head down, tail down, eyes averted, body shrunken against the floor. The emaciated cat stomped her paws when she walked, giving her a strangely heavy tread. Soon when Kierney heard the cat thumping in, she swiftly incarcerated herself under the table.

Only when Kierney was having a grand mal seizure would the cat approach in any other attitude besides hostility. Nose twitching, whiskers forward, she'd creep in a circle around this strange dog who galloped and went nowhere. She'd examine the fur, even taste it. Between seizures when the dog lay spent, she sometimes began to purr and to wash her as if she understood helplessness. But just as the cat couldn't accept Kierney's signs of truce, the dog couldn't accept the cat's tenderness, which only amounted to another indignity. As soon as she was able, Kierney winced and pulled away, distrustful, cringing as if chastened, as if humiliated, as if to inform the cat that, *Please, the best thing you can do for an epileptic is to look away.*

Over the months under Michelotti's care, epilepsy became routine. In our new house, hardwood floors allowed Kierney to piddle, paddle, and froth in any room with easy clean-up. And Delaney would trundle in on her scooter to announce, "Kierney having scissors." She skipped around Kierney's foul struggle, singing a song she picked up from a kiddy show, "Pocket full of posies, ashes, ashes, we all fall down," her sweet syllables invoking protection against swift and horrific illness. When the falling sickness took her, Kierney toppled and her legs went rigid, vibrating, reaching in four directions, her head lifting and straining like the craving face of Tantalus, as if near water which evaded her tongue, food which swung away from her grasp, a heavy stone above her ever ready to fall.

I'd step over her on my way to the computer or the refrigerator, and I'd make notes in the seizure log: "7-24-91, 8:32 a.m. grand mal 30 secs. Post-ictal amnesia 7 mins. Temp norm. Toe-dragging, pacing, 90 mins. 1 TB Karo, 10mg diazepam." So I wrote in tongues, a babble to keep Beelzebub at bay. My own pocketful of posies.

And Kierney would get up, drag her hind feet for a day, probably from the diazepam rather than nerve damage. The next thing I knew, she'd be stopping hearts on a Penn State campus lawn, the canine Michael Jordan, airborne, seizing a speeding Frisbee out of the sky. She couldn't miss. Just when it seemed she was running as fast as anyone could run and the Frisbee was sure to outfly her, her hindquarters bunched, her back sank lower to the ground, and her speed almost doubled—the cheetah's trick.

When friends came to the house she still rammed her nose into one of their eyes. "Look," I'd say when I'd caught her by the choke chain and wrestled her to the floor. "Why don't you go get your racquetball? I think you left it upstairs in the bathroom." Cocking her head, her eyes drifted as if she were thinking, "Yeah, all right, that's a good idea." Then I'd let her go, and she'd thunder up the stairs. She'd come skidding back with her ball, happy at a gallop. She'd toss it at me and spin away, *Throw it! Throw it fast! Throw it now!*

Delaney in her stroller, I'd walk Kierney downtown and we'd play Frisbee on the lawn at Old Main. People applauded and envied me. "Your dog's amazing. What kind is it?" they'd say. Sometimes someone would stop me at a street corner, even taking me by the arm to drive the compliment in nice and deep, "You're lucky you have such a good dog."

This comment always surprised me.

Kierney's admirer explained, "*My* dog is stupid. He'd never sit nice at a curb like your dog is."

"Thanks," I would say. "We've been to obedience school. There are lots of good trainers in town."

The stranger would say again, "Nah, *my* dog is stupid," seeming slightly annoyed at me for not being prouder, or at least fonder, of my dog. As the stranger left, I would have to wonder why it was so difficult for me to step outside my little pack and view it as was at that moment, a young woman rolling a darling little girl in a stroller, sauntering along a sidewalk with a trim black dog in perfect step, halting on a dime at the busy intersection, sweet and easy as pecan pie.

Sometimes when passing strangers praised Kierney and thought me ungrateful for her, I wished there were a way to explain: "Any dog can sit at the curb if his owner's willing to spend time training him, as I did. This one is neurotic and hyperactive, but sitting at my side is the least of her feats—she can leap six feet as soon as yawn, outrun a zipping Frisbee, catch a racquetball caroming faster than the human eye can see. She uproots trees with her teeth. She can metabolize three times the lethal limit of phenobarbital for a dog twice her size. She has a deadly disease and I've wrestled her out of the jaws of Leviathan. You haven't seen her convulsions. She hasn't bitten your bare hand."

There were no words for who she was to me. I couldn't say she was a good dog, nor that I was lucky. I really couldn't say with any substance that she was my "dog," a word that had barely contained my childhood fox terrier friend, Patches. Kierney had sometimes asked more of me than my husband or my baby did, but I wasn't her helpmate nor was she my daughter. To an old tune called, "K-K-K-Katy," Joe and I sang "K-K-K-Kierney, beautiful Kierney, you're the only d-d-d-dog that I adore," and the ditty somehow captured both the Kierney who galloped figure-eights on the night lawn and the one who carried branches half her weight and four times her length which she knew as "sticks." Her name and her nicknames, like "Sister Mary Kierney" (for her high-strung servility, her black-and-white garb, her ears always back like a wimple) captured facets of her, snapshots, none showing whom I knew best: the one jumping onto the bed when Joe and I invited her to sleep at the foot, then jumping respectfully off despite our disappointed protests; the one who reluctantly "kissed the baby" when told to do so; the one who slunk away when asked, "Are you begging?"; the one who careened off furniture yapping and snapping the air whenever somebody mentioned a "fly"; the one who matched the tippity-tap of my typing with the clack of racquetball-catching.

Once in a while somebody would say, "Hey, you've really trained that dog well."

In the company of somebody who could guess at the toil behind the show, I could laugh and say, "Thanks. She's a real piece of work." But even still, my heart would crowd my chest. "It's a miracle!" I'd want to cry, "A miracle! We're here takin' a walk and playin' Frisbee together, good and simple. She was dead, and is alive again." Make merry, and be glad.

A month passed, and then another, then several in a row, during which we thought nothing about epilepsy, for there were no seizures. We checked the log to be sure. Six months had passed, and we just had a really great dog, a well-trained four-year-old border collie. Who knew that contentment could be such an achievement? Not for the faint, the proud, the lazy, or the cruel. You stay awake past the point of exhaustion, kneeling on the bathroom floor while your little kid waits to vomit. Learn songs from Sesame Street and sing them. Confess, confide, cry. Put an album on the CD player and dance a silly dance. Throw the racquetball another thousand times. Turn your anger to the couch and punch it. Learn when to trade time for money and money for time.

"I love you today," I'd say to Joe and he'd grin. I love you today. I love you today. Today is all there is.

I marveled that I wasn't bored. Things that once fascinated me had lost their fascination, yet I was happy. The older Delaney got, the more she needed, and I was probably transfixed by her. I enjoyed watching the kittens, Odette and Albertine, named for Proustian sweethearts, free-fall into adulthood. Although they nursed for more than six months, they quickly became independent, and the mama cat left Kierney alone. The feline drama subsided into feline sleep. Rarely did I seem to notice Kierney. Still my All-Star, she continued to converse with us at a high level, but now her talk was old news, constant, and calm. She'd lost her hysteria.

However, there was a spell there, early on, lasting a couple of months, during which I was entertained to discover that the dog and the daughter shared similar language skills, their functioning vocabulary lists about the same length.

One day I pointed the comparisons out to Joe.

"But I assume they each have a different set of words," he said.

"True. If I say to Delaney, 'Your bone's in your food dish,' she can't quite figure what I'm talking about."

Kierney scrambled from behind me and stared, lips bunched and showing those tiny front teeth just under her nose.

"Oops!" I said and clapped my hand over my mouth. I should've known she was listening. She seems to be in every photograph of us exactly the way Daisy is in every frame of the Blondie comic strip.

When I failed to repeat the sentence, she whirled and launched away, knocking Delaney onto her diapered bottom, and blustered into the kitchen. We heard the empty food dish clatter angrily on the floor.

In a way, Joe and I had come to think nothing of her, just as we thought nothing of each other, of our being there. Our eating, talking, teaching, biking, writing, and our sleeping were all matters of course, the house and the yard and our paychecks all givens, our desires sated. We still wanted life improved for farm animals and lab animals and forests and political prisoners, but with the birth of our daughter, our activism dwindled to one cause: hers. To our surprise, we yearned for material things, like a log cabin playhouse for Delaney, a piano, a new mountain bike for Joe, a good bedspread, a sandbox, and a weekend at a sheep-herding clinic. These were beyond our budget, but pleasant to wish for, without urgency, no danger of despair. We figured once you acquired an object you wanted, another took its place on the wish-list, and you were back where you started. If where you started was pretty nice to begin with, why not just stay there?

I don't know exactly when it happened, but after years of active involvement in the Church choir and in Cursillo, a Catholic lay person organization, I gradually stopped going to Mass. Delaney wouldn't let me play flute for the choir anymore without knocking over my stand, wandering down the aisles, loudly requesting to nurse, so I had to quit. I was banished to the "cry room," where some parents chatted loudly with each other, their small children crying and clambering over the rubble of toys, while other parents like myself strained to listen to Mass over the crackling PA system. "I can baby-sit better at home," I grumbled. Mass, choir practice, and church meetings meant hours on the road and hours away from my house, my computer, my wide old windows and my dog. My daughter needed steady peaceful hours with me, just as the dog always had. It was a time to stay home, time to build up, time to dance, to embrace. It was a time to abandon words like "English Department," "Catholic," and "animal rights."

And "border collie."

The name had once impressed me. It impressed many people around me, and thanks to Stanley Coren's *The Intelligence of Dogs*, Donald McCaig's book and novel, and the movie *Babe*, the word was impressing more and more people. For me, it was a crystal ball that had made prophecies, pontifications, demands, but now the name "border collie" was getting thin and airy, just a soap bubble after all. It said that as a border collie owner my duty was to spend a lot of time and money on a dog sport, ideally herding, but if not that then fly-ball, tracking, agility, or obedience competition. The bubble said that as an unemployed border collie, Kierney was an abused animal. Unfit owners, Joe and I hadn't the time or money to meet these demands, except to take her running or to the slide in the kiddy park. Mostly what we did was let her herd tennis balls around the house.

A woman actually said to me, contemptuously, "Why do you even have a dog if you're not going to *do* anything with her?"

As a fan of Vickie Hearne, I felt it. I could remember the promises I'd made to George, to work Kierney, to show her, to earn a Utility Dog title. I had let go of many things.

That winter we had weekly blizzards, and we'd let Kierney out the door to hit the snow, leaping foxlike, plowing wolf-like, the blade of her chest cutting the drifts. Content she was, but maybe a tad depressed too. She slept more. I worried, but Kierney seemed happy enough at my side. The border collie soap bubble lifted and dried out before my eyes, fragile, veined, a sphere of dust.

I was once a woman whose daughter wore ruffled dresses and plastic necklaces and rode my hip. I was once a woman with a shadow in the shape of a quiet black dog, a dog some people didn't even notice, a dog that others were captivated by, a dog some feared. "She's got creepy eyes," the handyman said, and I promised to keep her locked up when he came. I was a woman knee deep in snow, casting sheets of birdseed and ducking out of the cloud of my own breath the better to watch my minikin Black Beauty run her white steeplechase.

I was also feeding gulls on an abandoned beach while Kierney cantered in the surf, neither of us awed by the Atlantic Ocean. What was the ocean to her as she ran beside it, proportion and perspective skewed on the wide-open shore—who could say which was the stronger, the louder, the more mercurial? What did the agile black dolphin enjoy that she did not? What did the obstinate tiger shark know of determination compared to hers? Did the great barracuda have teeth more menacing? She galloped along white breakers that hid sunfish, threshers, blue tangs, striped blennies, makos, batfish, porbeagles, torpedo rays, red hakes, croakers, ladyfish, mullet, wolffish, tripletails, white grunts, tattlers, shimmering silver lookdowns, and packs of flashing jack mackerel, but all together were they any more alive than she?

"You were always an adventuresome child," my mother said. Although never athletic, never graceful, I would climb to the once-unreachable tree branch, and, trusting the tree, I'd hang on with my toes and fingertips and dare the ground to fly up and whack me. On the New Jersey shore I collected bucketsful of stinging jellyfish and captured hatchling tiger sharks in paper cups. A languid, contemplative tomboy, I believed that if something was alive, like a rat or a vine or a body of water, it wouldn't hurt me. In the ocean, lured not by death but by wonder, by the lift of the waves as the sand dropped away from the tips of my toes, by the beach thinning behind me and the crowds shrinking to dots of color, by the horizon wrapping around me, I swam way past the breakers hoping to be the furthest swimmer out. More than once I got swept into riptides. Distantly, I'd hear a whistle. I'd turn and try to swim back. A crowd gathered to watch the rescue—not the crowd I had left, but another crowd a good mile down the beach—and some other lifeguard was swimming for me, an unwelcome hero, superfluous. Independent, spiteful, embarrassed, and a darn good swimmer, (to escape a riptide, swim shallowly) I always made it to shore without his help. As if I had every right to get swept away if I wanted to, I scowled past the crowd of concerned parents and envious schoolgirls who nightly dreamed of being rescued by that lifeguard, marched all the way back to my beach. I went straight back into the water and swam out past the breakers to flirt with the riptide.

In Africa, at four years old, I sat on our front step sharing hardboiled eggs with our night watchman, a Mossi who'd had his teeth filed into points. I once overheard my Ghanaian nanny convince my father that someone had used voodoo against him; whether for kindness, curiosity or jest, my father agreed to see the witch doctor. In Ghana we noticed I'd been born lacking a fear of snakes, which both Darwin and Freud cite as universal and necessary to our species. My father, a healthy ophidiophobic, remembers me in the city of Accra at the zoo, fascinated by the twenty-foot reticulated python. So that I could see it better, a laughing Ghanaian zookeeper lifted its body, which curved around him wide as the wheels of our pickup truck. Its head swung down his arm and came at me like the head of a Rottweiler, and I, a tiny fair girl with a headful of Shirley Temple curls, reached out my skinny tanned arm and patted it. I remember John, our cook, running when his wife shouted that there was a black mamba on the driveway, and I ran with him, hoping to catch a glimpse of the deadly snake before he hacked at it with the garden hoe, chopping it into twitching, bloody sausages and cursing it in Twi.

I tumbled with our friend's lion cubs and walked into the swarm of flying termites that rose from our front lawn, a hissing white storm cloud. When the millions shed their wings, we raked them, like so many autumn leaves, the yard lumping with hundreds of frogs and lizards all come to gorge themselves on the flightless worm-like bodies. I stood on the grass in my flip-flops, knowing there was nothing but a wedge of foam rubber between me and the hookworms. I stroked the tails of our angry, wild-caught parrots whose garden-lopper beaks were strong enough to clip off my finger. Dawn and dusk their cries smashed through the house, looting my very thoughts, an invading army of sound.

My fearlessness persisted through the years we lived in Indonesia. I lifted picture frames on the walls to scatter the gravity-defying geckos, and, never dare touching them, I pondered their ability to release their regenerative tails in exchange for their lives. We needed routine rabies shots, which hurt like the blow of a crow bar to the upper arm. Weekly I swallowed ground-up quinine pills, the sting only faintly tempered by a spoonful of honey. Impressively cavalier about malaria and most other dangers we faced living in Indonesia, my father would not take his pills. Then one day I found him lying on the couch chattering, muttering, twitching and sweating. "I have malaria," he told me, and then I knew that everything we feared about living there was *real*. I stared unflinchingly into the faces of noseless lepers—"Oh, look," I'm told I nonchalantly said, "that man has turned into a monster." Friends kept an angry monkey who bit and threw shit and ate his own vomit. My parents mumbled that it was wrong to keep monkeys, and I felt guilty for having enjoyed the sight of him shaking his bitter cage. Once our washerwoman got mad at me and splashed me with a bowl of her own urine. Running to the embassy compound swimming pool right behind our house, I dove in, swept away by the knowledge that I had made someone *that angry*. Poor and neglectful, the Indonesian zoo had one hairless kangaroo whose mange had become the pitiful animal's most intriguing feature, and I lingered at her pen, staring until the image of her flaming red skin against the yellow dirt was all I could remember of that place. The city of Djakarta was overrun with mangy, skeletal, crooked-tailed cats. I wanted to know about mange, about monkeys, about women who threw urine, about the nation's capital punishment for the killing of cats, about the sweet spiny fruit, rambutan, which I could pick and eat from the top of a fence.

Many years later, in Sana'a, Yemen, with my father, I climbed to the edge of a cliff five miles high. Standing toes to the brittle rim, I was certain that I wouldn't fall. On the rim of the cliff, in the shooting sunlight and the dusty wind, a passel of Yemeni men lounged, scarves wound round their dusky heads and their cheeks distended by *gat*, a leaf they chewed to get high. I sat down beside them and swung my sneakered feet over the edge.

People who obey their fear without question—what do they gain, what do they miss? Driving on a dirt road forty miles into Northern Pennsylvania forest, forty miles from any semblance of a town, I once, at dusk, saw an old rattlesnake, five or six feet long, crossing a dirt road before our headlights. Having a keen memory for information concerning living creatures, I knew that rattlesnakes aren't easily provoked and will lie still if approached, so I left the car and ran toward it, then slowed, then reverently crouched beside its head, gray in the white headlights. I studied the heat-sensing depression between eye and nostril, wondered what creatures the snake had stricken, what it had swallowed, marveled at the lay of its scales and its unblinking amber eye. I remembered a little Faulkner: *Oleh, Chief, Grandfather.* Having ceased its progress, the pit-viper lay patiently breathing, as if it had been paid homage by a dozen other literature students before. My new husband Joe was with me, or I should say, he was a good distance away from me and the snake, still sitting in the car, and I turned my head and waved to let him know I was okay, but when I faced the snake again it had in the span of a second furled its body into muscular petals, and a buzz shocked the air, not in fright, and not in threat, but in reprimand, for I had been crass by breaking gaze, by waving my hand. Somehow, defying the laws of motion and balance I bowed and backed away without making any forward movement to brace or propel my body, in a floating rush, as if the sound itself had blown me backwards, and yet, when I was a mere three feet away, I stopped, standing at my full height, and still under my gaze and still within reach it slowly unrolled itself until it once again made a straight line perpendicular to the road, bisecting the edge at a ninety-degree angle, out in the open like that, assailable by car, skunk, raccoon or deer, which will, like a Ghanaian, trample any snake, mamba or not, cursing in their own mute Twi.

Embarrassed by the reprimand, I nonetheless couldn't feel foolish, nor even lucky. I had merely been forced into alertness and obliged to make a correction, which I did and for which I was rewarded. The way I figured it, I'd have been foolish to have stayed in the car, as Joe had, Joe who in this case has nothing to tell. Within one stride of me, the head disappeared into the weeds, "fatal and solitary . . . evocative of all knowledge and an old weariness and of pariah-hood and of death," calmly leaving its smooth, aged body for a moment vulnerable and unsupervised by anyone but me.

A friend had us visit his homestead, a farm that had been in his family some hundred years, with a "Favorite" brand gas cookstove installed in the 1920's. One morning as we sat eating breakfast, he walked out the door, returned and opened his hands, releasing a winged creature four inches across, glowing pale green, pulsing, floating, pulsing, floating on the coffee-scented air, two long, delicate opaque tails trailing like dainty human legs. "A luna moth!" I cried. "There aren't many around anymore," he said. "Farm chemicals are killing them off." Translucent, it hovered as if holographic. He took it from the air and put it on my newspaper, where it lay docile and transparent enough to read through. Its plump, stubby, bright white furred body lay as if without legs, two big black eyes in a face as charming as an infant harp seal's. "They have no mouth parts," he said. "As soon as they hatch from their cocoons, they're dying. They hurry to mate and then fade." Trembling, it willed itself into the air again, a maiden of green light, and for a moment, I knew exactly what a fairy was.

In what passes as long ago in my short life, I came from the African continent and the swaying green blades of the Indonesian islands and found myself in a suburban New Jersey neighborhood where my desire to belong was matched only by my desire to thrill and be thrilled, to suffer the piquancy of being alive among other things that were alive. We'd traded lion cubs for Himalayan cats, cockatoos for blue jays, geckos for chipmunks, hippos for horses, pythons for rattlesnakes, white corn for rambutan, locusts for luna moths. But, if I could read Pippi Longstocking and Mowgli and White Fang, and if I could observe, analyze and imagine, and if could tell tales to myself, any neighborhood dog could be Buck, any wooded lot could be an uncharted continent. Wherever you find yourself, the creatures are exotic. In the living lurks adventure, awaiting rapture, in the guise of a poodle or a luna moth. Joy is a bird of prey.

In Michelotti's examination room, Kierney stood on the table the way she did—back flat, shoulders and rump level, tail long and low, head down and panting the pant of a weary wolf, with the smooth-skull shaggy-neck look of a Borzoi, or a vulture hot and hungry atop a telephone pole. She was all those things and everything beautiful and wise and horrible. She was alive and she would not hurt me. She nudged my hand.

"Six months," I said happily stroking her. "Six months and all's well." Kierney buried her face in the crook of my elbow, afraid Michelotti might try to squirt medicine up her nose.

"A remission," Michelotti said, folding his arms and frowning, "is no real sign that the potassium bromide has helped at all."

Chapter Eight

The Sidewalks of Heaven and Earth

There's a mattress on the floor in our living room, a pile of pillows at one end and the sheets loose and twisted. Delaney bounces on it and loses her toys in the folds. In the kitchen the tall brown bottle of potassium bromide is out on the counter, and the little snap-lid container, about the size of a canister of 35 mm film, stands beside it, the label reading, "Diazepam." It's early summer. Kierney has turned four, Delaney will turn three, and the heavy wooden front door is open. The torn screen door ripples in the cool breeze. The front porch isn't really a porch at all, but a step with a wrought iron railing guiding you to enter indirectly, from the side. Heavy rhododendron and yew crowd the railing, shielding it, so that even as you come up the walk you can't see the step until you're about to mount it. The old shrubs teem with sparrows, and a bird feeder hangs on the railing, a feeder I keep filled even though I rarely see the birds. I've peered into the dark city of branches and think those birds have a great set-up in there. I like hearing them, seeing the branches shake a little from their hopping. If I lie on the couch or mattress real still, I can hear their tiny beaks crack the miniscule orbs of millet seed. I remember Pavarotti and Rudy and Jill. The sparrows need never leave.

If you came up the walk you might not notice the wide deep shade from the maple tree, the birds in the yew, or the step, but you would see the front door's open. You might think you can come in that door, but you can't. As you pass the last yew bush you suddenly see a baby gate wired across the step and if you're lucky you just see a wet black dog lying there on a rumpled towel. "Come around to the side door," I will say, and when you come in, I'll tell you that my dog has been having seizures for two days straight, and she's sedated now. "It's a good place to hose her off," I say. "The weather's been great." I steer you away from the living room. "Joe sleeps in there so he can hear her. Come sit in the kitchen."

But nobody comes to visit. The mailman can drop a few "get well" cards from our dog-loving friends into the mailbox without using the step, and he never asks about the dog, but surely he knows this must be the same dog who usually charges the window. Her paws grip the back of the couch like talons on a branch, her body recoils like a cannon with each bark, and her voice shoves him off her land—it's the same with every other dog. Now when his shoes clop up the walk and he clatters the lid of the mailbox, there's no response anywhere but for a near-silent flutter through the shrubs. He can look down and study the dog if he wants to. But he doesn't. He's busy, and she's not easy to look at.

I'm one of five women carpooling to a meeting. In the front passenger seat, Marguerite, a good friend, asks about Kierney. "The last few rounds of seizures have been elaborate," I say, leaning forward from the back seat. "She sort of binds up sideways as if she's trying to get up, but she's not, and her head twists and then she flattens into these rigid tremors and then it starts all over. Afterwards she can't walk. She swims on her stomach on the floor like a frog. It's some sort of nerve damage in her hips, but it clears up and then she's fine," I say cheerfully. The seizures belong to us, and they're fascinating. Kierney is locusts and voodoo, mambas and mange, riptides and cliffs five miles high. I'm not afraid.

The other women seem tense, disapproving, and I suppose they're thinking, like so many people, that we should euthanize Kierney. Maybe they feel guilty for having euthanized their own animals in the past, and they want me to assuage their guilt for them by making the same choice they did. Or maybe it seems to them cruel and selfish to put her through this, as if I can't let go—as if she were mine to keep or discard. Ironically such thinking seems a cruel and selfish lie to one who has seen her dash a hundred yards in deep kicking sand, check the flight of the Frisbee over her shoulder, adjust her direction according to the ocean wind, then somehow spring straight up, turning, take the Frisbee in a tidy chop, and then skip back to us, loping, hopping, tossing the Frisbee to herself, ho hum, la-dee-da.

When we're at the veterinary hospital, the same lab-coated women who first greeted Kierney, who knelt on the floor with her and fed her from their pockets, they tell me, appreciatively, "Few people would put up with this." They know.

There's got to be some way to explain why I "put up with it," how in the world I learned to be upbeat about epilepsy. "After a couple days it'll be as if nothing happened. She goes weeks, sometimes months, between attacks."

"Great," the other women say feebly.

"Isn't there any way to stop the seizures?" Marguerite asks.

"We've tried everything. We're gonna increase the potassium bromide again, but it looks like it's not doing much good. At least with this weather we can leave her out on the porch and when the seizures jack her temperature up we can just hose her off."

"Oh, my God," one woman bursts out. "This is your *daughter*!"

"No," I say. "My dog."

The other women gasp, shake their heads free of bewilderment, and exclaim that they too thought I was talking about my daughter. "Oh!" they say. "Okay, then."

Leaning back in my seat, going silent, I ask myself, is it okay, then? Would I speak any differently if it were my little girl? I guess I wouldn't drag her to the porch and hose her off, but otherwise, if it were my little girl I imagine I'd speak the way people speak when they've lived in the culture of an illness long enough to acquire its indelicacies.

Joe's youngest sister has been caring for their oldest sister, who has cerebral palsy. "Her bowels aren't working properly," the youngest crisply reports. "Once a day I have to reach in with my hand and pull it out."

In her fifth year of metastasized cancer, Joe's mother is dying good-naturedly. "Forgive me for lying down. I've been putting in a full day at work," she says, just as triumphantly as she did the day she phoned me to tell me the beagle Jack had run away. Her voice is now only a musical whisper. The cancer crowds her lungs, but she's still free, free to work, free to earn, free, after a minute's rest, to tell another story. She straightens the front of her dress over her protruding belly. The doctors say the tumors are growing at such a rate that soon she will suffocate. They stopped chemo. "I only throw up for a few hours in the morning now," she sighs happily.

What does it matter whom you're speaking about? Your dog, your daughter, your sister, yourself? It's disease that's indecent.

Two days and Kierney's seizures end. She can't stand. My dog usually roars through the neighborhood like a renegade torpedo and usually completes her toilet daintily and privately in a shrub or a high stand of flowers or weeds. However, until the nerve damage heals I must take her out to the yard and prop her up. We're perhaps unable to comprehend the contrast: the peaceful days we usually share and the thrashing zombie who sometimes invades our kitchen and needs to be spoon-fed canned dog food because she can't hold herself upright well enough to eat from her dish.

From the first, I have understood that these seizures were deadly, just as I understood that a horse galloping over rocky ground can fall and kill you both. I understand that most people have their severely epileptic dogs euthanized. But the truth is, all I really believe is that she's our clever and gorgeous Kierney so much more often than she's a ghoul. During the spells, I see how they frighten her. I see how fiercely she wants to live through them. How can we not help her fight, how can we deny her the chance to have more clever and gorgeous days?

I look at it this way. Unlike the rest of us, Kierney's forced to give birth to herself over and over. We're her midwives. "You can do it!" we say, and then she's a newborn for a few days. We feed her and clean up after her and then there she is again, an adult. But she's not just any adult. On campus, when she plays Frisbee, people with places to go catch sight of her and suddenly have nothing better to do but watch and clap.

She's a border collie, God's own superstar.

My mother-in-law Barbara is dying of cancer and has thirteen children. She's also had two miscarriages. I once calculated that she'd spent a total of ten years pregnant. Why so many kids? "I love people," she answered, beaming with matter-of-fact generosity. Everybody feels good around Barbara, as if she were one of those sunny Saturday afternoons with breeze just cool enough and just dry enough, when there's nothing to do but tell stories about people who're heroes, people who're fools, people who're clowns, the day so taut and the telling so good you hardly notice you've cooked and eaten a meal, cleared the table, washed the dishes, pulled some weeds, pruned some tomato plants, and then helped carry Cindy in her heavy wheelchair up to the second floor for her bath. Barbara is fifty-three years old and she's big again, big like she was for a total of ten years, but she's not giving birth to another like she did thirteen times and not giving birth to herself the way Kierney does. This time she's not suffering for the sake of the life that follows. Or maybe she is.

Everyone gathers, her husband, all her many children, and the "outlaws," as those of us who've married into the family call ourselves. Everyone has gone to her, it seems, except me. I stay home the way I have been lately, for my toddler, who wouldn't tolerate so easily the long drive, the long and uncertain hours, the event itself. I stay home for the dog, who might seize. "Hold down the fort," Joe says as he leaves me. He calls every few hours, not crying, fairly talkative, reporting who's arrived at the hospital and in what state of mind, whether or not his mother's slept or ate, what they've talked about, how she's using her morphine drip. I start to feel like I'm missing an important event, a cross between the Last Supper and the Super Bowl. I'm grieving and guilty and lonely and left out. "Save yourself up," Joe says. "I'm going to need you."

So I brace myself for the hurricane of grief that will blow in with him when he arrives home. But he doesn't need me. After her death he's spiritually elated and I, bawling because I love my mother-in-law and I'll never see her again, am mystified, even resentful. "She wasn't afraid," Joe tells me, as if he's just witnessed the angel of the Lord roll back the stone, sit upon it and say, "He is not here."

"She wasn't angry. She talked and slept and sipped water. She smiled a lot. Then she slept for a long time. We could see her chest rise and fall. We all told her we loved her. We said we'd see her soon. And more and more time passed between breaths. Then her chest just didn't rise again."

Something's wrong with my husband. Denial. Or maybe he's cold-hearted and I just never noticed before. But at the funeral, you can distinguish between us easily—those sobbing have missed the death vigil, and those serene ones were with Barbara when she died. In the receiving line, as I approach Joe's father, I carry the full weight of my grief, my jealousy and my shame for not being with her at her death. Instead I lolled at home on the couch with my two-year-old.

Before I can speak a word, Barbara's widower looks into my eyes and says to me, "You're a good mother."

I'm thunderstruck.

"Barbara and I talked about you," he explains. "You're a good mother," he says as if Barbara speaks through him, as if reading my thoughts. Somehow, on her deathbed, she was with all of them and with me too. Is this wisdom? Is this love? Is this telepathy? Or is it Jesus? How I want to be like Barbara! How I want to live as she did, intuiting who will exalt when the chained beagle's set free, and to die as she did, leaving everyone with an unfaltering belief in an afterlife.

"Peace be with you," we say in the Catholic Mass, turning to shake each other's hands.

And also with you, Barbara, stranger, sister, priestess.

When we can tell the dying, "We'll see you soon," and believe it, grief has few sharp edges.

I'm packing for a trip, three days with Delaney in my old college town. My friend Judy, who went to visit her parents there and got stranded by premature labor at only six months pregnant, is bedridden for the next three months and bored. It would help her two-year-old son and her parents to have another woman around for a few days. As I pack, I hear Kierney's breath huffing and shooing and the clitter-clat of her nails. This fit's really strange, as if she's got a hook in her throat and somebody's on the ceiling trying to reel her in, but she's just too heavy. Then she goes limp and saliva spills from her mouth as if from a tipped cup.

"You want me to stay?" I say to Joe.

"The semester's over. I don't mind sticking around the house. I can rest and I got a million little things to do around here. Judy needs you. Go ahead."

It's June now, still bright and dry. As if he welcomes the change of pace from tutoring and lecturing, Joe whistles as he pulls the guestroom mattress down to the living room floor. The kitchen is just beginning to smell of her foamy breath and urine when he carries her out to the front step. He stands in the shade sprinkling her with the hose as if he's watering lilies. "She was getting hot," he says, and I remember the twig ladders he wove for Jill, the little white flightless finch, so she could hop from her favorite sleeping perch not just to the seed dish but to the bath and to the windowsill for sunshine. "She'll probably be through it by the time you leave."

By the time I leave, she's been seizing three days. "What if you need to take her to Michelotti's?" I say, because we only have one car.

"I've got everything I need right here," Joe says. "I can call a cab or I'll call Jim." Jim Morrow, the award-winning science fiction writer, lives just two blocks away, and he loves dogs, loves Kierney. Once when Kierney's epilepsy broke up a meeting of local writers at our home, Jim was the only one to stay behind. He sat on the floor resting his hand on her side, quietly lifting his white, wild-haired head to ask questions about her illness. Years later, in memory of Kierney, he was to end his novel *Blameless in Abaddon* with the image of a dying border collie named Crumpet, "born and raised in the concrete heart of Pittsburgh," finally having her feisty chance to herd sheep on a farm in central Pennsylvania, thanks to a Make-a-Wish foundation for dogs called the Kennel of Joy. Now Jim has his own border collie too, Pooka, his Princess of Peace.

So I drive three-and-a-half hours out of town, out of my present, into my past, my old college town, and into Judy's present, her parents' house, her son, her fears for the delicate creature bulging her tight, round middle. Stretched in a lounge chair in the sun, wearing white shorts, Judy straightens the front of her maternity top over her protruding belly. She closes her eyes, tanning her long lean legs, telling me her husband comes from their home in State College to visit her at her parents' house every weekend. "If I can just hold, like this, for another few weeks, the doctors say we can risk driving me back to State College."

She asks me to assist at her daughter's birth, and I'm touched. I happily agree. As it turned out, three months later all I managed to do was miss the storied birth by seconds. After enduring months of contractions, Judy arrived at the hospital more than ready to deliver her baby. In a breathtaking action sequence, the heroic emergency room orderly swept up to the front desk, shoved Judy into a wheelchair, and raced her down the hall. When he skidded to a stop in front of the elevator, the door opened, and there stood the obstetrician, who promptly knelt and caught baby Kira in the hospital's greatest Hail Mary pass.

A moment later, I arrived, lugging my boom box, massage oil, and a bulging overnight bag. I rushed to the front desk and, to the great amusement of everybody there, gasped, "Which way do I go? I'm Judy McKelvey's birth coach!"

But Judy and I don't yet know we're going to have such a story to tell. There are other stories unfolding even as she dozes in her lounge chair and I take her son and my daughter on a walk around the yard to pick dandelion blossoms. There are stories yet to come before Kira's born, and stories to follow, most without punch-lines.

Creaking the screen door open, Judy's mother waves the phone at me and shouts, "For you!"

"It's bad," Joe tells me. "Come home now."

Day five: profuse drooling, teetering head, locked jaws. Kierney's unable to eat or drink. I've been home since the previous evening. Now it's early morning, all the windows are open, but it's a little cool and dewy for this time of year. Having pulled sweaters on myself and Delaney, I put her in front of a Barney tape and go out to sit cross-legged in my favorite old torn jeans on the front step. I finger the fringed hole on my right knee—that knee because four years before I used to kneel on it to pick Shannon's hooves. Kierney's head sways the way our African gray parrots used to bob their heads when they were angry. "Back off," the movement said. But Kierney doesn't seem to be threatening anybody I can see. She's been an outdoor dog for four full days, sheltered only by maple branches, yew and rhododendron. By day sparrows must have cracked millet seeds inches away from her head. Flies and bees inspect. By night pill bugs trundle around her. The night before, I slept little, and lay under my upstairs window listening to the "*Seet! Seet!*" of the bats as they shot past the top of my head, a reassuring sound, friendly. It was good knowing somebody else was up and alive while I was down, asleep and unaware. Could Kierney hear them too? I wanted to tell her, "The bats are out, Kierney, and tomorrow you'll be well." I wondered if a passing skunk paused in the front yard, lifted a front paw, and flickered its keen whiskers in her direction.

She's not resting now, a sudden whimper as she struggles to get on her feet, her spine hopelessly twisted. The hook in her mouth pulls up, pulls up. No birds or bugs will linger here. Joe is a gray ghost behind the screen.

"So when did this start?" I ask him.

"It came on gradually. I guess I noticed it a couple hours before I called you."

"What does Michelotti say?"

"Brain damage." Opening the screen door, Joe sets the cordless phone on the concrete beside me. "He can't be sure." Joe leaves for his office.

After the previous few rounds of seizures this summer, she was partially paralyzed from the hips down, but the paralysis was temporary. This too, will pass. Over the next hour, the air gets warmer and drier. I pull off my sweater. Flies and bees hum past, and the shrubs empty of birds, gone to other feeders because of me. I rewind the Barney tape and Delaney doesn't seem to mind. "I don't like so much TV," I tell her, kissing the top of her head. "But tomorrow we'll take Kierney to the park."

Even though one neural blitz immediately follows another, tedium sets in. Then I find raw wounds on Kierney's skin where she has chafed against the cement. These could get infected! Busily I stuff a towel under her for cushion and fetch our antibacterial ointment. Meticulously, I comb over her body, her cheek, her shoulder, her elbow, her toes, her ribs, her hips. It seems it's been weeks since I've been this happy, since I've lost myself in something tender and hopeful, but of course, such are most moments with my little girl. But here my behavior's compounded, set in focus—what we thought was a blessing, what we thought was good, the weather, the cement, keeping her clean and cool and safe, has injured her, and I'm correcting, restoring. She rocks and huffs and shudders, and I wait for the seizure to subside, then reapply the ointment to an elbow that doesn't really need it. "You're just going to lick this all off, aren't you?" I say, and can almost see her sitting up, dipping her doe-like head to lick her elbow.

In the afternoon, I put Delaney near the screen door in a highchair with a snack and give Michelotti another report. A lozenge of sunshine has burst through the maple and touched down on Kierney's helpless hot black side, so I rig a blanket across the railings to shade her. Lowering myself to the cement and ducking under the blanket tent with her, my little black-furred girl, I tell her we'll go to the ocean again. I tell her we'll go to the woods of Alan Seger Park. I say, "Kierney will c'mon right here with Lisa from kitchen to upstairs, Kierney will lie down on Lisa's feet while I write, Kierney will taste toothpaste when Lisa brushes teeth, and Kierney and Lisa will watch bunnies from the upstairs window. Lisa and Kierney will ride in the car to go see Sweep and Toss and say, 'Hi!'" I say, using as many words as she knows. When a seizure's not riding her brain like a spring-horse, her ears cock to my voice, her tail thumps, and I almost fear I'm lying to her, since we can't do these things right away. But she knows. She likes thinking about it too. And it seems urgent, certainly reassuring, to maintain some connection, mind-to-mind.

Joe has an expression he uses when, after struggling with a difficult decision, he finally states what he's decided and follows the announcement with the proclamation, "There. I have said it."

Once it's been said, it will be done, for he's true to his word. Likewise I tell Kierney, "I'll call George and we'll go with Sweep and Toss to the sheepdog clinic this summer. I have said it." This I promise her, because part of me still believes that to herd sheep is a border collie's only true fulfillment. My mind's eye shows me Kierney on sheep, running as fast as she does on the campus lawn, a little black jet plane circling animated cumulus clouds on a sky of green.

The day is long. I sit with her, trying to get food and water into her clenched mouth, bathing her wounds, writing down every change, dashing to the phone when she manages to walk a few steps, leaving her side briefly now and then to get my daughter a meal and a few toys to play with, rewinding that tape. I can't make Kierney stay on the towel. Finally, decisively, preferring a soiled kitchen floor to sores on my dog, I move her off the concrete to the linoleum. It's time to make dinner.

Kierney is yelping with every breath, and the cycle of rocking, struggling to rise, and drooling repeats, each reprieve briefer than the one before. The sea serpent has dwelled in her five full days now and gains confidence. Hope and patience, my only weapons, grow dull. I am feeble. Choked with my own fear, I press my forehead against hers and swear, "After you get better, this'll happen again, weeks, maybe months later. But I swear, I won't make you live through it." There. I have said it. I can't stand my own sobbing. I call Michelotti.

"Can you hear her? She's cryin' and cryin'!"

Gently, he says, "Yelping is a form of seizuring. It doesn't mean anything. Remember that epileptics have no consciousness during seizures."

"But after five days it should be lettin' up, not expanding the repertoire."

He asks about other changes, then tells me that he's closing up for the day, that he'll be at his son's Little League game. "If there's an emergency you feel you can't handle, you can have me paged. Otherwise, give me a call in the morning and tell me how the night went."

I accept the sympathy in his voice, but I know Kierney too well: she understands her body, and she's afraid. She's afraid she's dying. She's pleading with me. She's yelping and yelping, stopping only to turn her head in strange rhythms, followed by that weak facsimile of an attempt to stand, a hook in her throat, and then a gush of drool. The series repeats—yelping, head turning, trying to stand, drooling. I cook dinner, pausing frequently to make myself watch her. "Kierney will ride in the car to the woods and spend all day," I tell her. "We'll celebrate. We'll go see sheep. And we'll go to the ocean, one more time. And then . . . and then when this starts again . . . Lisa will just stop it right away, okay?"

When Joe comes home, I somehow eat, even though Kierney's cries batter my heart like a newborn's wail, *help me live, help me now!* and with everything I am I want to run to her and *do* something. Joe and I stand over her.

"It's yours to decide," he says. "You'll be better at this than I am." He takes Delaney upstairs to play, and again I settle on the kitchen floor beside my dog.

There she is on the floor, my Kierney, my wild and wonderful and most troublesome friend. Panting, mouth a chute of drool, she teeters and whimpers, makes a haphazard clatter to stand, falls according to program, twists her head, pants and spills more drool. I marvel that so much fluid is in her when she hasn't been able to drink for hours. I pour water in her mouth. I think I see her swallow, but can't be sure.

Suddenly, looking at her, I see something different, or rather, there's something I don't see. For the first time, there it *isn't*. Nothing has changed over the last few hours, but something has stolen away, and I've only just now notice it missing. As if plunged into ice water, my muscles and bones shoot with cold. I rattle all over. Sweat pours under my arms like the fluid from her mouth.

Kierney's not in there.

I've swum out pass the breakers again. The sifting sand beneath my toes has fallen away and in one heave the sea has carried me a mile or more. I hang in the water, nose up, toes down, struggling for ground. I grab Kierney's face and hold her still. She's placid, unaffected by my sudden passion, by my touch. Her eyes don't fix on me. With my bare forehead pressed to the soft fur of her brow, my mind less than an inch away from hers, I say to her our most solemn word, a word to which she always responds swiftly and precisely, a word she *knows* is earnest: "Kierney, *come*."

But Kierney isn't talking. The only word capable of cutting through her brain's electric brambles, the command should've at least roused her, caused some visible anxiety, made her eyes turn my way, her tail thump, should've at least keyed up the seizure a notch, but there's *no* response, goddamn it, nothing!

Now I panic in the water, reach with the full length of my body and something brushes my toes, not sand, but scales, the passing back of a great, long beast. "Kierney, *come*!" I say again, pressing my face against her rocking head. I'm sobbing now, which used to send her into an attempt to comfort me so frantic that she scratched and bruised me. "Please, please, please, Kierney, Kierney, *come*! *Right here*! *Come right here*! Please come to Lisa," but if she hears me, she can't even respond in the subtlest way. I'm searching for any sign, I need some tiny, concrete indication that she's in there and that she wants to keep fighting—her zig-zagging eyes must briefly meet mine, her flattened ears tilt in the direction of my voice, a seizure lift her toward me when I call her. With all my heart I want a sign. When I see it, I'll know I can save her, just as I've done many times before.

But I don't see it.

All I see is a body rollicking into a sixth day of seizures, soiling my floor, mocking my hope, a savage reminder that Kierney has left me. Somehow my flashy sprinter has allowed this decrepit freak on the floor to eat her alive. It's just what she dreaded all along! She knew she would die young, yet how ferociously she fought to live! *For the thing which I greatly feared is come upon me, and that which I was afraid of is come unto me. I was not in safety, neither had I rest, neither was I quiet; yet trouble came.* Epilepsy has come, a stationary hurricane, and destroyed my antelope, my fox, my almost-chimpanzee. Kierney is gone and has left behind this revolting heap of muscles, tendons and misfiring neurons for me to clean up—

No, no, no, no! What if it's just as Michelotti said, that she's unconscious? She'll come around. I stretch out on the surface of the water, a good swimmer, smoothly tugging myself against the current. The whistle's blown and the lifeguard leaps from his stand. Michelotti said to tell him how the night went. A night! An impossible night! So many hours! Unthinkable hours! She's crying and crying and, seizure or not, it's a plea. If only she weren't making that sound! I rest my cheek on her side and beg her forgiveness for letting it go on so long, days and days and there may be days more, if not tomorrow, then next month, and there will be more each time. "No more, no more," I cry. I'm stunned to have come to this moment when the great serpent's side has rolled up between me and the shore, huge and hard, a coil of ice alive and undulating and so broad, so long as it circles that the scraping pain of its passing may never end. Leviathan's head rises up to paralyze me with the sight of its face, a face like so many familiar things, a reptilian hyena, a fanged horse; it opens its mouth and circles back. Immediate pain swallows the possibility of future joy.

I bury my face in Kierney's beauty, her intelligence, her solace in me, her rapture for running full-tilt, all our days together, our accomplishments, trophies won which only we could see. With these pieces I think to fashion a raft, lash it with the cord of my terror, grip it like a float and kick toward shore with all my might, but I don't. I can hear the methodical plunk, plunk of the lifeguard's strokes and the hiss of Leviathan's speeding chin.

Kierney and I just aren't strong enough. I stop swimming and wait in the flotsam of four years. The lifeguard and sea serpent converge.

I have Michelotti paged and weep on Kierney's freakish side until he phones. By the time he calls, I've been alone with my decision maybe thirty, fifty minutes, quaking as if I've dialed 911 and been put on hold.

He doesn't tell me, "Wait it out," or "Bring her in and we'll see if this is really brain damage," or "Let's put her under general anesthesia for the night and see what we have in the morning." He's calmly defeated, for the first and only time. What did I say? What changed?

"Meet me at eight at my office." We understand each other.

At ten-of, Joe carries Kierney's seizuring body out to the car. His back is broad, his arms thick and sturdy, and on either side of him I see her head and her legs, stiff and crooked and uselessly groping. She doesn't try to balance. She doesn't look down. Normally she'd be uncomfortable if big, strong, stern Joe, her Alpha, captured her, lifted her and held her too close, unnaturally, unnecessarily, nonsensically, but she doesn't crane her head and avert her face. *Status epilepticus* is a kind of animated *rigor mortis*. I watch from the shadows of house as he bends over in the bright evening sun and leans into the blue hatchback, touching his first dog for the last time. He returns to the house and to our daughter.

Sinking into my nightmare, I get in the car, helpless, slow-moving, resigned to violence, amazed. Her body fuddles behind me. Eight-o'clock on a June evening is so very bright and green, with clear air and long, distinct shadows. There are few streets and only two miles between us and Michelotti's syringe, but everywhere there are sun-splashed sidewalks, and on the sidewalks are healthy people walking their healthy dogs. I'm just lucid enough to be surprised that, rather than sear me bitter, the sight makes me happy. As if transported, I'm awash with peace, afloat on the swell of eternity, and I thank God for dogs. All the way to Michelotti's, I'm thanking God that I have dared love her. Her death is the simplest thing about her.

"She'll just lie in your arms and go limp," Michelotti explains. Within seconds, she does exactly that.

Wait!

Give me time to think! This is too final! I changed my mind!

Instead, I hear my voice dryly say, "Tomorrow when I wake up I'm going to scream."

I'm coming down, I'm losing myself, I'm ceasing, I've been tricked. I meant to save her, I meant to take her myself, this isn't me, this isn't Kierney, this isn't happening, this is no time, no place, the words Michelotti speaks are distant and alien. Nothing in me, nothing I know could possibly have led to this decision, this personal atrocity that can never be remedied. I could not possibly, of my own free will, have hired our rescuer to kill her. She's changed me so much that I won't be myself without her. I'm the person who promised to save her.

My knees buckle. I nearly fall. Clumsily, Michelotti tries to catch me. Our movements, our speech, our glances, all abortive, misshapen, inane.

"Can you drive? I'll drive you home," he says. "I can bring Joe back here to get your car."

No, I say.

He struggles to talk to me, even though he's familiar with this place and time and all these words. He's a practiced mercy-killer. I can hear the brave and sad and inadequate routine in his voice. Plunk, plunk. I yearn, I ache, I reach—blind, deaf, and numb—for that glimpse of sunny summer evening sidewalks where there's all time and all life, where, if not me and not Kierney, then some woman and some dog forever walk side-by-side.

Chapter Nine

Pippi's Bliss

I'd known for two years that epilepsy would try to kill Kierney quite young, and that, when she began to succumb, I'd rush in and kill her first myself. I'd understood that when I woke up the next day I'd scream like someone waking to severed legs. I'd fantasized about it countless times, I guess to prepare myself. But, when I actually did wake on that long-feared morning, I didn't scream. I simply slipped back into the nightmare I'd left when I fell asleep. The torture was this: I couldn't recall whatever possessed me to agree to that needle. The house was full of the terror that plagued Kierney all her short life—not being present at her own absence.

The absence was complete—there would be no ghost. She didn't visit me in my sleep the way my murdered friend Kim did while I was writing *Body Sharers*. Death had come to my house in a way that it did not come when my mother-in-law died. The grief roared in my brain until I was sick with it, diseased. As much as Joe's mother's death seemed to prove the case for an afterlife, Kierney's death proved the opposite. Maybe animals didn't have souls after all. Or maybe my sweet pious mother-in-law and her whole family had grieved themselves into a delusion. Or maybe that's what I was doing.

Nothingness stole upon me with a wide snout, like a hyena, and a hell of a breath. Kierney is not in the bedroom, she is not on the stairs, she is not asking to go out, she is not dropping her ball at my feet, she is not upset because I'm crying, Kierney *is not*. Her absence ran before me into every room, and when I rested, it sat heavily on my chest, crushing, stinking, suffocating.

One day, I, too, will not be. "Poor Kierney!" I wept, because she knew and she was afraid. Now I was afraid too.

Losing my dog, I was no longer myself. I would never be again. I was a forest cleared and subdivided. I was a city block washed empty by flood never to be refilled. I was Pompeii, buried running for breath. I was the trusting dodo, whose very name means "foolish," for I believed that if it was alive, it wouldn't hurt me. Kierney died on the very anniversary of our move into this house where we shared a year of genuine happiness; all around me snapped ironies and oxymorons, so that my every step was into the midst of their nasty mouths. The hilarities snarled at my ankles exuding their inescapable stink, the windows of universal malevolence.

Before eight in the morning, before twelve hours of not-Kierney had passed, I realized I'd forgotten to keep her collar. Michelotti's office didn't open until nine-thirty, so I'd have to wait before finding out whether or not he thought to take it off before he drove my dog's corpse all the way to the University of Pennsylvania Veterinary Clinic in Philadelphia. It baffled me, but apparently it was routine for him to drive his dead patients to the university's incinerator in the middle of the night. I was unable to question, unable to protest, unable to assert an alternative, and so her body had disappeared from me, which made her death all the more unbearable. I crashed around the kitchen trying to make coffee and breakfast, until the time when I could dial that familiar number and retrieve her collar. By nine-thirty I had convinced myself I had enough courage to call without bursting into tears. But I was wrong.

"It's right here," Shelley said. "Shh. It's okay."

And then I was right there at the vet's too, floating, in a shadowy reception room, cold, dim, as though it were cloudy outside, or there were a power outage. "I don't usually leave the house this early," I said, which was about all I could think of to say. How strange it was that I, a morning writer, was outdoors before noon. There were all these cars humming around and people keeping appointments as if Kierney hadn't died, alert and showered and dressed and accustomed to this hour, this slant of light, this play of pollen and dew, an alien and colorless world. I wouldn't have been surprised to see Rod Serling step across my field of vision in his dark suit and his grim emphasis, "Welcome to Happy Valley, a growing community of people and pets."

Shelley handed me Kierney's red collar. I saw it for what it was: a cheap, dirty strip of nylon that had nothing to do with me. Annoyed, I stuffed it in my pocket. This place was hateful. What the hell had I come for? To return to the scene of my crime?

Shelley was kind, respectfully distant, and busy. She and the other people were nothing but moths in a crypt to me, and I cared nothing about what they thought of me as I strayed like a crazy bag lady past the Pet Tabs vitamin treats in the great big glass jar, past the tin can begging donations for the no-kill pet adoption service, and lingered, wandering to the bulletin board. Tacked to the cork was a business card for a border collie breeder, Janet Lewis.

I whirled and almost fell against the counter. "Shelley, can I have a pen and paper? There's a border collie breeder in Huntingdon."

A voice behind me: "Janet has pups right now."

I spun around.

Michelotti didn't even look tired. "I talked to her last night."

I must've gaped, eyes brimming.

"I told her all about you," he said, taking the pen and paper himself and writing the information down for me. "I told her if anyone deserved one of her first-rate pups, it's you."

Kierney had been dead barely thirteen hours. It felt too soon to think about puppies. Collar and slip of paper in my pocket, I went home, and spoke hardly a word to Joe or Delaney. I was falling, falling, grabbing at dishes in the dishwasher, and sliding them onto cupboard shelves as if doing so would hold me up. Stirring a pot of white sauce for macaroni and cheese would keep me from stumbling over the empty space in front of my shins. Joe kept watching me.

I said, "I'm fine."

"You sure?"

He kept asking and I kept nodding until he left for work. I knew what I had to do.

When he left, I set Delaney up with a stack of jigsaw puzzles and crept away to the couch, lay myself down, and smothered my retching tears.

I heard the rustle of her diaper.

Sniffling, blinking, I lifted my head and smiled. "You finished your puzzles?"

"I have a present for you, Mommy."

Delaney was always bringing me "presents," sometimes a wadded flannel blanket, crinkled paper, or just her cupped hands. Sometimes the gift held one of her little toys, or nothing at all and we pretended it was one of those ceramic carousel horses that played music—she thought those precious but was too young to have one. The game required me to make the motions of unwrapping the present and to gush, "Oh! It's just what I wanted!" She'd beam and run off to bring me another.

This time my gift came in her rolled-up purple cotton hat.

Composing myself, I said, "Oh, thank you," and unrolled the empty hat. "I love it! What is it?"

She looked me in the eyes. "It's a baby Kierney."

Kierney had not-been for fourteen hours when I called Janet Lewis. Michelotti had indeed spoken to her about me, about the way I treated my border collie, and my loss. She gave me what I needed badly— recognition that I had been good to my border collie and the hope that I'd soon have another one.

"I have eight absolutely perfect puppies," she said. "It's an amazing litter. Any one of them would be right for you. Now, you need to know, I have eight deposits on them, but a couple of people're waffling. Somebody's sure to back out."

Lying on the couch, Delaney in the crook of my arm, and the light falling green through summer leaves, I read to her a book I knew by heart, "Hair, hair, it's everywhere. Some have a little, some have a lot." I found it absolutely terrifying that I could hold my little girl and read to her without thinking, my finger obediently tracing under each word because I was an over-educated, middle-class mother who'd been told that doing so prepares a child to read. How could my mouth pronounce words that my mind ignored? Was it some sort of seizure? All I could think about was the mind-boggling absence of my dog. It struck me like a tire iron, over and over, a repetitive blow to my head and gut. I stopped just short of recalling the previous day, the day I murdered my own dog for no conceivable reason.

Uncharacteristic of me, I called none of my friends. I only needed to know I'd soon have a puppy. That taken care of, now I only needed to cry.

Over the next few days, I sought time alone to sob, out of anyone's earshot. Like a secret tippler visiting hidden bottles of gin, I moaned into the chug of the washing machine, I keened on the floor of the shower stall, and I smothered Kierney's name into my pillow, upon which I lay in my clothes in the daytime, biting it hard as my body shook back and forth. It was like vomiting. It was like dysentery, or malaria—a burning, a purging. It was an illness I could walk away from, but to which I was obliged to return as if by some Faustian deal. Joe had it too, in his way. It bewildered him—his mother's death hadn't hit him like this.

"It's because Kierney lived in our house with us," I said.

He nodded.

"We're just so used to her being here."

In every ache and chill and burst of tears, there came a strange, sensual elation. I studied this elation suspiciously, and gradually realized that the pain and weakness were good. Sorrow was rightful testimony to the fact that, not only had I loved her, but I went on loving. I once rejoiced in her finesse, I once coddled her, I once condemned her, I once nursed her back to health, and now, all in proportion, I grieved her. Her life might not have been worth the torment, but my love for her—no, love itself—was worth more anguish still.

My mother told me about her friend, a woman with multiple sclerosis. Intelligent, well-educated and lucid, she was wheelchair-bound and deteriorating steadily. With no living relatives, she had no choice but to stay in a nursing home. She noticed that the orderlies were cruel to the patients who couldn't speak, and although she still could, she feared the day when she could not. She was cultivating their affection, trying to prepare for the day when she would be at their mercy. She had difficulty writing, and swallowing also.

"They're kinder after someone visits," she told my mother, and admitted that she wanted to kill herself. However, many years before, her only child, a son, had been killed in a motorcycle accident. "I'm Catholic, and I know my son's in Heaven. If I kill myself, I may never see him."

And so she hung on like that, hour after hour, year upon year, enduring a darkening nightmare, all for the thin sake of faith and the love of her son.

I'd met many older people who told me stories about the dogs in their lives. After listening to how much they loved dogs and how good they were with them, I'd declare, "You should get another dog!" And they'd just smile. I'd wonder what was wrong with them. Now I understood. As I leaned my head against the air conditioner and sent my moans whirring into its blades, I thought, "I can only love and then grieve like this maybe four or five more times in my life." I had glimpsed, for the first time, the end of my strength.

When I told her what I'd gone through, my friend Marguerite said, "I don't know how anybody ever dares love an animal when they just die."

Astounded, I said, "Because before that, they live!"

Besides, the same is true of people. They die. They leave. How do any of us dare love at all?

"I do not altogether blame sensitive people," Konrad Lorenz wrote, "who shrink from acquiring a dog in view of the final inevitable parting. . . . Well, actually, I suppose I do. . . . fundamentally I consider the man a shirker who renounces the few permissible and ethically irreproachable pleasures of life for fear of having to pay the bill with which, sooner or later, fate will present him. He who is miserly with the coin of suffering had better retire to some spinsterly attic and there gradually desiccate like a sterile bulb which bears no blossoms."

In my sorrow, I didn't think of love as a matter of duty nor of rightness, nor of courage; in fact, almost the opposite. The willingness to risk loving another dog was just a frank assessment of who I was: I was someone who accommodated a high-strung border collie, and the prospect of becoming someone else seemed too violent for me to survive it. In the same way, I knew if I ever lost Joe I'd eventually marry again, because I am a wife. Eventually, I'd become someone who was just too tired to be someone's wife or some dog's master, but for the time being, I wasn't myself without a neurotic, hyperactive dog poking me with a tennis ball.

I was also an animal rights activist, albeit a fading one. As such, I ought to have considered an SPCA mutt or Border Collie Rescue, but I just couldn't help myself. I was convinced I needed a purebred border collie puppy, a healthy one, from a trustworthy breeder. Dr. Michelotti himself had said so. He'd even prescribed one of Janet Lewis' pups and, as a doctor who understands he must *do* something, he took the first step himself to arrange my treatment.

In all honesty, I believed Kierney could be replaced, with improvements. Lorenz admitted, "Dogs are indeed individuals, personalities in the truest sense of the words, and I should be the last to deny this fact, but they are much more like each other than are human beings. . . . if on the death of one's dog, one immediately adopts a puppy of the same breed, it will generally be found that he refills those spaces of one's heart and life which the departure of an old friend has left desolate." At the time of Kierney's death, border collies were still bred primarily for their brains, and one was certainly very much like the other.

Janet's pups wouldn't be ready for six weeks, which, I told myself, would give me time to purge my grief. Believing that if I cried hard, I could love hard again, I eased into a dream of little black and white puppies, the smell of them, my palm against their tight, hot tummies. "A man cannot keep faith with an individual dog for obvious biological reasons [their shorter life span], but he can remain true to the breed," wrote Lorenz.

Just as the thought of Kierney outrunning a Frisbee once helped me endure her seizures, the hope that I'd soon have a baby Kierney helped me bear my grief.

Ninth in line for Janet's eight puppies, we three drove out to her house. On a large, screened-in porch in a portable dog pen, the pups were everything that ever broke a heart—big eyes, little noses, downy round curves, buoyant good health, the charming bumble of little babies with big ideas. With wide, regular white markings, they were each classic border collie beauties. Joe and Janet, who knew each other from Juniata University, talked about Juniata's English Department and how their careers were going while I sat in the pen with Delaney. Her long eyelashes brushed her round pink cheeks as she lost herself among the puppies, kissed them, pushed them away, laughed, crawled after them, and rivaled them for charm. Beholding a beautiful two-year-old playing with equally beautiful five-week-old puppies intoxicates, as Eastman Kodak knows, but it isn't the kind of moment that survives well in snapshot or on videotape, for a certain poignancy is lost when the action's not live. Here, today, on the floor in this porch, these puppies and this child share features and behaviors, the same domed foreheads, the same clumsiness and the same tooth-testing curiosity, all the more precious because the puppies, and not the child, will outgrow them in a matter of weeks. It's a fresh bouquet and, as the petals fall, they make a breathtaking cascade.

Showing Delaney how to handle the pups, I stayed close by, needlessly governing her every move so as not to worry Janet, who hovered as though the pups were her own offspring and she had never in her life met a gentle child. Proudly, Janet pointed out all the ways in which this was an extraordinary litter: without runt, without surliness or timidity. As she already had several times in various phone conversations, she detailed the parents' virtues and many obedience titles, and I enjoyed hearing about them again.

In fact, at this point, there was nothing about border collies to which I wouldn't listen over and over again, and these visits to Janet's were my only relief from sorrow. Not only did I get to hold these puppies, I got to be among her pack of five adult border collies. Any lover of border collies will tell you, and I suppose it may be the same for lovers of any breed, that when you're in the midst of a mob of them, it's like having free run of a theme park, wonders and joyrides every which way you look—a male's parading for a female, one sulks under a chair, two team up to search for a lost toy, one flashes fang at another. As if at a family reunion cleansed of ill will, I find few things more entertaining than watching border collies interact with each other. I love noting their similarities, their differences, the drama of creating and maintaining a hierarchy. Plus, to me, their distinctive white blaze and ruff is the familiar mark of a great and beloved beauty—when I see a crowd of them, I'm delirious.

Presiding in a folding chair, Janet spoke, bestowing her dog training and breeding knowledge upon us novices, sometimes providing more corrections or qualifications to whatever we said than was welcome or necessary, but, accustomed to academics, we knew how to keep from getting steamed. No doubt we were the same way on certain topics. Besides, we wanted one of her puppies.

Weeks passed and we visited Janet's pups several times. Between visits she and I shared long telephone chats about the puppies' progress and about the people who had come and made their choices. Luckily, the litter was so uniformly well-tempered, whichever pup was left over for us would be just right. As Janet predicted, a couple of people who'd left deposits on puppies were waffling in their decision. "We'll know in a few days whether you have two to choose between or just one."

Then Janet called, almost in tears. Eight takers had taken eight puppies. "It was such a perfect litter," she said. "It was too good to be true."

"It's okay," I said. Really, I felt nothing. Except maybe steeliness. I *would* find myself a dog.

"A friend of mine moved and couldn't keep her sheltie. She gave her to me," Janet was saying. "She's a beautiful merle and she's got her U.D. title. Her name's Fawn, you know, for Fawn Hall? You'd love her. And she's a good size for your daughter, not so rambunctious as a border collie. She's a well-mannered house dog. She's four and she's in excellent health with a champion pedigree. She's sweet—oh, she's an unusual color, a red merle, sort of a pale, brindled sable. I love her and I love having her here, but I feel just awful about this. And you've been waiting for weeks, it's about time you had your dog. You can have Fawn. She's a valuable animal. She's been fixed, though, so you can't breed her, but you don't want to do that anyway, do you? Why don't you come meet her?"

Her offer almost touched and tempted me, but my teeth were clenched and I was fighting the urge to hang up and start dialing other breeders. "Let me think about it, okay?"

Days went by. Joe, who'd been grim since Kierney's death and grimmer since we lost Janet's pup, wanted the quick fix of Fawn. Delaney, from what she could understand, wanted the Princess Fawn. I pictured Fawn prancing on her tiny sheltie toes across my kitchen floor, her luscious blonde coat flowing. Fawn "dancing" with Delaney the way Kierney had, only laughing and gentle. Fawn begging at the table and then politely ducking away when scolded. Fawn and I doing obedience work in the yard and me realizing there's no work to be done, except on me.

But Fawn was a four-year-old sheltie and a Utility Dog and did not belong in my house.

I wrote Janet a heart-wrenching "thank you" note, explaining, probably unnecessarily, why I was going to continue searching for a border collie puppy.

I called several breeders, a few recommended by Janet, who'd kindly called me when she got my note. I ran into a problem Michelotti must've anticipated when he called Janet and made my case for me. Good breeders didn't want to sell a border collie to a homemaker.

It wasn't long ago that few people even knew what a border collie was. In fact, the definition of a true border collie had been under hot debate. Recently, despite protests, the border collie was welcomed into the American Kennel Club. Roughly speaking, the A.K.C. regulates a breed by defining its physical attributes—color, coat, ear set, height, weight. A border collie, the herding fans growled, is not a dog that *looks* a certain way, but a dog that *acts* a certain way. Their concern was that as physical appearance took priority over the behavioral characteristics, the herding instinct would be diluted and the availability of reliable stock dogs diminished. It stood to reason that the more kinds of people there were who wanted border collies, the more kinds of border collies would be bred. Some people were understandably rankled to think that with the A.K.C. in charge, border collie bloodlines would turn out "Barbie collies," mincing black-and-white fluffheads with just enough gumption to dither at the end of a show lead, their only instinct an uncanny ability to turn their good side to a judge.

Fans of the border collie's herding ability pointed to the horror stories of other breeds, such as the German Shepherd. When form took priority over function, the great war dog's hind legs became so angulated that some could hardly walk. The bull dog, whose blunt face is no longer employed in the sport of bull baiting, can hardly breathe. However, the hope was that the genetic crap shoot would roll up both looks and wits, and that most "Barbie collies" would be born with properly computing brains that included the fabulous synaptic sheep-herding chip.

However, at the time I was puppy shopping, one of the border collie's most significant characteristics was that it was a popular dog. "I'm glad *Babe* didn't win Best Picture," a border collie breeder told me. "Things are bad enough. Publicity generates greed and there will be people who buy up border collies and breed anything to anything just to churn out cheap dogs." While it had always been true that some people turned out border collie puppies by the dozens in barns and basements with very little foresight at all, now that border collie mania had set in, more would be bred irresponsibly, disregarding brains, beauty, health, availability of good homes, or anything else, and more would end up burning in the Humane Society holocaust.

Many breeders felt that people like me were at fault. Almost every reputable breeder I called asked me snottily, "Are you looking for a *pet*?" Pet was a bad word among many border collie people, and how I responded to this question determined whether or not the breeder was going to hang up on me. Responsible breeders usually only sell to people who have owned border collies before: to sheep farmers, to those heavily involved in dog sports, and to each other. Sometimes it seemed as if border collie people were members of some canine Masonic order, complete with impenetrable ironies and contradictions. Venturing into border collie circles of all sorts, I found plenty of people with generous hearts and clear minds, but I also ran up against people adamant that a border collie should not go to a pet home because the vigorous, intelligent animal would just end up clapped in the pound or tied to a dog house going insane.

Further inspection revealed that they themselves often had two dozen kennels and two dozen caged dogs, more than they could properly care for, many of their own dogs bored out of their minds. Border collie zealots often assumed that, because border collies have been bred to herd, they were happiest toiling among sheep all day and sleeping chained up alone in the snow all night, but were criminally abused following their owners around an apartment, taking a run in the park, chasing a Frisbee, and sleeping at the end of a warm bed. Even some of those who bred for obedience shows believed that life on a sheep farm was a border collie's heavenly ideal—and yet to many actual sheep farmers border collies were nothing more than a cross between livestock and farm equipment, and the only consideration they got was work, fuel, and cost-effective repairs.

Most sheep farmers didn't care what I did with the dog, and leapt at the chance to sell me one. "I got a box of 'em out in the barn right now. Come 'n' get 'em."

"Have they had their shots? Has anybody spent any time with them?"

"Well, they're in a box in the barn. I check on 'em 'most every day."

Thanks, but no thanks.

The breeders whose dogs I wanted were inclined to refuse me a dog. I had to prove that I was a rarity, a homemaker who understood that you couldn't buy a good dog the way you do a good food processor, that I was not an All-American mom who usually bought her purebred, designer dogs in malls or from specialty dealers, never questioned the limited guarantee, and returned them whenever she liked, if not to the seller then to the pound, a free disposal service. Breeders feared that when Stanley Coren's *The Intelligence of Dogs* came out rating border collies number one, that shoppers would think it a kind of *Consumer Reports* rating.

I had to be concise, which isn't always easy for a novelist. In a few swift lines, I had to say I had a border collie once, and I understood that owning one meant making a commitment that in some ways exceeded that to my own child. Children can watch TV. They go off to school. Eventually, they make friends and enjoy activities that don't involve you. But for the entirety of her life, almost every waking hour, Kierney had nagged me to do something with her, anything—play Frisbee, chase squirrels, heel, track, run obstacle courses, learn to lead the blind—craving not so much the action as the interaction. I promised I would not leave my border collie alone in a house for eight or nine hours a day the way are many American dogs, because a border collie will find something to do: pluck the fur from your cat, gut your sofa, shred your carpet with her bare nails, eat the leg off your antique roll-top desk, or break loose and direct traffic or try to herd the neighborhood kids. Left alone in a dog crate or a pen, she will, sometimes noisily, sometimes quietly, go insane. The border collie gusto is the unflagging, undeniable power of genetics. I had to say I understood that by refusing me a border collie, the breeders weren't protecting sofas, carpets, neighborhood kids, traffic patterns, or trying to keep me out of the Border Collie Country Club. They were trying to keep the dogs they loved from getting shot, euthanized, smashed on the road, or chained to a dog house year-round, day round, with nothing for their considerable brains and bodies to do but snap at flies, worry a rump full of fleas, and pace a miniature baseball diamond of packed dirt. Every time I met a rude border collie zealot, I figured I was meeting someone with a broken heart.

It was the same confrontation I'd had four years before with George. He had just wanted to make sure, before he sold me a pup, that when I came back overwhelmed by my dog, he could say he told me so. I got the breeders telling me so, and I got them to hear my plea. "I want a dog with a type A personality. I want an upwardly mobile dog." I wanted a border collie, because in order to command a herd of sheep, they must be highly interactive, opportunistic, and eager to assume the upper hand. If, feeling cozy one evening, you let her cuddle on the couch, you could wake in the dark to her striding across your bed, I knew. If you let that intelligent face soften you into putting your plate on the floor for her to lick, you might walk into your dining room to find her standing right on your table, polishing off your casserole. Fluent in body language, she'll note any sign of fatigue, boredom, or illness, and she'll win the next round of tug-of-war (she always could), growl the next time you dare pick her rawhide chew off the couch, or even claim the king-sized bed as her own exclusive territory. To maintain alpha position myself, I had to be ever vigilant. Most of us, in a normal home, especially one with children in it, would rather take human dominance for granted, but not me. Thanks to four years with Kierney, mine was not a normal home.

After making this speech, convincingly, several times, and after getting my name on lists for the puppies of bitches who hadn't even been bred yet, I started to rethink the matter. Maybe I wanted a long vacation from border collies—but how I loved them! Maybe I wanted a border collie crossbred. Mutts seem to inherit the best of both parents. So, briefly, using the classified ads, I checked out blissfully clever and agreeable border collie/golden retriever crosses and border collie/husky crosses. They turned out to be border collies stripped of their vigor and lunacy, which wasn't quite what I wanted. I will say, perhaps in more and more towns all over the country there are genetic seamstresses trying to tailor the border collie brain to fit family life. In fact, some "Barbie collie" breeders' goal may be to produce a dog who looks like a border collie, carries the designer A.K.C. label and the mystique of a border collie, but doesn't show the behaviors undesirable in suburban households.

I wish them well. It's unlikely, but they may discover the genetic pattern for the elusive Lassie personality, which sure isn't a border collie. If they ever do discover the Lassie recipe, then anybody could own an All-American companion dog—as long as he has the money. No one would ever again need to mop piddle off the floor, throw out a favorite pair of shoes 'cause they're all chewed up, spend fifteen minutes a day practicing ninety-degree turns, or rush a puppy to the vet when it's swallowed a pound of chocolate, a pound of gravel, and a razor blade. Lassie doesn't run away, so no one will ever have to spend thousands of dollars on a fence only to have the dog learn to climb it. No one will have to wake up and go outside in the middle of a cold and rainy night or leave a great party early because the dog needs to pee—Lassie can really hold it. Lassie is born understanding that a flower bed is not a play area nor is it a toilet. Lassie respects your television viewing and won't keep standing in front of the tube with her Boodabone in the middle of *ER*. When you get a hankering to win a sheep dog trial or an obedience match, you and Lassie will team up and clean up as if you're in a dream. As soon as your children are of an appropriate age, Lassie will show herself mysteriously pregnant, fastidiously she will offer five gorgeously healthy purebred puppies for the pleasure and edification of you family, and then, when the charm has worn off, she'll make them disappear. And if you want to go away for a long weekend, Lassie will thoughtfully curl up and slip into a coma. No need to feel guilty—she'll rouse herself in time for a sufficiently energetic welcome home.

Janet had given me the name of a sheep farmer whose pups were among the most sought-after in the northeast, Walt Jagger. After grilling me, listening to my story and hearing me drop a few names, he agreed to sell me a pup, not one of his own, for which there were long waiting lists, but one his daughter Cheryl, an accomplished shepherdess, had bred. Out of the bloodlines of Walt's own dogs, hers were winning trials. Cheryl's pregnant bitch hadn't whelped yet. I called her, had a good chat, and was told I was first on her list. I mailed her a deposit right away and relaxed into an easy few months' wait.

One afternoon, I got a phone call from a shepherd's wife. I'd called her husband a week or two before, but nothing had come of it. I'd learned that he only had two male pups available, and they were five and six months old (out of different litters). Not only that, after calling him I had heard his name spoken with contempt by other breeders, shepherds and obedience people alike, and so I had many reasons not to take one of his half-grown pups.

"I'd like you to reconsider," the shepherd's wife said. "Please just come meet the one. He's five months old and a black-and-white smooth-coat. He's very handsome and good with children."

Never having encountered a hard sell, I got immediately suspicious. "I'm afraid I'm looking for a younger dog, a female, with a rough coat."

"He'd make a good pet," she said. "My little boy and I love him, but he's soft on sheep. My husband says he has to go. Look, his testicles didn't descend, and two of his toes got cut off in a mower."

I didn't want a soft dog, nor did I want one with birth defects and a gimpy foot. Besides, the husband had already told me about the missing toes, but *he* had said the bitch had accidentally chewed them off with her over-vigorous licking. "I'm sorry. I already have a deposit on one of Cheryl Jagger's pups," I said, inwardly thanking God. "Thanks anyway." And that was that.

Grief and hope chased tails in me so fast that they took on one distinct form, the immediacy of the moment, the tug of my own breath. I was dynamic, mutable, transient. One day I would cease to exist. Kierney's fear lived on in me.

I made an appointment with a priest on campus. On the given day and time, I found him in his office, a trim, handsome man in his early forties, packing books into a box. Sliding an armload off a shelf, he greeted me and said, "So what's this about?"

There wasn't any place to sit. Awkward in the doorway, I confessed my born-again atheism and my fear, expecting if not alarm at least a serious frown.

Lowering the heavy box to the floor, he smiled slyly. "It's no sin to stop believing in God." He clapped a fresh box on his desk and lowered another book into it. "What makes you think God doesn't exist?"

I started to tell my tale, but he interrupted.

"There is no evidence for the existence of a creator," he said, expecting me to gasp in shock that a priest would say such a thing. He seemed to relish the discussion as if we'd begun a game of chess together and I was about to blunder away my queen. Pausing, he hefted both boxes into his arms. "Come with me down the hall," he said, proving he could carry on a sparring match while walking, carrying two boxes of books, and flipping his wit over his shoulder like a lock of hair.

I followed him out of the room, not just down the hall but down the stairs and around a corner and down another hall and through a swinging door into yet another hall. Chasing after him, I barely had time to wonder how I got tricked into playing "Angels on a Pinhead" with a man who couldn't help gloating that he was sure to win.

My interest in the game flagged fast. Any other time I would've loved the intellectual exercise, but today it wasn't what I needed. "Look, you were nice to meet with me," I said as he unlocked his new office door. "But you're busy, and I . . . I gotta go." And I left.

Two weeks later I tried again with an older priest, plump and balding. We sat side-by-side in a pew in the empty campus chapel. I told him that Kierney had died and now I didn't believe in God.

"It's no sin not to believe in God," he said.

"The thing is, I love *everything*—" I made a vigorous swoop with my arms as if to take in the chapel and the campus and the valley and the mountains and even mighty things, such as my daughter and my new puppy still turning in her mother's belly. "And, now that I know what I seem to know because of my dog's death, I'm, I'm *terrified*. All the time." I pressed my lips together to stop the sting in my eyes.

He examined my face a moment, and then, he knew that I had seen the Leviathan of Job.

"There's this sonata," he said thoughtfully. He named it. I thought he hadn't been listening. Sinking against the pew back, he crinkled his eyes at me. "Perhaps you know it?" he asked as eagerly as if he'd named a woman he'd loved and lost, and he hoped for word of her.

I was sorry—I didn't know it.

"When I listen to it, I cry, and it's the most beautiful music I've ever heard." The rims of his eyes reddened.

By now I had gotten hold of myself and was thinking maybe this sweet guy was prematurely senile.

"I have the CD," he confessed, choked up.

"You poor fellow!"

He chuckled, then said, "Sometimes I can't bear to listen to it. Other times I can't stop myself." To my distress, he tipped his head back and droned about that sonata a long time, and I tried frantically to find the connection between faith and fear. "It's a glorious day." He cocked his eyes toward the open chapel door. The leaves of the elms cast green light and spangled shadows.

"Yes." On my walk to the chapel the sun had come and gone and come again as if swinging overhead on a pendulum. Everywhere I'd looked, whether at a robin or a rhododendron, I saw a life throwing itself headlong into its own beauty, risking everything.

"It's no sin," he said again, "to doubt." And he gave me a bemused smile, as if we were sharing a subtle but very silly joke. "Right?" he said, prodding me with a nod. Didn't I get it?

Frowning hard, looking into his eyes, straining to understand, I suddenly grinned. Look how my nihilism had floated me right into a pew! Honest doubt would save me. I could doubt the nihilism too. Nothing, not even my despair, had been amiss. Isn't it wonderful that I weep? Hasn't the music been beautiful? I didn't need to fight my doubt; doubt was auxiliary to faith—when you wear a lifejacket you'll float even if your boat sinks.

A few days later, as I was putting food on the counter to prepare a meal, the shepherd's wife called back. "We're only asking one hundred dollars. He's got excellent papers."

"This is the dog that's missing toes?"

"He was born that way. It's his only defect. It doesn't affect his gait at all."

"Uh-huh. Like I said, I already have a pup on the way." I was on a cordless phone, but I hovered by the cradle, poised to hang up.

"You could have two dogs!"

"I'm really sorry." I hung up shaking my head and turned—to see Joe standing behind me.

"You could bring that pup home today," he said, pained.

"I can wait." I opened the refrigerator. "We don't need a mutilated anorchid half-grown male bred by desperate people who can't keep their stories straight." In my mind, I held Cheryl's puppy. I put my palm on her bare, freckled belly and rolled her back and forth. But unlike me, Joe couldn't see Cheryl's pup, hadn't heard the good will in Cheryl's voice, hadn't seen the check slide into the envelope. He hadn't licked the stamp.

"We could just go see," Joe said. "Wouldn't it be fun to see dogs?"

"I don't know." I drew a knife and chopped a zucchini.

"Let's drive out there," Joe said, sliding sideways into a kitchen chair, wearing his summer vacation mood. He had time to kill. "Call her back. Get the directions. It can't hurt to look."

But I didn't want to call her back. "They're all the way out in Bedford!" I didn't want to see dogs. That is, I certainly didn't want to dignify these charlatans by driving an hour out to see their defective wares.

"It'll be fun," Joe said. Was he relaxed or tired? "You don't have to take the dog. But you don't *know* that you'll get one of Cheryl's pups."

I set down my knife and looked at him. I hadn't thought of that. "There's no reason to think I wouldn't get one." I threw the chopped zucchini in a colander and rinsed it.

"It could be Janet Lewis all over again."

"I'm *first* on the list this time."

"You and who else?" Joe said, turning in the chair to confront me directly. "And suppose a friend of theirs or some big sheep-trialing winner wants one. Will you still be first? How many pups is she having? What if she doesn't have any, like that one bitch who turned out not to be pregnant after all? The pups could all die. C'mon. It'll be fun to see dogs."

I gave the colander two quick shakes, then set it down and leaned over it. Oh, I was still so tired. Honest doubt or not, I was easy prey for despair.

Delaney rolled in on her scooter. "Are we going to see the puppies again?"

So, with a knot in my stomach, I called back and got directions.

"My husband's a carpenter and he built our house himself. You can't miss it." I'd obviously made the woman very happy.

"We're just coming to look," I said firmly. I steeled myself, and by the time we got there, I was certain I wasn't buying that dog. It was as if I'd driven all the way with Cheryl's sweet-smelling pup napping in my lap.

We drove an hour, west toward Bedford in the early summer evening, straight into the sinking sun. We pulled up the sweeping drive of a huge, glowing redwood home with a full wrap-around porch that stood out like a paper lantern against the dark green pasture land. Sheep blew like giant cotton balls across the hillside. By contrast, against the bonnie land and beside the opulent home stood a scrappy lean-to with ten shallow, open-air stalls in it. In about half the stalls, attached to four-foot chains, were border collies. Spiritless, they gave us trespassers a few muffled and hesitant barks, head and tails down low. A small wedge of packed earth before them showed me they had just enough chain to touch noses with each other, and no more. The high, narrow roof would provide little relief from blowing rain and no relief from cold. Flies were winding in the air and the stink of dog crap came and went with the intermittent breeze. At the end of the yard in a chain link pen stood a Great Pyrenees and her brood, each month-old babe as big as my old fox terrier Patches. No doubt, the shepherd had built her the pen because she'd pulled her lean-to down.

As we stepped out of the car, through a screen door a woman clattered out to greet us. "I don't know where he is," she said, and whistled. "Here, puppy, puppy, puppy!" she called, just the way Janet Lewis used to. Behind us, the chained dogs whimpered.

Her husband joined her and whistled.

"You built this yourself?" I asked, tipping my palm toward the house. "I'm impressed."

Thanking me quickly, he went on calling for the dog.

"Why isn't he chained here like the others?" I asked, picking Delaney up and settling her on my hip.

"Oh, you know," the shepherd said. "*You* were coming. He's usually there," he said, pointing to the last stall where a short chain lay in the dirt. Each stall had a hay bale in it, so at least the dog could get off the ground. I looked, but noticed no water bowls, which the dogs probably, in their narrow confinement, habitually spilled. Maybe there were buckets hung on the walls—I strained to look.

"Here he comes."

Out of a stand of trees tottered a gangly adolescent proudly carrying the severed leg of a deer. Three times as long as he was, it reminded me of Kierney carrying a branch that was bigger than most trees growing in new suburban developments, but still, I recoiled: he was so far from my memory of Kierney and from my vision of Cheryl's pup. Cursing, the couple bickered about where he might have found the uncouth object—"Did you leave that carcass—How long's it been there—I told the kids—" As if we hadn't heard, the shepherd turned to us and said, "We have poachers," as if poachers were something we city slickers would accept unquestioningly without attaching any onus to him. Then, with a shout and a swoop, he relieved the pup of the severed leg and threw it on a log pile, where, at least, it blended in.

I was ready to leave. I shot Joe a look. Still carrying Delaney, I strolled toward our car, Joe followed me, and the shepherd followed Joe, talking to him on and on, despite Joe's protestations that *I* was the dog person in the family.

"Hey, Pippi."

Who had spoken in such sweet, unconscious tones? I turned, and there, as if in tableau, I saw behind us the shepherd's wife stoop to greet the young dog. He stumbled and tottered toward her, rump swinging. He sat before her, tail tucked so far under him that it came up between his front legs and wagged there like a furred and unruly penis, and he most innocent, most innocent indeed. She loved him.

Suddenly I shared the urgency I'd heard in her voice when she'd phoned me. I let the men walk on.

"Pip," I said.

Pip ran to me and sat front as he did for her, looking up, nose to the sky, frightened and thrilled, slightly crazed by my attention. When I touched him, he ducked away to search for that great stick that had meat, hide and bone in it—maybe I'd throw it for him. He ducked away as Sweep did for her soccer ball, he ducked away as Kierney had for her racquetball, he ducked away as a border collie will.

But he staggered and wheeled. "There's something wrong with his hind end!" I cried.

Nobody said anything.

The shepherd was now focusing particularly on the awards he'd won with Pip's parents.

Joe was nodding that nod that tells me he'd stopped listening long before.

"And we're only askin' one hundred dollars," the shepherd said.

"May I meet his parents?" I asked.

"Just sold them both," he said. "Sold the bitch two days ago, as a matter of fact."

Delaney struggled, and I put her down. Although he'd easily found the severed deer leg, Pip abandoned it and raced back to greet Delaney, careful not to frighten her, swinging his tail low, keeping his head down. He sat and gently licked her hands. But then, abruptly, busy boy that he was, he ran to the wood pile again.

"Pip is real sweet," the woman interrupted, patting her thighs. Once again careening away from the wood pile, he tottered into her arms, and she pinned him in a hug. "Great with kids." She called her son off the porch to demonstrate, but the boy ran right to the Great Pyrenees and let them out of their pen. Overjoyed, Pip broke free and romped with the puppies, one-fifth his age, half his size. "Pip's a great pet," she said.

Wincing, I looked at Pip, obviously a gentle socialite, and at the woman watching him too with a sad furrow across her brow. Remembering scraps of things the two of them had said—the inability to place this dog with farmers, the sale of several of their most valuable dogs—I turned toward the row of shanty-kennels, then looked at the cedar house, gleaming, handsome and huge. I saw the row of remaining border collies, silent, heads low, eyes curious, nervously watching the shepherd, tails wagging between hind legs, gazing at him the way dogs did at the fearsome Bob Martin.

Without quite knowing what I was doing, I pulled out my checkbook, and the next thing I knew I was riding home in the car with that oversized goofball Pip on my lap.

"You saved him," Joe said as we left Bedford. "You did the right thing."

"What if he's got hip dysplasia?"

"We know how to take care of a handicapped dog."

"I don't want to take care of a handicapped dog. I don't want to go on emptying our savings account into Michelotti's pocket." Kierney's illness had set us back years. I was thinking maybe I could find another home for Pip. I could list him with Border Collie Rescue. Uncomfortably, I shifted his weight on my lap, missing my small, fragrant dream puppy. Maybe we could keep two dogs. "That puppy deposit with Cheryl Jagger is non-refundable, you know."

"Even still, the way I figure it," Joe said, "we've saved two hundred dollars."

We arrived home, a trace of sunlight lingering in the sky. Unfamiliar with a leash, Pip cringed and halted and apologetically licked my leg. I unhooked the leash and he stayed close to me all the way to the side door. When I opened it and invited him in, he sat down, wide-eyed, and wouldn't budge.

"Go on," I said. "It's okay. In." He started to enter, then stopped and prostrated himself, as if doorways ejected bolts of lightning.

"It's okay," I said. "C'mon in, good boy." It felt strange to say "boy." I took his collar, gave him a heave through the door, and slammed it behind him. He cowered on my feet. "It's okay, Pip."

He jumped up, mauled me with kisses, then dashed from room to room, up the stairs and down, galloping and skittering on the hardwood floors. Suddenly, airborne, he sailed to the couch and stuck. He collapsed, sprawled and panting, as if succumbing to an orgy of sensual bourgeois delights: a roof and walls, air conditioning, a couch, and a carpet. One of life's lottery winners, Pip tore around again, knowing, the way Kierney had her first day in our home, exactly what was his.

Chapter Ten

Going Canine

The morning after Pip came to live with us, I took him to be examined by Michelotti. I had made the shepherd and his wife understand, nothing was final until my vet had examined those hips. I could cancel the check.

"Well, he's packed end-to-end with worms," Michelotti said. "He's emaciated. But his hips are sound. The problem with his gait is that his muscle development has been stunted, probably from malnutrition and from being chained while growing. All that's reversible."

"What about the missing testicles?"

After palpating a few moments, Michelotti frowned. "They're in there somewhere, but I can't feel them. They'll have to come out. He's sterile, but retained testicles produce excess testosterone and they're prone to cancer."

"Excess testosterone?" I said. "We don't want *that*." I asked about the toes and related the varied and contradictory explanations the shepherd and his wife had given.

While Pip lifted his head, nervously licked his own nose and swallowed, Michelotti lifted and turned Pip's half-foot, pressed the scar with his fingertips, scratched it with his nails, squeezed the bones between his fingers, then gently set the foot down on the table. "It's not a birth defect. Nor did a mother dog do this. The scar looks surgical. Either a vet removed these digits or machinery did."

"A lawn mower?"

"A lawn mower could have done this." Bending close to the table, he peered at Pip's foot bearing weight. "The missing digits do make his step slightly unstable."

"I knew it!" There. I'd have to get rid of him. I'd soon be driving out to Hop Bottom, PA, to take my pick of Cheryl Jagger's puppies.

"Well, it shouldn't slow him down. These guys can outrun you on three legs." He showed me how other parts of the foot were developing pads to compensate for the missing toes. "Perhaps when

169

he's old he'll have a little joint pain."

"So, I'm not raising another handicapped animal?"

Dr. Michelotti shook his head. "He's going to be a fine dog."

I hated Pip.

When you have a roly-poly baby, you expect to teach language. There's the big-eyed, twitchy-nose, wobbly-headed curiosity. You expect verbal skills to mount along with physical skills. However, raised to adolescence in his lean-to, Pip had no idea that the sounds coming out of human faces might mean something. He wearied me. I longed for Kierney; I mourned for my imaginary puppy, Cheryl's little treasure, a pup whose many possible names I'd penciled in the back of a baby name book: Mitchie, Moss, Trixie, Mist, Caper, Spright, Jet, Fling, Flirt, Dally, Bess, Coquette. Gone. I'd even gotten my fifty dollars back.

Pip—that name for a border collie is the equivalent of Bear for a big shaggy brown dog or Kitty for your average cat. His name was another sign that no thought had gone into him, and, because it was the one word he knew, I had to call him by this name, empty of imagination, empty of affection, a syllable I could fill with my disappointment. He followed me, fawned over me, and groveled for forgiveness—for what, I didn't know, for being alive, for being in my house, for not being Cheryl's pup. He tried. Joe and my friends pointed out how hard the young dog tried. It pained me that Pip wanted something more from me than cuddles, and I tried to give him what he wanted. I threw the ball. He stumbled after it, then left it, ran back to me, and sniveled on the floor.

"He's no border collie," I sighed. Half-heartedly, because I had no other choice, I spoke to him the way I once did to young Kierney and still did for my little girl, repeating the words for all the people, places, things and actions in his life, but he didn't catch on. "He's stupid," I groaned. "Besides, he's ugly."

"No, he isn't," my friends would say.

But he was. He had a thin, flat coat, a big head, floppy drop-ears, legs too long for his short, xylophone-ribbed body. Young and new in town, he understandably carried himself abjectly, but I had so dearly dreamed of a forthright dog. This fellow seemed to think his good fortune was beyond belief and was telling me over and over, "I don't deserve all this."

I was beginning to believe him. "He's soft on everything," I complained. I shared the shepherd's disdain.

Grudgingly, I admitted he *might* be bright enough. One household accident his first day with us was all it took to housebreak him. Pip did have border collie eye in his favor—that is, he was born with the inherited urge to stare down moving objects and head them off, stop their progress. As he gained the assurance that he was in our house to stay, he chased down racquetballs and Frisbees and became so obsessed with playing catch that I eventually regretted having coaxed along the trait. Perhaps he had a shot at earning my respect after all.

Although I sometimes dejectedly passed many days without speaking to him at all, I did clap a leash on him and work him in obedience. Like most border collies I've known, he learned formal commands within one or two repetitions and never forgot them. Any more practice and he got bored and resentful. But as soon as he heard me exhale in exasperation, he threw himself on his side and lay there, stiff, holding his breath, one eye watching me. "Had enough?" I'd say, and, to avoid encouraging that kind of behavior, I'd work him a few minutes more to make sure that *I* was the one to end the session. But I was no power-monger—I made a mental note to try to keep things more interesting for Pip. Considering that his first few months of life had passed with little human interaction, I had to give him a crumb of credit. And in fact, once he'd learned a few basic verbal obedience commands, he did transfer the skill of language acquisition to routine matters: "dinner time," "get off," "upstairs," "go find your ball," "back," "mine," "ride in the car."

Over the months, more and more days passed during which I spoke to him absent-mindedly, and he spoke to me, as he did when he'd had enough of obedience work, or when I asked him to poop and he didn't have to go—he sat directly facing me, just as Kierney did. After some time, I realized he was telling me when he had to go out by flinging himself in my lap as if to say, "Help, I'm about to shame myself!" Between us, we had new words, such as "hug"—Pip was much more affectionate than Kierney ever had the nerve to be. He slept alongside my body all night, he lay on my feet as I worked, he shadowed me through the house, and when Joe was around, he placed himself always on the opposite side of me, as if to make a statement of protest, a statement of loyalty. Or as if, for some reason, he harbored a fear of men. To run with Joe, Pip had to be dragged, lying flat on his side, out the door. Sometimes in pity and disgust, Joe'd say, "He loves it once you're out of sight, but forget it."

Finally, I ordered him, "Go for a run with Joe," and led him out the door, handed the leash to Joe, gave Pip's trembling nose a kiss, and off they went. We handled it this way for over a year, and now, when Joe grabs the leash, Pip explodes into joyful, shrieking song.

Slowly, I found myself liking the sight of Pip. Worm-free, on a good diet, and getting exercise, Pip flourished. His coat filled out, he developed sinuous limbs and powerful contours, his proportions came into balance, his coat thickened and glossed, and, as his muscles deepened, his gait steadied. He "beautied," as Delaney says. Maturity improved his countenance and became less servile, eventually taking his new home for granted. In fact, around other dogs and animals he got downright cocky, as if that excess testosterone had left its mark on his brain. Head up, ears forward against regal cheeks, chest ruffled and thrust out, white toes trotting high, tail high as a flag, Pip would strut for any female who took his fancy. He looked every bit the charming bachelor, the well-to-do gentleman, Mister Pipster, Esquire. People would croon, "Oh, he's beautiful. What is he?" Because of his smooth, short fur, nobody recognized him for a border collie.

After we'd left him alone in the house for a few hours, he'd greet us with a little "Roo-roo!" song, which soon earned him the nicknames "Roo," "Rooper," and "Pip-a-Roo."

I loved him.

Then, Pip wowed us. Most ball-crazy border collies I know have to solve the problem of how to give the ball to a human and get into "catch" position simultaneously. Some try to hand it over, but are afraid to let go, because the human might throw it before they're ready. Kierney used to toss it at me and spin away. Pip solved his problem with brilliant politeness. We were slow to figure it out. After teasing him with a few hypnotizing sweeps of the ball, I'd throw it, he'd dive for it, and then go off and lie down. I'd shrug and go back to my writing. A moment later, I might notice he'd gotten up, trotted out to me and then trotted back and lain down again in the same spot, ball in his mouth. One day Joe and I were sitting in the kitchen and Pip was lying at the far end of the hall. We heard a racquetball bounce, and a moment later, the ball hit my foot. I looked up to see Pip "pointing" at the ball border collie style, belly down, pantherine.

I reached down; Pip tensed. I tossed; he caught, then lay down, delicately placing the ball on his outstretched forelegs. Gently he nudged it with his nose, and it rolled a few inches, but he quickly retrieved it, then realigned his front legs. Several more times he repeated these dry runs. Then he gave the ball a serious snout-shove and it bounced, rolled, and tapped my foot, stopping beside it, exactly as it had a moment before.

Fascinated, over the next few weeks Joe and I positioned ourselves in various places and marveled to see Pip adjust different surfaces, angles, and inclines. The living room offered a particular challenge, because the floor not only sloped, but the surface changed from hardwood to area rug. Pip had to get the ball to roll fast enough to maintain its course after bumping over the edge of the rug. With this ball-rolling act, Pip began to monopolize our friends' attention as much as Kierney ever did.

One morning, while he was shooting his ball down the kitchen hall to where I sat at the table, our fully grown, full-bodied kitten Odette flopped down in the hallway, rolled over, showed her glorious, shaggy white belly to the air and meowed shamelessly. Pip lifted his head to stare at the cat, at the hallway, at me. Sharply, he yapped once. The cat righted herself, then dozed where she was. Several times, Pip sent his racquetball straight into her plush side. She only flinched when, with a great show of annoyance, he charged over and snatched it out of her fur. Finally, taking his racquetball in his mouth, he squeezed it thoughtfully, returned to his spot and lay down again, but this time he shifted about twenty degrees, pointing his front legs at the wall. I watched. He tried a couple of dry runs, then shoved the ball. It passed the cat at an angle, caromed off the wall, and rolled to a stop, gently tapping my foot.

As a sign that I loved him, I bought Pip a rolled, oiled leather collar, a rich brown promise ring, gleaming like the polished wood of my grandfather's best pipe. I chose rolled leather because it seemed more comfortable and didn't interrupt the line of his elegant neck. He never needed a choke chain.

One crackling crisp autumn weekend, when the mountains were quilted red, orange, and yellow, and the newspaper provided maps for foliage tours, I took Pip to a hillside sheep farm for a herding clinic run by Cheryl Jagger, in honor of the promise I'd made to Kierney but couldn't quite keep. There, to put the final lie to the shepherd that bred him, Pip, still only about eighteen months old, proved himself anything but soft on sheep. Easily the most aggressive pupil there, Pip bit the sheep—called "gripping"—and independently rounded them up against the fence rather than bringing them to Cheryl and me, as if he didn't trust us to help control them. Or, more likely, he wouldn't presume to trouble us.

There, at that clinic, I realized what I should've known all along, that border collies have complex inner lives, and it's a failure of human imagination to suppose that because they're sheepdogs they need sheep. Pip was no more fulfilled by them than by his racquetball. He didn't prefer herding them with Cheryl to playing Frisbee with Joe. Like humans, border collies have a brain for relationships; in particular, they herd. They'll herd anything, happily, just as we'll interact with anything, alive or inert. We'll program a computer, ride horses, knock a golf ball around a gigantic grass game board, or invite friends over for a *McHale's Navy* marathon. Unlike us, however, border collies don't seem to tire of their pastimes. Sitting in the bright autumn sunshine, remembering how Kierney stared with complete absorption at the racquetball she'd placed in my lap for the millionth time, I finally forgave myself for letting her die before she'd ever moved a sheep.

That weekend on an autumn hillside, lost and delirious in a crowd of dog lovers, border collies, and sheep, I sat back, lolling in my happiness. It had always seemed overtly poetic that the wildfire that was Kierney, the extreme of wit and speed and passion, should have a deadly character flaw and a serious illness, a death force commensurate with the force of her life.

I've seen myself and my friends attain peace and stability, only to discover that these beatitudes are mere breathing places, vistas, or diving boards, from where we collect our psyches, examine our lives—and then jump off, risking it all. And so it was in just such a mind-frame that, at the sheep herding clinic, in our shared felicity, Pip and I fell in love with a border collie bitch.

The daughter of Walt Jagger's own glorious Kit and Celt, a relative of the pup I almost bought from Cheryl, Dee was a lean, light, feathered imp of a dog, flirtatious, furious, unforgettable. She was everything I'd dreamed that Mitchie-Moss-Trixie-Mist-Caper-Spright-Jet-Fling-Flirt-Dally-Bess-Coquette would be. Kierney had died and had taken that razzle-dazzle with her—how and why had we lived so long without it?

Within the year, we brought home the next best thing to Dee, one of Dee's own female pups. A few weeks later, I got a letter from her breeder saying, "I sold the puppies' beautiful mother, Dee. She was so stylish, strong and talented . . . I had to give her to a sheep dog trainer capable of developing her full potential." I knew this was just a diplomatic way of saying, "I adored her but I was at my wit's end with that maniac." Naturally, just like George had done with Sweep, the woman, knowing that she couldn't handle her dog, had bred her—duplicated her—and sold her pups to dazzled dodoes like me.

I remembered the last time I'd seen Dee, the day I went to buy one of her pups. In a specially reinforced pen, Dee slammed back and forth, back and forth, back and forth, like a black-and-white Fury, a gorgeous griffin, a lethal and unearthly beast. And so after reading the letter, I looked down at my dull, crumple-eared pup and thanked God that I had been spared having a wild animal in my home.

I seemed to have nothing to fear. Besides adding to our vet and feed bills, the new pup did little more than bring a bolder note of complacency to our home. In fact, I sometimes wondered why I'd bothered getting a second dog. Warm-hearted people at the sheep herding clinic had smiled at me, squinting in the sunlight, "You only have one border collie? Nobody ever has one border collie for long." Now I had two, and I still didn't know what they were talking about. Never underfoot, never yapping, never shredding furniture, she had an eerie knack for going unnoticed among us. She was stout and unpleasantly-marked, with bizarre pleated ears, folded fan-like and limp no matter her mood. I kept rubbing the cartilage in her ears, trying to iron them out. Before I could name her from my precious list, Delaney had dubbed her Casey, and I added Jane for "plain Jane." She was like something computer-selected, pH-balanced, sugar-free.

However, as humdrum as Casey Jane was, Pip could barely tolerate her. The Felix Unger of dogs—if Pip had hands, he would've been wringing them. Fastidious Pip was a dog of the old *sit-stay-heel-hush* school, a good boy who knew his place. He slunk toward me, ashamed of his urge to bite her when she lapped from his water dish, chased his Frisbee, or curled beside him on his mat. I thought her youth annoyed him, but the problem amounted to more than a generation gap. When Casey piddled on the freshly-upholstered window seat, Pip bore her shame and bore it inordinately, as if by her refusal to repent she had stained so much more than the new brocade. Often in those early days he looked up at me as if trying to communicate something rather like dread.

As Casey approached her first heat, I began to notice we had a second dog. "C'mon in," I'd call from the kitchen door, and, if the weather was fine, she'd look straight at me, then bounce in the other direction, shaking her tail like a pompom. Aghast, Pip would snap into a voluntary *heel*. If she wanted to play catch, she'd not only drop the ball in my lap, but ram into me with front legs like twin javelins. I had paw-shaped bruises on my ribs. In the space of a few weeks, she became a tireless terror, a perpetual-motion machine with the pain threshold of an anvil. As intractable as a feral animal, by nine months she was so exuberant she shattered her own shoulder—repeatedly— and only began to show a faint limp when bone fragments inhibited movement. Thinking I was overreacting, I had taken her in to have Michelotti examine her. He'd thought the visit to his office was unnecessary too, until he took the X ray.

"How am I supposed to take care of an animal that can't feel pain?" I said. "How will I know when she needs me?"

"You won't," he said. "If she shows the slightest hesitation, bring her in. Something will be very wrong."

Not only was she insensitive to her own pain, she was insensitive to everyone else's. Pip would line up one of his graceful racquetball rolls, tap it with his pool-cue nose, and she would swoop by, scoop it up, then spin around with her graceful plume high over her back, taunting. They brawled, screamed, and drew blood—mostly Pip's. Casey just didn't give a damn.

While it was dawning on me that neither I, nor Delaney, nor my noble Pip-dog could tolerate another week with Casey, one day Joe came back from a run with her, panting and sweating happily. "Thank you, Lisa," he said and kissed me.

"For what?" I said.

"For Casey." She was the first of our dogs to obey him fearlessly, to look him in the eye, and to stand unflinching at the sound of his voice. She obeyed him, she preferred him, she was *his* dog, and he loved her.

Then, Joe went off to work, and I had a wild animal in my home, to stay.

I called my friend who trained Rottweilers and won national obedience championships. After listening to me describe Casey's demonic sass, she recommended I try the dominance roll. So, the next time Casey jabbed me, I leapt on her, and after about ten minutes of sweat and foul language I finally pinned her spindly, seventeen-pound body. Triumphant, I said, "Ha!" then wondered what was next, how long to hold her there, why no one was clapping. As soon as the fight had started, Pip had burrowed into the hot air vent. But Casey wasn't even breathing heavily. She was bored! In a throb of hatred, I knew myself capable of betraying every hour I'd ever spent advancing the cause of animal welfare.

Then, it was Casey's turn to wow us. Soon after I had made it clear to her that any political and athletic acts of self-expression would be squelched, Casey Jane, left alone and loose in the kitchen for ten minutes, decorated the entire linoleum floor with an intricate brown-dot pattern. At first I thought she'd spilled and arranged some kibble; then the odor told me no. Casey hadn't had any ordinary bowel movement. No one could call it an "accident." I stood some moments considering it as if I were the first person to behold crop circles. Deliberate, ordered, brilliantly offensive, the crap-pattern told me that an alien and intelligent mind was trying to communicate with me. Maybe she was possessed. I looked at her. She *looked* possessed. Horror novels from my teens came to mind, *The Amityville Horror*, *The Exorcist*. Didn't the Devil like shit? But maybe she wasn't evil, maybe she was creative—the two are easily confused. More recently I'd read what I had thought was a spoof of the art world, *Why Cats Paint*. Looking at my kitchen, I reconsidered the seriousness of that book. For a few minutes, I pinched my nose and thought about art.

Defying my authority with more than a flair, Casey Jane had transformed the room by undermining all preconceived notions of kitchens and their association to hearty, sanitary meals. Her multi-sensory work achieved expressionistic simplicity in its technique, as every dot had been neatly dropped, not crudely paw-stamped. The artifact made the viewer simultaneously aware of the work and of its execution. I couldn't quite believe it, nor could I deny it, but Casey had produced the first of her daring works of art, *Scato Logic*, and catapulted herself into the family limelight.

Pip ran. He tore upstairs as if sucked out of the house by a passing tornado.

Tail wagging high, Casey looked up at me in happy anticipation, as if she were sure I would show a more appreciative reaction than had Pip, if for no other reason than I was taller and therefore had a better view. But Casey was still just a dog and didn't understand the meaning of a dropped jaw. Actually giddy about what she'd done, she wanted to run to me, but then realized that she had committed a serious design flaw—the artwork was a physical barrier between herself and her audience. She had literally painted herself into a corner.

Before I could get to her, I was going to have to deconstruct the piece. The kitchen had to be cleaned in a cautious and systematic fashion. As if she enjoyed watching me unravel the design, Casey stood in her corner, following my every minute criticism, grinning and intent. Then, when I was finished and catching my breath in the lingering stink, I discovered the puddle spreading under the kitchen table, pooling under the legs of the chairs, draining into the seam in the linoleum, an appalling *coup de grâce*.

My act of censorship had given me an unexpected intimacy with the painting. On my hands and knees, nearly nose to the floor, I could study it closely, contemplate it, and attempt some interpretation. First, was it really art? Experts on the subject have said that normally dogs are moved to paint immediately after defecation. Canine artists dab their paws in their chosen medium, then print by running on the canvas, be it grass, gravel, linoleum, carpet, or cement. Some behaviorists hypothesize that these dogs are not expressing themselves aesthetically, but merely widening the area in which they've deposited their personal scent, leaving a strong visual marker along with the olfactory. On the other hand, anthropologists argue that human artistic self-expression has its roots in territorial marking behavior. Wolves and wild dogs, for whom territorial markers are crucial for survival, never touch their own feces, and without touching hers, Casey had dropped them in an uncannily regular pattern over a large space, obviously a deliberate, territorial act. And no question about it, for forty-five minutes, the kitchen was hers. And the *Scato Logic* was original—at least I'd never seen anything like it before. In the home where Pip had for years charmed and exasperated everyone with his fastidiousness, it seemed almost inevitable that the young, shrewd, upstart daughter of the maniacal Dee rise to the challenge of self-assertion and drop dime-sized turds at four-inch intervals, creating a malodorous grid—the perfect rebellion against the impeccable Pip.

In rage and admiration, as the family cook and fellow artist, I had no idea how to react to what had happened in my kitchen. Naturally, I fell back on my dog training experience and treated the whole event like a lapse in housebreaking. Except for play time under surveillance, frequent walks and training sessions, Casey Jane was back in her crate. However, it was during this period of repression that she created her subsequent and most remarkable works.

Casey crapped in her crate, but she did much more than defy the traditional view of the denning behavior of dogs, particularly of females. Her first crate work, *Pip in Hell* featured a hard, round plastic food dish squished into a soft, swirling pile of feces, which contrasted markedly to the sterile, straight lines of the crate bars. To add humor to what would have otherwise been a mere exercise in juxtaposed shapes and textures, she had wittily worked herself into the piece, stepping on and mashing the medium between her toes, stamping whimsical paw prints on the metal floor, lying down and working it into her own coat like a rank brown lather, and, in a final stroke of irony, sitting the very rump that had produced the feces right down into them. To underscore the mocking tone, as I entered the kitchen and got walloped by the stench, she stood up, wearing a turd on her chest like a lumpy brown corsage, and wagged her tail. The humor, while bawdy, had a maturity to it, aware of and well in control of its many dimensions.

Pip rolled over on his back and begged me to rip open his throat right there.

Again, I couldn't be certain the work was aesthetically motivated. It might have been happenstance, the result of a vigorous caged dog suffering full and immature bowels. But hadn't I *just* taken her out? There was no question she knew better—she was the pup that had learned *sit, stay, come,* and *heel* all in one brief training session and never forgotten them. Here again was the deliberation, the defiance, the sass in her eyes. I had never seen her happier.

Now a dog who's unloaded in her crate and up against her food dish, then made herself right at home in it all, is as much a challenge to clean as to punish: do I bathe her before or after the dominance roll? Do I scrub the dog or the crate first? Should I get her a studio? What do I do when her long feathered tail has become a big sweeping paint brush and the walls have been done in merry brown swirls? Did she have an anal fixation? Could she be a closet coprophiliac? Could she be some kind of canine visionary, above and beyond the bounds of decorum and my priggish conniptions? Should I give her to an art instructor capable of developing her full potential?

In the biographies of influential artists, it's not uncommon to read about times during which the surrounding community suspects them of illness and insanity. *Pip in Hell, Daisy Daze* and *Sheep Dog Scream* marked for Casey her most difficult and misunderstood times. She was forced to make distressing trips to see Dr. Michelotti. Even he, the doctor who always knew what to do, could think of nothing to do.

Daisy Daze represented a deeper plunge into expressionism, similar to the vibrancy and furor of the world-renowned Bootsie, feline painter, the winner of the 1993 Zampa D'Oro (Golden Paw) Award and a featured artist in <u>Why Cats Paint</u>. *Daisy Daze* marked a brief period of experimentation with a new medium—bile. A collage obviously created with intense concentration and little forethought, grotesque blossoms of bright yellow vomit were slashed by long blades of semi-digested grass, evoking a bizarre vision of spring. With jarring colors of the sort favored by James Sidney Ensor, the ghoulish flowers evoked a palpable sense of despair. The fancy, foamy, spring-like colors and the natural blades of grass were undermined by the bile, which hinted at disease, decay, and repugnance for the forces which withered the bloom of a young sheepdog's life. The quaint yellow paw-prints achingly recalled the homey, faded wallpaper in the farmhouse where she was born. Finally, the combination of the yellow fluid, which strongly mimicked urine, and the fresh grass of the outdoors made the devastating point that those with the bourgeois habit of "going outside" to do their business are despicable for their hypocrisy.

Sheep Dog Scream could be called an obvious tribute to Edvard Munch—I was teaching Munch's famous painting to a class of Humanities students at the time, and the writers of *Why Cats Paint* would say I must have inadvertently left my text lying open. Bearing nightmarish similarities to *Pip in Hell*, turds were herded into the corners of the crate like little round, brown sheep. The central figure, a lone turd cut from the herd, seemed to be on the verge of mental collapse. Swirling fecal smears radiated from the central figure, echoing into every corner, turning the very crate into a mute shriek of terror. This haunting portrait of pending sheepdog madness captured Casey's own sense of isolation in the face of repression, obedience work, and death. *Sheep Dog Scream* was an existential cry against a household in which canine creativity—time and again—met with nothing but hostility from both the blasé and the housebroken.

Finally, after about three months of intense productivity (nearly two years in dog-time), Casey showcased her most mature and contemplative piece, the neo-classic *The Ark and the Flood*, with a large, tapered heap as the focal point, paw prints and turdlets as the gathering animals, and a touch of performance art in the still-streaming flood. She wagged her tail, puzzled, as I entered the room. "Boy," she seemed to conclude, turning her back on me, "have you got a problem." Through my tears of frustration I couldn't help but notice that energy and idealism defined this ingenious marriage of tradition and the cutting edge. The orderliness was off-set by the deontological tension of the scene—some animals will be saved, most will not—and yet the arrangement was peaceful, accepting, showing that the artist was coming to terms with the demands of domestication.

That winter was unusually cold. Half of January and all of February, I lay coughing and shivering in a twilight of fever. For weeks, I was too sick to take Casey out on a leash, and, although she wouldn't run away, she galloped wide loops around me, loops wide enough to zig the neighbors' yards and zag the roads. I stood hunched on the back step, for it was too cold for me to stand upright. I discovered that I could control her if I hissed, "Case!" and twitched as if she'd just caught me in the act of sneaking away. She'd roar and charge me, somehow managing to look as though she weighed four times more than she did. When she was nearly upon me, I'd say, "Poop," or "Tinkle," depending on what needed to be done. On a dime, she'd pivot and lope away. Task completed, I'd hiss, "Case!" and duck into the house just as she brayed past me, skittered on the linoleum, and bit Pip in the head.

One day I lay down on the couch, which I didn't usually do when I was sick because the window above it was drafty, but there was going to be an eclipse of the sun and I was hoping to see it from there.

"Mommy, Casey pooped on the kitchen floor," Delaney announced. Casey had created *Still Life With Bacteria*.

I replied that I'd come see in a minute. Hours later, Delaney was making reports, "It's like Play-Doh on the floor," and I was still waiting for the eclipse to begin.

Usually Casey Jane passed her days at two speeds: trot and rocket. She never walked; she rarely napped. But, the entire time I was sick, she lay curled on my torso in a foxlike orb of bone and pelt. At first, cynically, I attributed the behavior to her metabolism. Casey burned herself down to the bones and shivered if the temperature indoors dropped below seventy. I reasoned she was warming herself with my fever.

As I watched the moon seeping across the face of the sun, Casey lay on me, the stink of *Still Life With Bacteria* fading as it dried. I studied her little face, snipe-nosed and bunchy-lipped. Was she cold, was she sleepy, was she ill, was she sweet, was she bored? No, she was alert and absorbed in an inert task, like a sitting hen. She was determined— determined to do what? Warm me? Protect me? I had to admit, the only time I stopped shuddering was when she lay on me. Weak and clouded, I let myself be gratefully fooled into believing that weeks of synchronized breathing would fuse us.

I was right.

After the day she painted *Still Life With Bacteria* and I did *not* come yelling, knock her down, and pin her to the floor, Casey never really defied me again. And she never had another accident, either spectacular or drab, proving that her housebreaking lapse and been no accident but an elaborate act of attention-getting. A dog who always knew exactly what she was doing, she matured into a border collie beauty, well-feathered, eagle-sleek, nimble-witted, fast and high-leaping, perpetually mesmerizing.

Whenever I was out, Casey waited by my office chair. When I was upset with her, she didn't collapse the way Pip did, but tried to figure out what made me unhappy so she could avoid doing it again. Her charming combination of spunk and shyness made her irresistible to our friends. She and Pip reconciled, and, in a way, it was our loss— Pip's spectacular racquetball rolls with his pool-cue nose were over, replaced by efficient border collie teamwork, amazing in its own way. He'd nose the ball to Casey, and she scooped it up and delivered it to a human, whose job it was to throw the ball to Pip, completing what would be an endless loop if not for the limits of the human link.

While Pip was making the catch and settling back into position for the nose roll, Casey zoomed back and forth several times between him and the ball-tosser, huffing her hot breath as if to say, "You still with us?"

When she wasn't part of the racquetball circuit, all day long, while we dressed and cooked and talked and walked, our crumpled-eared artist watched us, dancing back and forth, back and forth, gorgeous and unearthly, panting that pant that sounds like soft laughter. And whenever we fell sick or sorrowful, she slept on us, keeping her funny little watch, warming us with her shivery bones.

So we became a pack. Casey found her place in it. She had been craving intimacy, but couldn't at first get past Pip to be close to me, except by infuriating me. The bond between me and Pip, it was true, was formidably deep. When I traveled to visit my mother, she sometimes remarked, "You miss your dog more than you do your husband." Never really having had a dog of her own, my mother couldn't know that for those of us who spend every waking—and sleeping—minute with a border collie at our sides, the attachment can bet profound. Primordial.

Black magic.

In late autumn high in the Appalachian Mountains, the leaves rust and redden and brown and yellow and yet they cling, while snowflakes float in the air like ash from some distant bonfire. Night falls abruptly, mornings are gray, and at dawn the grass crackles underfoot. By Halloween, the mountains lie hunched and bare. Looking up at them from the bottom of Happy Valley, you can almost see through the trees to the rocks. Thin and frail, the trees rib the mountainsides like delicate fish bones. This is the join between two seasons, between harvest and the long barren months. Rainfall flickers to snow and back. The join is loose.

They used to say that on Halloween night the join between the living and the dead was loose too; there was a tear in the fabric of space-time. On that night fools walking in the dark might follow a will-o'-the-wisp, slip through the tear, and disappear. On that night the souls of the dead wandered among us, witches took the shape of beetles and passed through the keyholes of locked rooms, cows were heard to speak in their barns, bats swooped and ate the souls of the dead like so many gnats. Come autumn in the mountains of Pennsylvania, when the wind blows hot, then chilly, then hot again, when plants that had browned suddenly bloom, you can feel the tear in the fabric howl wide open.

The week before Halloween, when Casey was still only five months old, Delaney, Pip and I drove out to the Mennonite farm where we always get our pumpkins. From the highway we could see that the pumpkin fields had lost their broad leaves, and the great vines had crumbled and left behind the big tilted orange heads, nodding off like an audience dozing before a big-screen sky. The farmhouse was charmingly old with its wrap-around-porch awry, laden with Mennonite handicrafts for sale, and on the back stoop stood a rusted 1950's Frigidaire bearing the sign, "Take eggs and leave money." Nearby, as if trained to open the refrigerator and lay their eggs inside, hens roosted and cooed on the stump of an ancient grapevine. High on the gable of the barn hung a Pennsylvania Dutch hex sign, either to ward off evil spirits or to beckon tourists—maybe both.

Ignoring the hens, Pip dashed about the farmyard, nose to the ground. Delaney and I reached the edge of the pumpkin field where pumpkins had been trucked over, unloaded, and sorted according to size. Several other families were there, running their hands over the orange grooves. Refusing to examine the one his mother preferred, a boy straddled his favorite. A man toppled a pumpkin and peered at its bottom as if checking its sex. Planning to flank both sides of our front walk with jack-o'-lanterns, Delaney and I chose six noggins, set them in the trunk of our Toyota, called Pip, and drove off, swerving under the new ballast. All the way home, Pip, who usually bounced from front seat to back, calmly twitched his nose on the edge of the open window, eyes closed. At home, looking unusually black and lanky, he serenely drank his water dish dry and then slipped off for a nap. I lined the pumpkins up on the counter, where they stood hugely incongruous, making the kitchen into a barracks for six squash soldiers. We still had to go to the grocery store. Through the bars of her crate, Casey had her eyes fixed on me. I took her out to the yard to tinkle and then locked her back up.

As we drove out to the grocery, afternoon slumped toward evening without the sky changing at all, just a pale, blank, steady gray, a sheet thrown over the dead face of the day. An hour later, I fumbled at our front door in the sudden dark, noticing that Pip didn't greet us by sticking his nose through the mail slot, clacking the brass cover and roo-rooing his high-pitched banshee song the way he usually did. Grocery bag on my hip, snapping on lights as I went, I headed for the kitchen. There, I stopped.

The kitchen was still mobbed by pumpkins, but somehow, oddly less so. One was missing. Delaney counted five, counted again, and began to cry.

A pumpkin was missing, and so was Pip.

Picking Delaney up, I kissed her, gave her a tissue, and said, "Twenty-pound vegetables don't just waddle away." Look—a smear on the linoleum—the glistening trail of a giant orange snail. We followed it into the dining room. There, on the rug, was the stem and a wedge of shell. Seeds lay scattered amid whorls of pumpkin entrails.

"Oh, no!" Delaney cried.

In tottered Pip, belly distended, hanging his head. Slowly, he belched, just loudly enough to make Delaney giggle through her tears, and then he broke wind, so loudly that he spun around to examine his own rear end. As if from the maw of an outhouse or from the syrupy innards of a great vegetable corpse, an odor rose up and haunted the room. Pip slunk away.

Long ago, in Salerno, Italy, families spent Halloween day preparing banquets. They set out the food, then left it steaming unattended while they went off to church. They believed that while they were out the souls of the family's dead were dining. When they returned, the food in fact was gone—eaten, they believed, by the dead.

Of course, it must have been the doing of the town dogs. But either way it's rather mystifying—Pip had eaten a vegetable half his weight.

Coincidentally, this was the year Delaney wanted to be a border collie for Halloween, and it did make some spooky sense to dress her as the family scavenger, especially in light of the dogs of Salerno. Earlier that fall I'd designed and sewn an oversized costume out of fake fur, thick as a parka, with furry white spats, white fur mittens, and a white fur ruff. Using Pip's head as a pattern, I'd made a black fur hood with two drop ears and a white fur blaze on the brow. Should the night be colder than forty degrees, there was plenty of room in the outfit for more insulation, which I figured we'd need since the previous Halloween we'd had sleet.

The morning of October thirtieth, the day before Halloween, a warm, heavy rain fell. I woke to summer weather in a late fall landscape, the trees stripped of leaves, the lawns brown and puddled. So plentiful were the fallen leaves and so very wet that when the rain stopped no one bothered to rake them. Water and rotting leaves slithered along the gutters, rain spouts clogged and overflowed, scarecrows sagged, ghosts hung in trees like forgotten laundry with their Magic-Markered faces smeared, and ducks appeared where ducks had never been before and paddled across back yards. Bees, flies, and mosquitoes, risen from the dead, circled rooms where the window screens had already been removed for winter.

And so it was that on Mischief Night, which the town officials had cleverly replaced with a Halloween parade, Delaney stood in our living room, sweating under black-and-white fur and face paint. The face paint turned out well. I'd blackened her brow, cheeks and nose tip, and dabbed a white blaze that met with the fur blaze on the hood. I whitened the area around her mouth and her lips as well, then drew a cartoonish doggy mouth, complete with freckles and a lolling pink tongue down one side of her chin. Except for the tongue and the fact that my daughter's muzzle is pretty short compared to Pip's, she looked uncannily like a border collie standing on hind legs. The tongue violated the verisimilitude enough that I almost erased it, but when Joe first laid eyes on her, he burst out laughing and declared the tongue hilarious.

However, as Delaney and I headed out to the parade, Joe stopped me at the door. "I know you've worked hard on this," he said tactfully, "but people might not know what she is."

It was true. In fact, even people who knew border collies didn't always know what smooth-coated Pip was. Even if you already knew what a border collie was you might puzzle over Delaney's costume; with the white bib you might think she was a cat or a panda. "Oh, I'll just bring Pip—that'll clue people in," I said, and put on my rain coat, stuck my camera and a couple of compact umbrellas in my pockets, handed Delaney the plastic, glow-in-the-dark, trick-or-treat pumpkin that I was going to end up carrying, and took up Pip's leash. Joe and his wild animal stayed home.

When the parade stepped off, the cadence of the high school band rapped against the stone store fronts, rumbled under the street lights, and thumped through the throng of soft bodies, a river of sound under the wide, warm night. Time slowed; hands and faces floated. Spectators made a long wall of grinning faces, all of them, it seemed, straining to see Delaney and her dog. Over and over we heard, "Look! Two dogs!" followed by laughter. People stooped and said to my daughter, "Which is the real dog?" and my daughter's blackened face beamed behind its white stripe. People shouted and pointed to make sure their friends didn't miss the sight of a little child dressed exactly like her dog. Some looked me right in the eye and said, "It's wonderful" or "I love the tongue." I passed friends, neighbors and colleagues who laughed and congratulated me with a heartfelt "Wow." Looking down at the two, I realized the effect could never be so perfect again—this fall they happened to be the same size, both forty pounds. Delaney carried her plastic trick-or-treat pumpkin and people dropped candy into it. "Thank you," she said, and people laughed all the harder, surprised to hear her speak, because really, she looked quite a bit like a dog.

Pip was there to prove it. Person after person looked at him, guffawed at the walking punch line, then reached to pet him. Having noticed that people had brought bags and bowls of candy to toss to the marching children, Pip darted from one to another, his nose a missile guided at their hands. A few recoiled, but most grinned to have been touched by one of such an uncanny pair. To some, Pip quite simply *was* another child. "Well, hello, there," people said to him as if he wore a particularly ingenious costume, "how are you?" With his characteristic gentility, he rose on his hind legs, hooked his paws over a candy bowl and peered at the tiny packets of Butterfinger, Krackle, Mounds, as if to say, "I'm only three-and-a-half years old." As soon as people had noticed his nudge it was over, and for some it was over too soon—they whistled to call him back and slapped their knees, they strained to stroke his side with their fingertips and settled for a swipe of his tail, as if he were something rare for Central Pennsylvania, a leopard, a swami, a real-life leprechaun, as if touching him might cleanse their conscience, improve their karma, add positive ions to the chemistry of their souls.

Like the dogs of Salerno who gobbled up banquets left for the dead, Pip had fooled his town. People weren't simply mistaking his thieving nudge for friendliness the way strangers mistake a baby's gassy grimace for a smile. They were spellbound, bewitched by the little dog-child and her twin who presumptuously "shook hands" like a campaigning politician. Neither creature was what it seemed; the two merged in the eye-duping commotion of white and black, loosened the join between animal and human, created the electrifying possibility that at any moment one of the passing gorillas or zombies or space aliens or trolls might be the real thing.

On the next night, Halloween proper, I spent a couple of hours whittling, then set out my five intricately carved jack-o'-lanterns in a row to light my front walk. Within the hour, all five had disappeared, perhaps turned to a convoy of magic carriages—or eaten by a passing dog. Smarting, I dressed my daughter in her deep plush dog costume, painted her face again, and took her and Pip into the warm drizzle for trick-or-treat. Store-bought, pumpkin-faced paper lanterns lined front walks, defied the rain, and, I couldn't help but notice, did not get stolen. Styrofoam ghosts swayed under the bare limbs of dogwood and Japanese maple trees. Slouching under umbrellas, shadowy troupes of parents and children scurried across the street, a cape or two trailing behind. The bell of Old Main rang the hour, echoing like sorrow against the wet stone faces of the houses, echoing like the clang of medieval bell ringers who long ago wandered the streets on Halloween, warning that the spirits of the dead approached.

The trick-or-treaters seemed to feel that the parade was the real holiday, this rain-soaked event but a miserable afterthought. Trudging across front porches, children muttered their line and declined invitations to take more than one piece of candy. A surprising number of houses were closed up dark with a large bowl or basket of treats left out as if to appease something too fearsome to face. With their slippery thick layer of unraked leaves, the sidewalks were treacherous, but the neighborhood streets, free from cars as if by unspoken community agreement, had been washed clean. People walked down the middle of the streets and crossed without looking, the way they do after a disaster—a blizzard, a bombing, a tornado—has made roads impassable by car. In the gaps between the slate roofs and elms, summer bats crisscrossed. On front stoops, the faces of jack-o'-lanterns leered in their slow rot.

With a lanky black dog at my side, the desolate night seemed a most convincing Halloween, much like the original ones, during which people, in fear that the waning sun might snuff out altogether, built bonfires to boost it. I could almost imagine these might be the last warm breezes we'd ever feel, this the last sweet rain. The final harvest was over, decay had set in; and now, in our last hours, in darkness and mourning, we faced a never-ending night of want and isolation, of fits and agues, of cantankerous ghouls who threw shoes and ashes, of yellow-faced goblins gawking through our window panes, of witches with their packets of blood, bones and hairs, their naked bodies greased and blackened with flying oils made from the fat of little children. Our only protection was to light candles in carved pumpkins, leave sweets to appease angry phantoms, nail horseshoes above our doors, cook meals backwards, and throw salt into fires. Pausing here, crossing there, wandering back, the bewildered people on the streets might just as easily turn their pockets inside out, tie knots in their bed sheets, or pour milk over graves to feed the dead.

Or, they could disguise themselves. They could dress as dogs. They could walk with dogs. Centuries ago, afraid of the evil spirits All Hallow's Eve unleashed, villagers sent decoys out, dressed as demons, to parade them to the town limits. They wore disguises themselves in the hopes of being mistaken for a demon and spared as one of them. Having dressed and painted my own daughter to look like Pip, *to be him*, she and I were one with the black animal that trotted along, head slung low, long white teeth gleaming from shining red gums, a familiar of the dead. The animal that shared my bed moved comfortably through the gloom, bony shoulders rolling, lean as a mummy, blacker than a shadow on a moonless night. He would trot the same way whether on suburban sidewalks or on the sands of the Sahara, where other toothy, skeletal canines tear at rats. In his flickering silhouette I saw a creature made to thrill over the offal on the outskirts of Istanbul, to swill in the gutters of Cairo, plunge his head into a wild boar's rotted gut on the bank of a Siberian lake. No leash was necessary; Pip would stay beside me; in the fabric of space-time we were woven across Asian plains, across the tundra and the Great Lakes, the Alps and the African deserts—across the twelve thousand years since the day when, in the land we now know as Israel, a woman was buried with her hand resting on the body of her dog.

Chapter Eleven

Everything Moves

During those first few weeks after Kierney's death, I felt a painful leaching from the cells in my body. When I brushed my teeth she didn't come beg for a taste of toothpaste, when I rose from the computer she didn't pop from under the table and shadow me, and when I put the baby to bed there was no one to talk to in our sign language. I put all of Kierney's things into an old tool box—her leash and collar, her chew rope, little bottles of pills, a disintegrating squeak toy. Even now, years later, when I open that box, a ghost rises in a vapor, and she's upon me, rocketing into my face. So powerful is the link between scent and memory that a few cells from Kierney's body can float into my nose and I'm besieged by her mouth, her paws, her illness, the oily fur around her ears. She's alive. During the first months after her death I opened that box often.

The worst moments were in the night as I slept in the waterbed, the humidifier spitting by the door and the yellow Pennsylvania night spilling around the blinds. The air was different. I was restless. When I stirred and lifted my head, she wasn't there on her floor mat lifting her head too so that we could tell each other, "Yes, we're still alive together."

I didn't know when Kierney was alive that her body might have been encoding itself daily into my brain as I breathed. And I wonder now, what is Pip's body doing to mine when I sleep in the amniotic vapor of our bedroom? We inhale each other's molecules all the time, and some of them, the pheromones, affect us physically. Breathing day by day the pheromones of my dog might have some subtle physiological effect on me. Maybe that was why, since we'd gotten Pip and I was sleeping with two male animals, my menstrual cycle had shortened. Have I become a Pip addict? Maybe all of us are, on some level, whether we like it or not, addicted to the aroma in our homes. If an element in the air changes suddenly, perhaps we go through withdrawal. Perhaps this withdrawal is part of the stress of travel, what we call "homesickness."

I wonder whether or not, as my little family funneled more and more of its relationships through answering machines, fax machines, and electronic mail, we aren't starving ourselves for the physical presence of other people. There's no substitute for old-fashioned visiting, for sitting and sharing food and talk, together drawing through our bodies the air of a family room or an office or a restaurant, breathing each other in, together growing sleepy in the steam of rain or frisky with an autumnal cold snap, the clock on the wall speeding or slowing according to our pleasure or boredom.

When my little daughter and I talk, we usually sit saturated in the fragrance of our couch, a bed, or in the kitchen, which is no doubt charged with the molecules of the meals we eat, the very stuff that fuels and forms our cells. Sometimes when I listen to her, I find myself watching the way her eyes dart or how dimple winks by her mouth, I catch whiffs of her breath, and I listen to the musical babble of her conversation, which at age five is a medley of magical images, like luminescent fairies darting from bough to bough in a pink and tinselly tree. I say to myself things like, "This is my daughter at five and myself at thirty-two, here and now."

Noticing the mist in my eyes, my intuitive little girl assures me, "We'll be old together, Mommy. I'll never leave home."

I almost believe her, so forbidding is my heart's question, "Who will I be without you?"

Pip sleeps at the end of my bed at my feet. Lying still all night, we float heavily on the waterbed, rarely needing to turn, breathing well-humidified air in a room shut tight, blinds drawn against the glowing mist that saturates our Pennsylvania nights year round. The humid air reflects the streetlights, so it's never perfectly dark; Pip and I can see each other. If I get up in the night, he lifts his head, his eyes seek mine and we share brief, near-motionless, but somehow urgent reunions, as if by slipping in and out of sleep we risk forever parting.

"We're still alive together," we say. "Yes, we're well."

Sometimes Pip sneaks up to rest his head beside mine on the pillow. I sleep better when I can smell him. I wake in the night, reach for him, bury my face in his fur, breathe in, and fall right back to sleep.

One day Joe said, "In the morning the whole bedroom smells like one big, square Pip."

"*I* can't smell it," I said. "That's impossible."

Almost solid black, smooth and lean as a greyhound, Pip could not possibly stink.

"He's beautiful," a golfer once told me as I jogged the perimeter of Penn State's Blue and White course. Pip cavorted alongside me. "You must bathe him every week."

A friend of mine said, "The first time I laid eyes on him I thought, he reminds me of Fred Astaire." People hug him—that's the kind of dog he is—and never, even in the most potent stages of unwash, has anyone turned a nose away from him.

In fact, one day I was walking Pip, and a neighbor knelt right down on the sidewalk, nuzzled his face into Pip's shoulder and crooned, "He smells wonderful. I wish we had a dog."

Jim Morrow once said Pip's scent should be made into a cologne for men.

Yet whether his odor was good or bad, powerful or faint, finally seemed to be beside the point. The real point is rather unnerving— Pip's body odor matters to me.

Pip's odor has become an integral part of my bedtime ritual—we say goodnight by brushing faces, I lift his popcorn-smelling paws to my nose, and gather his whole silky self into my arms and breathe all of him in. When she's in my lap, I do the same with my daughter, close my eyes and let my nose drift through her hair and over the skin of her cheeks, but so often she just smells like shampoo and soap, the enfeebled traces of her scent buried along her scalp. But what am I doing, sniffing my daughter's head and using my dog as an aromatic sleep aid? Now I'm worried I'm becoming one of those kooky dog ladies who "go canine" the way explorers and missionaries sometimes "go native."

To what have I acculturated myself? I have two dogs in the house, which means I have two scavengers in the house, and scavengers never learn to be quite as discreet as humans. Between them Pip and Casey have eaten crayons, gravel, a bunch of bananas, Play-dough, tree branches, carpets, an entire bag of jelly beans, Barbie doll extremities, a tin of Crisco shortening, the contents of a litter box, lipstick, and whole cakes of Dove Moisturizing Body Bars. The problem is this: scavengers will swipe Pop-tarts off the counter, moldy cottage cheese out of the garbage, a raw onion off the cutting board, a dirty casserole dish out of the sink, top it off with a little rabbit doo in the yard, and then, a couple of hours later, they unashamedly allow their rear ends to trumpet the change in diet. Most dog owners can't even begin to describe what they have smelled.

Maybe my olfactory cells have dulled. So I asked some of my friends whether or not my house stinks like dog. They're frank and they convinced me no. Although reassured by my friends, I had to admit that my husband was right about the bedroom in the morning. Closed up for eight hours like a teacup with a lid, the room was well steeped with Pip-scent by dawn. It wasn't a bad smell, a stench, but it was strong and definitely Pip. So I bathed him in a gentle oatmeal dog shampoo, and at first he seemed to have no odor at all. Then, slowly, his fragrance returned. I caught myself burying my face in his fur almost hungrily, as if something in me had been starved.

And so it is with Pip and Casey, who dive into me when I come home as if I'm nothing but a pool of scent. To them, reunions are literal— bodily plunges with as much commotion as possible. They beat the scent out of my coat and out of their own so that whatever we've experienced during our separation can permeate and unite us. If I were a dog a reunion might tell me, "Oh, while I was gone Pip napped on the couch," but I imagine the telling wouldn't be just a sterile verbalization, but an immediate transference of the experience, better than virtual reality, as if I too had curled on the couch with the sun on my rump. Although he never came with me when I taught my writing classes, I can imagine Pip knew my classroom, my office, my students, knew them potently, in ways that I didn't. With over forty million times the scent receptors a human has, Pip enjoys a life profoundly suffused by my own. Sometimes when I'm writing, he gently rises on his hind legs, slips most of himself into my lap, closes his eyes, and lifts his face to mine. It reminds me of Wendy's horse Shannon, who slowly moved his nostrils to mine and blew softly as if an exchange of breath were the equivalent of soul searching.

Now I love all of Pip—the sharp, oily smell of his ears, the hint of weeds and dirt that sometimes whiffs off his belly, that first hot morning-breath smooch to start my day, and most of all his coat, full of our home's odors, its dust and cat dander, plus a trace of our last run on the golf course, as well as Pip's own body odor, light and alive, skin and scant doggy oil. His cheek against mine is like a gulp of smooth whole milk. His fur, soft and warm, almost buoys my hand like bath water. His glossy little black body is made of water, as is mine, and so it isn't any surprise that there should be some faint, airborne transfusion, one body of water to another. It makes me think, when two or more live together, regardless of species, they may in some ways truly have one flesh.

In the beginning, at the creation of heaven and earth, the Spirit of God moved upon the face of the deep. Perhaps the Spirit of God still moves upon the deep and upon creatures made of water. Perhaps in seen and unseen ways Creation is still in progress, the earth persists somewhat without form, and the division of light and darkness remains incomplete. In the lingering darkness, humans don't see well, but they can learn to grope. Human beings may be blind, fallen, Douglas John Hall wrote, explicitly because of their "frightened but arrogant refusal . . . to accept and rejoice in . . . their own creatureliness." We are creatures who do not know what we are. Perhaps we're afraid to know and afraid to peer beyond the beam of our own lamps, where the implications of nothingness and of somethingness are equally fearsome. My fear is that beyond the beam there may await the kind of appalling revelation that Mark Twain unleashed upon his readers in *The Mysterious Stranger*, a book written toward the end of his life: we are each but "a vagrant thought, useless thought, a homeless thought, wandering forlorn among the empty eternities!" I'm aware that for those who hope in God there may await a jilting, as Katherine Anne

Porter wrote, so cruel that we can "not remember any other sorrow because this grief wiped them all away." Invading our sadness and our sleep, the darkness beyond the light of reason is very like the night sky which our eyes can't penetrate, the very same dark breeze that blew hooting through the skulls of Golgotha: there will be betrayals, there will be death.

Maybe the faith of a dog, the quintessential wise fool, is the way to go. My poor foolish dogs greet me leaping even though I've let them go hungry and bored, accidentally slammed their tails in doors, and smacked them for reasons they couldn't fathom. Again and again, they come to me like small children—trapped in the eternity of the present, trusting, exuberantly affectionate, ignorant, irrational, desperately self-interested, and full of wonder. I'm running through the house to answer the phone! Casey blusters and tries to block me, long teeth laughing. Someone new, fresh for a game of catch, has come to visit! Pip sings a deafening song and rolls a ball with his nose. When I was a child first falling in love with dogs, I knew that what fascinated me most about them was that they were *lovable*. Why not study them and learn to be lovable too? At least I will have been loved. And if God exists? Ultimately, isn't that what I want most—to be lovable in the eyes of God?

If there is a hierarchy of souls, it probably isn't graded by intellect—from the protozoa to *Homo erectus*, plankton to professor—but by anima, the animating force, the breath of life, by how much energy a being has for fear, for compassion, joy, rage, and play. "Will its new heart be strong and stubborn enough to snap the tethers of nothingness that break so grudgingly?" Beryl Markham once asked upon the birth of a colt. "Will it breathe when it is meant to breathe? Will it have the anger to feed and to grow and to demand its needs?" How much soul will it have? Ethereal, yet also brutishly visceral, the anima is what intends to keep on living, even in the face of certain death. In *Dead Man Walking*, written by a spiritual advisor to death row inmates, Sister Mary Prejean observes, "holding a rosary is a physical, tangible act. You touch and hold the small, smooth beads a while and then let go. 'Do not cling to me,' Jesus had said to Mary Magdalene. The great secret: *To hold on, let go. Nothing is solid. Everything moves. Except love—hold on to love. Do what love requires.*"

A lawyer in a crowd once tempted Jesus with the question, "And who is my neighbor?" and Jesus replied by telling the tale of the Good Samaritan. Had I been there, I might have asked a follow-up question: "Are other animals our neighbors too?" Many of us dismiss other creatures "for their incompleteness," as Henry Beston put it, "for their tragic fate of having taken form so far beneath ourselves. And therein we err, and greatly err. For the animal shall not be measured by man. In a world older and more complete than ours, they move finished and complete, gifted with extensions of the senses we have lost or never attained, living by voices we shall never hear. They are not brethren, they are not underlings, they are other Nations, caught with ourselves in the net of life and time." Alien as they are, they're neighbors in the net, and no matter how hopelessly foreign they may first appear, they are not beyond our empathy. The way of man is not in himself, but in mercy, in imagination, in understanding that when something happens to the least of them, it happens to the others.

Our empathetic nature is why we watch movies and sporting events and the news; it's why we read books. And we're not the only creatures with this capacity. It's why, when Bob Martin punishes one dog in a room full of dogs, all of them cringe. The anima recognizes itself in people and sea birds, dogs and horses, rattlesnakes and luna moths. It recognizes itself in the strange, the poor, the sick, the deranged, and the hateful, and knows it must go on living, it must let go and reach for the next bead of life, if not in ourselves, in other secret nations inside other heads, whether larger or smaller, furred or scaled, full of blunt or jagged teeth, dreaming their alien dreams.

This summer half of the Hetzel Union Building lawn has been bulldozed to make way for an expansion. As we arrive there, it seems we're the only ones around, the cranes and dump trucks silent behind the blue-and-white fence. Joe releases the dogs from the coupler, a leash in the shape of an upside-down "Y" on which they heel together like a two-headed, eight-legged dog. Freed, they skitter away, then crouch, glaring at us like starved wolves after a rough winter. Joe tosses them the Frisbee, which is all they hunger for. Under a cool, shiny sweetgum tree, Delaney, Joe, and I climb the steps to the gazebo. I am newly pregnant with our second child.

Casey blasts up the steps and drops the Frisbee clattering at our feet.

"Can't reach it," Joe says, and in a good-natured zap, Casey snatches the Frisbee and spits it on the bench beside him. Tar black, Pip crouches on the grass in the spank of late afternoon sunshine. Joe flings the Frisbee, and Casey sweeps after it.

Delaney hangs on the rail pretending to be a sportscaster: "Welcome back to the Double-Duty, Bubble-Trouble Frisbee Tournament! Cannonball Casey is the Penn State favorite!"

A black mound in the grass, Pip just lies there, watching Casey hit the sky in a slow-motion arc. High up, her long back makes a wild flip, her tail flares above her, and she hits the ground, Frisbee captured.

I worry Pip's getting old.

"Pip's getting old," Joe says, although I haven't spoken.

"You always say that," I scold. Pip is only five. Border collies can live as long as fifteen years. "He's just pacing himself," I say. "Everybody looks old and slow next to that rocket-butt."

Delaney leads the invisible crowd in a cheer, "Cannonball Casey, yea, yea, yea! Triple-A Casey, A, A, A!" Delaney naturally prefers Casey, who willingly joins dress-up games and slumber parties. Pip grumbles whenever she her and her friends clamp a tiara on his head.

For a moment, I worry how he'll handle the sticky pinch of a baby's hands, but immediately I can see it: the baby pulls his fur, he ducks his head, points his nose at the pain, flattens his ears, rolls his black eyes pleadingly toward me, rapidly wags his tail down low, and waits, breath held, for me to pry the baby's fingers off. I can trust him.

"I thought it was cooler out," Joe says. "I wish they'd drink." He takes the Frisbee from Casey, sets it aside, and pulls from his knapsack a dog dish and water bottle. "Water," he says, pouring it out. Indifferently, Casey bolts over and laps once.

"Champagne for the winner!" Delaney cries.

Refusing to drink, Pip crouches emphatically, shoulders lower than rump, head to the ground, almost bowing, eyes locked on the Frisbee, which Joe has set on the rail. Pip is making a point. *Get on with the game already.*

Overhead, a breeze pulls on the trees. Joe taps the water dish and says, "Thirsty?"

In the beating heat, Casey doesn't move except to shiver with anticipation, one paw raised, eyes following Joe's hands so she'll be ready the very second the game resumes.

Joe fills a cup with water and holds it out to me. "Thirsty?"

Smiling, I shake my head.

"Water," he commands, tapping the cup, delighted in so many tiny ways that I am pregnant.

It's still hard to believe. I take the cup and gulp the water down.

"Well, I can't make *them* drink," Joe says.

I grab the Frisbee. "Pip catch!"

I launch it over the rail. Pip breaks into a bunch-and-stretch gallop, measured and deft, devoted to the sport and to me. Right behind him, Casey snaps at his tail. A hundred yards away, we can hear her teeth clack.

Unhindered, Pip catches the Frisbee and lopes back to his crouching spot, long-legged, fluid, efficient, fierce.

"Persnickety Pip pulls up, but never fear, Cannonball Casey fans! It's not over yet!" Delaney shouts into her paper-cup microphone.

"Well, well, well," Joe teases. "Pip caught one."

While Pip meticulously lowers his body into position, Casey dashes to Joe, as she does single every time, shaking her pompom tail, and giddily pants as if making a report. Joe speaks for her, "All is well, Captain!"

With his nose, Pip flips the Frisbee like a stiff pancake, a sign to Casey that she has his permission to deliver it to us. On her way out, she hesitates just before leaving the sweetgum shade and looks back at us, her tongue as long as a red necktie.

"They're hot," I say, stepping down from the gazebo. "We'd better go." I pick up the leads and call out, "Collar!" They come running. Side-by-side they sit straight in front of me, chins up.

Pip, a mama's boy, veers away from Joe and sticks close to me, asking to be excused from heeling with Joe and Casey on the coupler. "Wanna heel with Lisa?" I say, snapping him on a separate leash.

Grateful, he thumps me in the chest with his front paws.

"He's such a baby," Delaney complains.

Together we head home. The humans stride, the dogs trot, a little pack, alive together, walking sidewalks, every alternate step one of hope, the other of fear, there is a God, there is not, together sheering into the riptide of blood and weather and food.

Ahead, Casey heels with Joe, precise yet zany. When a small "house for sale" sign stuck in a lawn suddenly sways, she spooks like a foal.

I think of how she wriggles and flattens herself when she approaches puppies and small children, how when Delaney had pneumonia she wouldn't leave her side, how she drops her toy and joins me for the afternoon naps my pregnancy has caused, how she will never have her own puppies.

Lagging with me, Delaney holds my hand and intuits my thoughts. "Who do you love better?" she asks.

"You," I say, although I know what she means, as well as what she doesn't know she means, that I am divided by four, however unequally and erratically, and soon to be divided by a fifth who will take far more than a fair portion. She means the newcomer will be a treasure as well as a sacrifice, that we are wondering who the child will be and who we will become in response, that this transformation is something she has been craving for years, begging to add herself and her family to a brother or sister, another puppy, a lop-eared bunny, an albino corn snake, a jar of potato beetles, any other life that will undo us and enlarge us.

"That's not what I meant," she says. "Casey or Pip?"

"Can I say both?"

"Yes." Dissatisfied, she runs ahead to ask her father.

"Casey," he promptly declares. "She's the winner."

Taking his hand, Delaney sings a song about a legendary dog named Cannonball Casey.

I look down at Pip. His jogging back bumps the side of my knee. With his domed head and flopping ears, he seems small, fragile. Together, on the wide sidewalk, as we pass beneath a new high-rise student apartment building and one of the last hundred-year-old elms on this street, Pip and I both seem rather small.

"Hey, Pippi," I say.

He glances up, immediately sees I've got nothing planned, and snaps back to the thrilling business of sniffing his universe.

I look around too, enjoy the feel of the slack lead between us, a sweet trace of my daughter's warm hand on my fingers, and, as we reach the bluff of the street, for a moment I can see across the valley to the next mountain.

Pip, I tell myself, seems to know he has a lot of time.